PARTY POLITICS IN
CONTEMPORARY WESTERN EUROPE

PARTY POLITICS IN CONTEMPORARY WESTERN EUROPE

Edited by
STEFANO BARTOLINI and PETER MAIR

FRANK CASS

First published 1984 in Great Britain by
FRANK CASS AND COMPANY LIMITED
Gainsborough House, 11 Gainsborough Road,
London E11 1RS, England

and in the United States of America by
FRANK CASS AND COMPANY LIMITED
c/o Biblio Distribution Centre
81 Adams Drive, P.O Box 327, Totowa, NJ 07511

British Library Cataloguing in Publication Data

Party politics in contemporary Western Europe.—
    (West European politics, ISSN 0140-2382)
    1. Political parties—Europe
    I. Bartolini, Stefano   II. Mair, Peter   III. Series
    324.24   JN94.A979

    ISBN 0-7146-3271-6

This group of studies first appeared in a Special Issue on
'Party Politics in Contemporary Western Europe' of *West
European Politics,* Vol. 7, No. 4, published by Frank Cass &
Co. Ltd.

Printed in Great Britain by John Wright & Sons (Printing) Ltd.
at The Stonebridge Press, Bristol

Contents

Notes on Contributors

Stefano Bartolini is Assistant Professor in the Department of Political and Social Sciences of the European University Institute in Florence. He is the author of *Riforma istituzionale e sistema politico* (1981) and of several articles on political parties and electoral development which have been published in Italian as well as in international periodicals and books. He is currently carrying out research on the comparative historical development of the European left.

Peter Mair is a Lecturer in Government at the University of Manchester and was formerly an Assistant Professor in the European University Institute in Florence. He is the author of a number of articles on Irish and comparative politics, and of the forthcoming volume, *The Irish Party System*. He is co-editor of *Western European Party Systems: Continuity and Change* (with Hans Daalder, 1983).

Franz Urban Pappi is Professor of Sociology at the University of Kiel, Federal Republic of Germany. His research interests include voting behaviour, stratification, local elites and models of collective action. He co-authored *Networks of Collective Action* (with E. Laumann, 1976), edited *Sozialstrukturanalysen mit Umfragedaten* (1979), and has recently published articles on collective action of community elites: *Zeitschrift für Soziologie* (1984); *Kölner Zeitschrift für Soziologie und Sozialpsychologie* (1984).

Philip Norton is Reader in Politics at the University of Hull. He is the author of *The British Polity* (1984), *The Constitution in Flux* (1982), *The Commons in Perspective* (1981), *Conservatives and Conservatism* (with A. Aughey, 1981), *Dissension in the House of Commons 1974–1979* (1980), *Conservative Dissidents* (1978), *Dissension in the House of Commons 1945–74* (1975) and editor of *Law and Order and British Politics* (1984).

Leonardo Morlino is Associate Professor of Comparative Politics at the Institute of Political Science, University of Florence. His recent publications include comparative essays on democratic transitions in Italy, Spain, Portugal and Greece, and the books *Come cambiano i regimi politici* (1980), and *Dalla democrazia all'autoritarismo* (1981).

Diane Sainsbury teaches politics at the Department of Political Science and the International Graduate School of the University of Stockholm. She is author of *Swedish Social Democratic Ideology and Electoral Politics 1944–1948* (1980). Her recent articles include 'Theoretical Perspectives in Analysing Ideological Change and Persistence' (1981) and 'Functional Hypotheses of Party Decline: The Case of the Scandinavian Social Democratic Parties' (1983), both published in *Scandinavian Political Studies*.

Antonio Bar is 'Profesor Titular' of Political Science and Constitutional Law at the University of Zaragossa, Spain. He was previously Lecturer at the University of Santiago, Spain, and Research Associate at Harvard University. His publications include *Syndicalism and Revolution in Spain* (1981), *La CNT en los años rojos: Del sindicalismo revolucionario al anarcosindicalismo* (1981), *El Presidente del Gobierno en España: Encuadre constitucional y práctica política* (1983), and numerous articles on political science and Spanish politics.

George Th. Mavrogordatos is an Assistant Professor of Political Science at the University of Athens. His publications include *Stillborn Republic: Social Coalitions and Party Strategies in Greece, 1922–1936* (1983), *Rise of the Green Sun: The Greek Election of 1981* (1983), and several articles in volumes and journals.

Introduction

Stefano Bartolini and Peter Mair

The literature on parties and party systems in Western Europe in the 1960s was primarily concerned with explaining persistence and stability; in the 1970s, by contrast, the literature has focused on discontinuities and on what many see as a process of party system transformation or even breakdown. At this stage it therefore seems appropriate to review the present state of European party politics and to see if the expectations of large-scale change have been justified, or whether traditional patterns of electoral competition have now begun to reassert themselves. To do this, it is necessary to look at the parties and party systems of Western Europe in some detail, identifying the forces of change as well as those of continuity, and assessing the extent to which traditional models still hold true.

The purpose of this special issue of *West European Politics* is to provide just such an up-to-date account of party politics in contemporary Europe. Of necessity, this cannot be a comprehensive survey. Limitations of space prevent the inclusion of many of the 18 party systems in Europe, and a number of the small or 'middle-range' countries have been excluded from this volume – countries such as Finland, Iceland, Ireland, Luxembourg and Portugal, as well as the consociational democracies of Austria, Belgium, The Netherlands and Switzerland.[1] This present volume does include the four major countries or so-called 'pattern states' – Britain, France, Germany and Italy – as well as Spain which, in terms of size alone, deserves parity with these four. There is also a single chapter combining analyses of Denmark, Norway and Sweden, as well as a briefer study of Greece, a country often neglected in the comparative literature. The final chapter does not have a single-country focus, but assesses the extent to which there has been sub-stantial change in European party politics.

Rather than systematically analysing each different aspect of the indi-vidual party systems, which again would be impossible given the limited space available, each author has chosen instead to emphasise those specific questions which are most relevant to the discussion of change in his or her individual system. In this sense, the contributions are not intended to be cumulative; rather different problems or themes emerge in the different countries, and while certain questions recur again and again as one crosses the frontiers from one system to the next, nevertheless the essential focus remains country-specific.

In the *German* case, the key question clearly concerns what has been called 'the new politics' and whether a new cleavage has emerged to chal-lenge the established bases of the traditionally dominant parties. Pappi identifies two distinct phases in the development of the West German party system: the first, from 1948 to 1961, representing the concentration of the system, and the second, from 1961 to 1983, representing a stable three-party system. The success of the Greens in the 1983 election may mark the beginning of a new period in that, at least at the level of the Bundestag, there is now a four-party system. At the same time, however, Pappi is at pains to emphasise the presence of stabilising tendencies and the persistence and continued relevance of the established cleavages, and he suggests that the political as opposed to socio-structural protest which gave rise to the Greens may yet be absorbed by the SPD. What is particularly interesting is his refutation of the conventional unidimensional representation of the German party system in favour of a triangular one based on the changing interplay of the two basic and still dominant cleavages. Through an analysis of second party preferences of the electorate, he convincingly argues that this party system configuration can better account for past and future changes in party alignments in Germany.

In *Britain* the problem is less one of identifying change as explaining its nature. The decline in popular support for both major parties in Britain, and particularly for the Labour Party, is ably documented by Norton, who also reviews three potential explanations. First, a decline in class voting; second, the emergence of new issues and/or a growing dissonance between popular preferences and partisan policies on particular issues; and third, the performance of the parties in office and the operation of the two-party system. He suggests that the applicability of the classic model of the two-party system is now very questionable, but also argues that the present state of British party politics is better described as one of 'perplexing flux' rather than as a transition to an alternative type of party system.

If in Britain the problem is that of explaining political change in a context of relative social stability, then in *Italy* the problem is almost exactly the reverse. As Morlino argues, the striking feature of the Italian party system is its persistence and stability in the face of massive societal changes. The quite extensive activation of new political movements between the middle 1960s and the 1970s has not found autonomous political institutionalisation, nor has it been integrated successfully in the existing parties which have found themselves castled in a system-defence position. This lack of political integration of newly mobilised electors has possibly resulted in a growing dissatisfaction with the parties as such and a growing gap between the political system and society. At the aggregate level, however, evidence of such growing dissonance is not very clear. Morlino provides an interesting explanation for this. Faced with a decline in their representative role, he suggests that the parties have tried to compensate by laying greater emphasis on an expanded clientelistic politics which includes a tightening of party control over much of the recruitment to state and para-state agencies. What Morlino's analysis seems to suggest is that political parties may deliberately respond to the weakening ideological and organisational ties with electoral segments by strengthening their distributive capacity in the society at large through a progressive 'colonisation' of its vital nerve centres (mass media, welfare institutions, etc.). This may allow them to substitute a declining identification vote with a growing exchange vote.

The most important question to be asked in the *Scandinavian* case is whether Social Democracy is in long-term decline. In an extended discussion of the experience in Denmark, Norway and Sweden, Sainsbury assesses developments in the 1970s in the light of the classic Scandinavian model of a stable politics dominated by Social Democratic parties and finds that the trends differ in each of the three countries. For instance, the 1970s have witnessed a decline in class voting, but the Swedish evidence suggests that this might now have been arrested, while the shift from the Social Democrats in Denmark has been somewhat compensated for by a growth in support for other parties of the left. What is perhaps most interesting in Scandinavia, however, is that the high level of unionisation has acted to stem the tide away from the SD parties, in that it is principally among the unorganised workers that the class–party nexus has suffered its greatest decline. What is also interesting to note is that there appears to be no general secular decline in levels of party identification, but rather that the pattern is more cyclical, declining in the 1970s and regaining strength in more recent years.

The major problem in *France* is to see whether in fact there has been a real trend towards a *bipolarisation* between the left, represented by the Communists and Socialists, and the right, represented principally by the Gaullists and the UDF, and whether party strategies are consistent with this trend. Bartolini analyses patterns of party competition in the Fifth Republic, emphasising the crucial role played by institutions, and particularly the electoral law, in constraining the strategies open to the various parties given the spatial distribution of the French electorate. The essential point is that the new electoral and presidential institutions have afforded enormous weight to the behaviour of electoral sectors which are ideologically marginal with respect to each block and individual party electorate, pushing the parties to emphasise their responsiveness towards them in particular. Such an analysis suggests that the conventional description of the French party system of the 1980s as bipolar may be oversimplified and too influenced by the evident bi-coalition context, and does not explain fully the PCF strategy and the internal conflicts in both blocs. The system is better characterised as a 'mixed' case, combining low fragmentation with a multipolar distribution of opinion.

Finally, in Spain, as in Greece, the key question concerns whether existing typologies offer appropriate models for these new party systems. In his discussion of the *Spanish* case, Bar emphasises the high degree of polarisation and the reduction of fragmentation, but cautions against seeing the system as one which is already stabilised and consolidated. The immense turnaround evident in the last election, which witnessed the virtual disappearance of the once dominant UCD and the gaining of an overall majority by the PSOE, is itself sufficient to emphasise that the party system in Spain remains in the throes of formation.

In *Greece*, on the other hand, as Mavrogordatos emphasises, the new party system bears a remarkable structural similarity to its predecessors. Though also arguing that it is difficult to fit the Greek case to existing typologies, in that it represents a mix of limited pluralism with polarised competition, Mavrogordatos does suggest a certain consolidation, in that the current division into left, centre and right is one which represents a continuity with divisions which have dominated Greek politics throughout the post-war period.

Although the discussion of persistence and change leads to different aspects being emphasised in the different cases, nevertheless there are also a number of concerns common to all, or some of, the countries. Certain themes tend to recur, while at the same time what are seen to be problematic areas in certain cases seem hardly in question in others. One obvious example of this is the problem of *party system models or typologies* – and the modes of operationalisation of these – which is still the key concern in the emerging party systems of Greece and Spain, as well as in the cases of Britain and France. The reason for such an emphasis in the Greek and Spanish cases is self-evident. Both are new systems, each of which has experienced just three elections since the demise of dictatorship; in both cases, the central question concerns whether they have settled down to a stable pattern of party competition which at the same time is identifiable in terms of typologies devised for the more established party systems in Western Europe. The concern with models in the British case is also to be expected, since for so long Britain has been seen as the archetype – if not the only real example – of the classic two-party system, and yet the recent period has witnessed the immense electoral as well as organisational decline of the two major parties. In France also, the degree of change has been such as to raise questions concerning how the party system itself might now be defined. In Germany, Italy and Scandinavia, on the other hand, despite electoral changes in some instances and a growing disaffection from party in others, the question of whether the party system itself may need to be redefined is not really considered relevant. While the entry of the Greens into the German Bundestag may yet have a very lasting impact, even in this case the evidence of stability is such that existing models continue to prove viable.

A second common concern is obviously the *persistence of cleavages* and in particular the persistence of the class cleavage, a topic which has been the focus of much discussion in the contemporary literature on European parties and party systems. Yet, as is evident in a number of the studies in this volume, and as is also evident in the general chapter by Mair, there is little substantial evidence of a decline in traditional cleavages. Pappi's discussion of the German case is perhaps the most forceful statement in favour of persistence, in that he lays convincing emphasis on the continued capacity of the two traditional cleavages in German politics, class and religion, to structure contemporary voting patterns. From a different perspective, Mavrogordatos also offers strong evidence for the persistence of cleavages in the Greek case, despite the suppression of democratic politics under the Colonels' regime. Norton's analysis is also interesting in this regard, in that while demonstrating the declining relevance of occupation in the structuring of the vote in Britain, he nevertheless also shows how other class-related variables, such as housing and trade-union membership, continue to play a major if not an increased role in the formation of partisan preferences. Sainsbury, on the other hand, employing the Alford index, finds a decline in class voting in Scandinavia but, as she herself points out, shifts in this particular index of class voting bear little relation to the electoral success or failure of class parties.

What is perhaps most important to understand in this context is, first, that evidence of a decline in class voting is necessarily dependent upon the definition of class involved (contrast the approach of Pappi with that of Sainsbury, for example); and second, that the measurement of the class cleavage cannot be reduced simply to the measurement of the relationship between social stratification and party choice. As we have argued elsewhere,[2] and as Pappi also underlines in his definition of a cleavage as 'an enduring relationship between a population group and a political party', the very concept of cleavage is particularly complex, and involves an understanding of organisation and identity as well as of social stratification. The coalition which a party builds up with a group of the population depends not just on the type of work in which that group is involved, but also on the organisational and cultural infrastructure through which the group defines its own identity, an infrastructure which itself is partly sustained by party. As such, to define class simply in occupational terms, and then to measure its relationship with party, is not to measure the strength or weakness of the class cleavage. The concept of class, and therefore of a class cleavage, must of necessity go beyond this. In this sense, though there may be evidence of a changing association between occupation and party choice, the evidence from Britain, Germany and Scandinavia does not point to any significant waning of the class cleavage as such.

The third major theme to be highlighted by a number of the chapters is *the role of institutions* and, in particular, the importance of electoral law. The question is of particular relevance in three of the cases, France, Greece and Spain, all of which are also characterised as 'mixed' systems in terms of Sartori's typology.[3] They all combine the features of limited pluralism (low fragmentation of the party system) with a high degree of polarisation. Yet each of these countries is also characterised (as is Britain) by a more or less reductive electoral system which favours large parties and/or parties which can forge effective pre-election alliances. The obvious point of contrast here is with Italy, which combines a large number of parties with a high degree of polarisation in a classic polarised pluralism model; yet what also distinguishes the Italian case from the others is the absence of a reductive electoral system. Such contrast in fragmentation among countries which are ideologically polarised in a similar way therefore seems to be determined by the differing constraining strengths of the electoral systems.[4] It is not by chance that, in the three countries which are mixed in a typological sense, fairly disproportional electoral arrangements were introduced in phases of democratic inauguration (Greece and Spain) or of regime change (France) which allowed prominent leaders a significant amount of freedom in political and institutional engineering. The most interesting theoretical question related to the future development of these party systems is therefore whether the basic ideological polarisation will foster party system fragmentation notwithstanding penalising electoral systems or, on the contrary, whether the latter will prevail in helping to maintain limited multipartism and perhaps also fostering ideological depolarisation.

Other general themes are also highlighted, but with less emphasis. The Italian and British data, for instance, as well as the Eurobarometer data which are discussed by Mair, suggest that *party identification* may be in decline. Here, though, it is worth noting Sainsbury's data which point to a possible strengthening of party identification in Scandinavia. Another question concerns *party organisation* which, though touched on only briefly by most of the papers in this collection, would also appear to be generally weakening. Here again there is an exception, however, in that Bartolini points to a strengthening of party organisation in the French case in the last decade. In addition, as Sainsbury and Mair emphasise, and as is also evident from Norton's discussion of the British case, the role of such party-associated organisations as trade unions should not be overlooked when cataloguing the organisational resources available to parties. Yet another theme concerns the impact of *deconfessionalisation*, which Pappi suggests may have been responsible for a shift of white-collar voting support from the CDU to the SPD and/or FDP in Germany, and which Morlino also suggests may be in part responsible for disaffection from the DC in Italy..Interestingly enough, none of the studies of the individual countries evidence any real concern for the possible challenge to parties posed by *new modes of interest-intermediation*, though this is taken up in the final chapter which concerns the problem of measuring and explaining change in party politics in general. But despite the rapidly growing literature on neo-corporatism, this phenomenon is not seen in this particular context as being of any major relevance to the discussion of change in European party politics.

What is emphasised again and again by all authors, however, is the actual strategy adopted by the parties and the way in which they respond to different political circumstances. A single thread to be drawn from these contributions, therefore, is that parties are still primarily *active* agencies, adapting to change and forging new methods of maintaining their predominant role. Obviously they do so in each case under different institutional, governmental and social constraints, and therefore, in different ways. But their continued capacity to do so belies to a certain extent the impression of the vulnerability – if not of the obsolescence – of parties prevalent in much of the contemporary literature.

NOTES

1. For a recent assessment of the continued validity of the consociational model, see M.P.C.M. van Schendelen (ed.), *Consociationalism, Pillarization and Conflict-Management in the Low Countries* (special issue of *Acta Politica*, Vol. 19, January 1984).
2. Stefano Bartolini and Peter Mair, 'The Class Cleavage in Historical Perspective: An Analytical Reconstruction and Empirical Test', paper presented at the Annual Meeting of the German Political Science Association, Mannheim, 1983.
3. See Giovanni Sartori, *Parties and Party Systems: A Framework of Analysis*, Vol. 1 (Cambridge: Cambridge University Press, 1976).
4. According to the figures of Mackie and Rose, the French electoral system is 79 per cent proportional, the Greek 88 per cent, the Spanish 83 per cent and the Italian 95 per cent. See T.T. Mackie and Richard Rose, *The International Almanac of Electoral History*, 2nd edition (London: Macmillan, 1982), Table A.5, pp. 410–11.

The West German Party System

Franz Urban Pappi

I. THE POWER OF THE PARTIES IN THE FEDERAL PARLIAMENT

In every parliamentary system, the power of the parties in parliament offers conclusive information about the character of the system. If the system is democratic, then the success of the parties in general elections, due to the one-man, one-vote principle, will be the main determinant of party strength in parliament. Institutional rules for vote-counting procedures and the formation of governments are important additional determinants of party systems.

When these institutional rules were formulated for the new Federal Republic of Germany in the late 1940s, the Western Allies and the politicians of the major parties were most anxious to avoid the fragmentation of the party system of the Weimar Republic and they aimed at strengthening the parliamentary system. Two institutional devices were – and remain – of special importance. One is the strong position of the Chancellor, who is no longer an appointee of a strong President as under the Weimar constitution, and who, once elected by an absolute majority of the federal parliament (Bundestag), can only be dismissed by a 'constructive vote of no confidence', that is, through the election of a new Chancellor. The other device is the five per cent threshold of the federal election law, which guarantees that only parties which gain at least five per cent of the votes can enter the Bundestag. Otherwise, the electoral system has the effect of a proportional representation and not of a majority system of single-member constituencies, even if one half of the candidates are elected in the constituencies.

In 1949 the five per cent clause was already in effect, although not at federal level, as was the case from 1953 on, but only at the level of the *Länder*. Originally this constraint was not a German invention but was included in the first federal election law by request of the three military governors. It is sometimes overlooked that from the very beginning the military governments of all four German occupation zones were responsible for a certain concentration of the party system. The Soviets were the first to permit political parties with their famous Order No. 2 of 10 June 1945. The Western Allies followed soon after and licensed the same parties in their zones which were already founded in the Soviet zone, that is, the organisations of the Communists (KPD), the Social Democrats (SPD), the Christian Democrats (CDU/CSU) and the Liberals (FDP or LDP). In the British occupational zone two additional parties were founded early and gained some importance in certain regions: the Catholic Zentrumspartei in Westphalia and the secular conservative German Party (DP) in Lower Saxony. Other regional parties or right-wing parties were not licensed until 1948. The

KPD lost many of its former voters due to the policy of the Soviets in their occupation zone and, with the exception of the two parties with regional strongholds, the licence policy of the military governments gave the SPD, the CDU/CSU and the FDP 'a head start which . . . they never lost'.[1]

The main German contribution to the concentration of the party system was the founding of the CDU, or CSU in Bavaria, as a new political party. The idea was to overcome the traditional confessional cleavage between the Catholic Zentrum and the diverse national liberal and conservative parties of the Protestant right. The CDU/CSU was supposed to be the major *Sammlungspartei* against the socialist left and was successful in this respect in the first *Landtag* elections of the southern and northern states.

In 1948 and 1949, the Parliamentary Council formulated and debated the new West German constitution. In this same period many new parties were founded and after the results of the first federal election in 1949 became known it looked as if the fragmentation of the Weimar party system was again prevailing against tendencies towards a concentration in the years before. At that time it may have been difficult to foresee that only the three *Fraktionen* of the Parliamentary Council were the forerunners of the later West German party system, and not the eight parties in the first Bundestag. In the Parliamentary Council the members of the CDU/CSU, the SPD and the FDP had the official status of *Fraktionen*, whereas the KPD, Zentrum and DP did not have enough members to form *Fraktionen* and did not therefore possess the same rights as parliamentary parties.

The basic information about the development of the West German party system is presented in Table 1. For a parliamentary system it is not sufficient to know how many votes were gained by each party in an election. The more crucial information is the strength of a party in parliament. And this latter variable is also determined by the election laws.

One can distinguish between three periods in the development of the party system. The first period, from 1949 to 1961, is characterised by a general trend towards a concentration of the party system. The second period, from 1961 to 1983, is the period of a stable three-party system. Whether a new period was started in 1983, when for the first time since 1961 a fourth party was successful in entering the Bundestag, is too early to say. But at least for the present Bundestag, a four-party system has been established.

The first period began with a highly fragmented Bundestag. For eight parties more than ten candidates were elected and were, therefore, able to form *Fraktionen* in the Bundestag (parties 1 to 8; cf. Table 1). The core of the right-wing members were five candidates of the Deutsche Reichspartei who were elected in Lower Saxony. This group could not stabilise itself and was in constant flux due to a coming and going of individual members of parliament. One of its former members lost his mandate when the Federal Constitutional Court declared his party, the extreme right-wing Sozialistische Reichspartei (SRP), to be unconstitutional because it undermined the democratic order of the new state. This ruling was based on Article 21 of the Basic Law which restricts the area of freedom for the parties in that anti-system parties can be declared unconstitutional and can be dissolved. Even if

TABLE 1

THE GERMAN FEDERAL ELECTION RESULTS 1949-83

Parties [1]	1949 V	1949 S[2]	1953 V	1953 S	1957 V	1957 S	1961 V	1961 S	1965 V	1965 S	1969 V	1969 S	1972 V	1972 S	1976 V	1976 S	1980 V	1980 S	1983 V	1983 S
	%	%	%	%	%	%	%	%	%	%	%	%	%	%	%	%	%	%	%	%
1. CDU/CSU	31.0	34.6	45.2	49.9	50.2	54.3	45.3	48.5	47.6	49.4	46.1	48.8	44.9	45.4	48.6	49.0	44.5	45.5	48.8	49.0
2. SPD	29.2	32.6	28.8	31.0	31.8	34.0	36.2	38.1	39.3	40.7	42.7	45.2	45.8	46.4	42.6	43.2	42.9	43.9	38.2	38.8
3. FDP	11.9	12.9	9.5	9.9	7.7	8.3	12.8	13.4	9.5	9.9	5.8	6.0	8.4	8.3	7.9	7.9	10.6	10.7	7.0	6.8
4. DP	4.0	4.2	3.3	3.1	3.4	3.4	–	–	–	–	–	–	–	–	–	–	–	–	–	–
5. Zentrum	3.1	2.5	0.8	0.6	–	–	–	–	–	–	–	–	–	–	–	–	–	–	–	–
6. WAV	2.9	3.0	–	–	–	–	–	–	–	–	–	–	–	–	–	–	–	–	–	–
7. BP	4.2	4.2	1.7	–	–	–	–	–	–	–	0.2	–	–	–	–	–	–	–	–	–
8. KPD,DKP	5.7	3.7	2.2	–	–	–	–	–	–	–	–	–	0.3	–	0.5	–	0.2	–	0.2	–
9. Right Wing/NDP	1.8	1.2	1.1	–	1.0	–	0.8	–	2.0	–	4.3	–	0.6	–	0.3	–	0.2	–	–	–
10. GB/BHE	–	–	5.9	5.5	4.6	–	–	–	–	–	–	–	–	–	–	–	–	–	–	–
11. Grüne	–	–	–	–	–	–	–	–	–	–	–	–	–	–	–	–	1.5	–	5.6	5.4
12. Independents	4.8	0.8	–	–	–	–	–	–	–	–	–	–	–	–	–	–	–	–	–	–
13. Other Parties	1.4	0.3	1.7	–	1.3	–	4.9	–	1.6	–	0.9	–	0.1	–	0.1	–	0.1	–	0.0	–

Notes: 1. Party names: (1) Christian Democrats, in Bavaria Christian Social Union, (2) Social Democrats, (3) Free Democrats, (4) German Party, (6) Party for Economic Recovery, (7) Bavarian Party, (8) Communists, (9) since 1965 National Democrats, (10) Refugee Party, (11) Greens.

    2. V = Valid votes (since 1953 second ballot) cast for the parties.

        S = Elected Members of the Bundestag.

Sources: P. Schindler, *Datenhandbuch zur Geschichte des deutschen Bundestages 1949 bis 1982* (Bonn: Presse- und Informationszentrum des deutschen Bundestags, 1983), pp. 34–9; Statisches Bundesamt, 1983.

the KPD was the second party to be dissolved by the Federal Constitutional Court in 1956, one should not forget that Article 21 was also an effective weapon against the formation of a new Nazi party. The ruling of 1952 against the SRP was merely a highly visible indicator of the many restraints upon extremist right-wing parties after the war.

The smaller parties of the first Bundestag had one characteristic in common. They had powerful regional strongholds, and did not compete in every state. But there was the one exception, the KPD. This party nominated candidates in every *Land*, but because it received more than five per cent of the votes in only five of the ten states, its share in parliament was two percentage points less than the percentage of valid votes.

One cannot directly derive from Table 1 the weight or power of the parties for forming coalitions. I shall use the Shaply/Shubik index to measure the power of the *Fraktionen*. To compute the index, all possible voting sequences are considered and those sequences are counted in which a party is pivotal. When a Chancellor has to be elected by an absolute majority, one assumes that every party in a sequence votes in the same way and that the one which enables the coalition to exceed 50 per cent is pivotal. The more often a party is pivotal in the possible voting sequences, the more powerful it is. This index has been interpreted as the probability that a given party, 'by casting its votes, establishes a winning coalition of minimum size in any voting sequence ...'[2]

Even in the first Bundestag, when the power of the parties was not yet very different from their share of the total numbers of members, some characteristic differences existed. One was that the SPD had a power index of only 0.27 compared to the 0.33 of the CDU/CSU. Thus the parties were less similar in their power than in their size. The more characteristic difference concerned the FDP as the third largest party with a relative size of 12.9 per cent in parliament. Its power index was 0.23.[3] In this situation the leader of the largest party, Konrad Adenauer, decided to form a coalition of CDU/CSU, FDP and DP.

The result of the second Bundestag election in 1953 was quite astonishing for those who in 1949 had predicted a fragmented party system. The CDU/CSU almost gained an absolute majority of the seats, due mainly to the decline of the small parties which had not participated in the coalition. The coalition party DP and the Zentrum were able to enter the Bundestag again because in some constituencies the CDU did not compete with those parties. But there was a new party which was able to surmount the now *federal* five per cent threshold. This party, the GB/BHE, attracted the votes of the huge number of refugees from the East in West Germany.

Even with this new party being represented in the Bundestag, the prospects for coalition formation were quite different in 1953 in comparison with 1949. Before the first session of the newly elected Bundestag one member of the Zentrum joined the *Fraktion* of the CDU/CSU. This meant that this party on its own had an absolute majority of seats and a power index of 1.00. In this situation, Adenauer decided to include all parties but the SPD in a coalition government. Only the FDP survived as an independent party; the others were destroyed by their own strategy in parliament.

In short, the concentration of the German party system in the 1950s was caused by the head start of the CDU/CSU, SPD and FDP after the war, the successful strategy of the parliamentary party CDU/CSU as a *Sammlungspartei* in parliament and in general elections, and its dominant position in the Bundestag from 1953 to 1961 with a power index of 1.00. No coalition government against the CDU/CSU would have been possible.

The consequence of these developments was not a two- but a three-party system. This was not a historical accident but was based on the rather stable ideological and social structural framework of the German polity. I shall outline a model of the German three-party system in the paragraphs below. This will help to evaluate the change of the party system in 1983 when for the first time since 1961 a fourth party, the Greens, was successful in a federal election.

In every federal election since 1961 the votes cast for the CDU/CSU, the SPD and the FDP accounted for at least 94 per cent of the valid votes. With the exception of 1972, the CDU/CSU always gained a relative majority, the SPD remained the second largest party with a percentage between 36.2 and an exceptional peak in 1972 of 45.8. The FDP as the smallest party was several times in danger of not reaching the five per cent threshold. This weakness of the smallest party was interpreted by some observers as an indicator for a two-and-a-half party system and not a fully-fledged three-party system.[4]

When one takes the power of the parties in parliament into consideration, the period from 1961 to 1983 can be better interpreted as a period of a stable three-party system. The power index of each party was exactly one third over the whole period. In all these years, a two-party coalition was necessary to elect a Chancellor and form a government. With three parties, three different two-party coalitions are logically possible, and it is a characteristic of this German three-party system that each logically possible coalition did indeed occur. From 1961 to 1966, CDU/CSU and FDP were in coalition, from 1966 to 1969 the two largest parties worked together in the Grand Coalition, and from 1969 to 1982 SPD and FDP together formed a government which they labelled the social–liberal government. From 1982 on, CDU/CSU and FDP again formed a government which some label a bourgeois government.

The entry of the Greens as a fourth party to the Bundestag changed the power of the parties for the first time in twenty years. The CDU/CSU as the largest party gained power, its index going up to 0.5. The SPD and FDP lost power. Their index is on the same level now as that of the Greens, 0.17.

II. A MODEL OF THE GERMAN THREE-PARTY SYSTEM

The ideological dimension underlying the German party system is often interpreted as a left–right dimension with the SPD on the left, the FDP in the middle and the CDU/CSU on the right.[5] During the period of the social–liberal government this may have been a plausible interpretation, but it is quite time-specific. If one assumes a tendency towards minimum connected winning coalitions,[6] the Grand Coalition would not only have been a falsification of the size principle, but also of Axelrod's principle of a small dispersion of the policy preferences of the coalition partners on the supposedly relevant left–right dimension. The Grand Coalition would have been a coalition of strange bedfellows each of which would have had greater similarities with the FDP than with each other.

One may doubt whether parties change their ideologies as fast as they do their coalition partners. In the period immediately after the war, the FDP was the only party which favoured a market economy, whereas parts of the CDU had sympathies for socialist solutions. Given the importance of the economic discussion, it is easy to understand that the FDP chose to sit to the right of the president of the Bundestag. And there it stayed until today, whereas the CDU/CSU was supposed to be a party in the centre of the political spectrum.

I think one should give up the simple framework of a left–right dimension underlying the German party system. I suggest instead the model of an isosceles triangle, where the points represent the three parties and the sides the coalitions (see Figure 1). Even if this is a party-defined space, the stability of the space should depend on the ideologies which are advocated by the parties. The parties manoeuvre within this space by forming coalitions, but they should advocate a general political *tendance* in normal times which they do not give up easily.

FIGURE 1
THE TRIANGULAR GERMAN PARTY SYSTEM

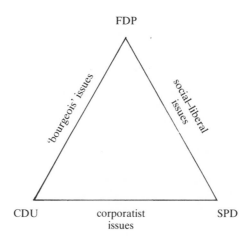

The stability of the West German party system after the Second World War can be explained within this framework by the stability and boundedness of the system of political *tendances* and the continuing advocacy of a certain *tendance* by one and the same party. The single *tendances* are, of course, no German speciality, but the ideological boundedness of the system was accomplished in Germany after the war and was maintained afterwards by avoiding the fragmentation of a multi-party system.

The following *tendances* may be distinguished: socialism represented by the SPD, liberalism represented by the FDP, and Christian conservatism represented by the CDU/CSU. This last *tendance* may look like an erratic block in the political landscape, but it is historically the most important one because it could be combined either with corporatist ideas or with the advocacy of a market economy. The religious traditionalism of the CDU/CSU antagonised the two secular parties, thus creating one major cleavage during the SPD/FDP government. But, at the same time, it opened up alternative options for the economic and welfare-state policy of the CDU/CSU.

Many Catholic members of the CDU/CSU are influenced by the social doctrines of the Catholic Church (*katholische Soziallehre*) and are, therefore, inclined to favour corporatist solutions to channel the process of interest aggregation and policy formation. In this policy area, CDU/CSU and SPD have some important joint interests, because the Social Democrats always tried to strengthen the position of the unions, which are not fragmented in Germany, but united in the German Federation of Unions (DGB). During the first major recession after the war, the CDU/CSU and SPD formed the Grand Coalition and took some initiatives to overcome the pluralist system of interest intermediation. The most spectacular outcome of this policy orientation was the creation of the Konzertierte Aktion as an informal steering committee for economic and social policy. In this committee the most important voluntary organisations of employers and employees were represented besides government officials.

Corporatist tendencies did not completely disappear when the social–liberal government took over in 1969. One can interpret the passing of the law of codetermination in 1976 as the last major success of a corporatist policy. This law guarantees that one half of the members of supervisory boards (*Aufsichtsräte*) of German enterprises are representatives of unions. The FDP raised many objections against regulations which were supposed to strengthen the power of union leaders to the detriment of the employees of the enterprises. The coalition parties finally reached a compromise to which, characteristically, the CDU/CSU also consented. Other corporatist initiatives of the unions failed, like the plan to introduce an Economic and Social Council into the constitutional order.[7] If my interpretation of the triangular party system in Germany is correct, a corporatist policy can be implemented successfully only by a CDU/SPD government.

The most important decisions regarding the basic political, economic and social institutions of the Federal Republic were made either by the Parliamentary Council in 1948/9 or by the first coalitions at federal level. The Basic Law did not regulate the economic system in detail, so that it was logically possible in 1949 to move either into a more socialist and corporatist direction or to favour a liberal market economy. But the first federal government had had a decisive forerunner, the directorate of the Bizonal Economic Council. In contrast to the prevalence of CDU/SPD coalitions in the *Länder*, the SPD did not participate in the 'government' of the Economic

Council.[8] A 'bourgeois' coalition was formed by CDU/CSU, FDP and DP, with Ludwig Erhard as economics director, and it was this coalition which was responsible for all the basic decisions in favour of a market economy. The CDU/CSU and FDP have a common stock of economic policy preferences they can use for a steady economic policy. In this 'bourgeois' coalition, the CDU/CSU has to pay more attention to welfare politics in favour of the less affluent citizens. It advertises its compromise politics under the label *Soziale Marktwirtschaft*.

To corroborate my interpretation of the German party system it would be necessary to compare the concrete policies of the different coalition governments in order to see whether their political contents really fit the interpretation I have just given. I assume that public opinion, which is only partially shaped by the parties, focuses on different issue scenarios in different periods of time. These different issue-emphases should have consequences for the formation of coalitions. Whenever liberal economic issues are emphasised through public opinion the situation is conducive for a CDU/FDP alignment. As a consequence the SPD is forced to counterbalance this climate of opinion with a vocabulary of class politics. During the time of the SPD/FDP government a type of reform politics was advocated which antagonised the CDU/CSU – perhaps last, but not least, on the religious dimension. One has only to recall the legislation regarding abortion and divorce. The different political contents of the dominant conflicts can always be unfolded on a left–right dimension during a certain period of time, but then one has to concede a frequent change of what it means to be left, middle or right. Since I do not assume a development of the system in one direction, I think the circular movements on the outlined 'party triangle' are a more promising hypothesis about the character of the German party system.

III. THE PARTY SYSTEM FROM BELOW: PARTY PREFERENCE RANKINGS OF THE VOTERS

When we have three parties to consider, not only is the first preference of the voters important, but also their second preference. It should be an indicator of the coalition preference of the voter, whereas the first party would be a measure of partisanship in its normal sense.

We interpreted the parties as representatives of certain ideological *tendances*. Ideally, we should have data about the ideological leanings of the voters and their distances to the parties as representatives of the three ideological *tendances*. The ideological space would be fixed and the parties would maneouvre in certain regions of this space. The voter would nominate the party which is closest to his or her present ideological position, followed by the second and third closest. Actual voting behaviour would occur on an analytically distinct dimension and could be determined also by short-term political influences which are not related to the ideological structure of the party system.

This blueprint for an ideal investigation would be difficult to realise because in reality the analytically distinct dimensions are enmeshed. In this situation we have to rely on conventional data on party rankings for which the ranking criterion is either sympathy or liking.

Among three parties, six preference rankings are possible. In Table 2, the relative frequencies for these six preference types are presented for all election years since 1961. Two latent types of voters should be responsible for the ups and downs of these figures.

Voters with a clear partisanship will be the dominant type. They will adjust their second preference to the governing coalition. Thus for every two-party coalition, voters whose first choice is one of these parties will have the other governing party as their second choice.

The other type is more interesting for our interpretation of the party system. These voters do not adjust their second preference to the coalition behaviour of the party elites. For this type it is possible to infer their ideological position within the system of political *tendances* and basic political orientations.

One problem with this interpretation is that we are unable to distinguish the two types among the adherents of the opposition party. But for those voters who picked the opposition party as their first choice it should be interesting to ascertain whether they anticipate the next coalition with their second choice or not. This anticipation would become possible for those adherents of the opposition who are sensitive to changes in the climate of opinion.

With the aid of the data of Table 2, we need to discover first how the voters adjusted their second preference to the coalition behaviour of the parties. This may be observed most clearly in 1969 when the coalition changed during the period covered by the surveys. During the pre-election surveys, the Grand Coalition was still in government and among the supporters of both CDU and SPD the respective coalition partner was the second choice for a large majority of the adherents. Immediately after the election, SPD and FDP started negotiations for a new coalition. This made the FDP more attractive for SPD supporters, but caused some irritation among FDP supporters, especially among those who had picked the CDU as their second choice. It is interesting to learn that the highest percentages of SPD and FDP supporters who ranked the other social–liberal coalition partner as second choice were gained in the post-election surveys of 1972 and 1976. Thus, satisfaction with the coalition reached its highest level when it turned out after the election that the party elites were successfully negotiating a continuation of their collaboration. After the election of 1980 this pattern did not recur. For the first time since 1969, SPD supporters were less in favour of the FDP after than before the election, but this anomaly may have been caused by a change of the first-party preference of former SPD sympathisers to the FDP.

During the election campaign of 1961, the CDU/CSU with its absolute majority was the only party in government. But among its supporters and those of the FDP, the other 'bourgeois' party was already the preferred coalition partner, whereas SPD followers were split in their second choice. The situation was different in 1965, when a majority of SPD supporters favoured the CDU/CSU, thus 'anticipating' the Grand Coalition. Since 1976

TABLE 2

PREFERENCE RANKINGS OF CDU/CSU, SPD AND FDP 1961-83[1] (PERCENTAGES)

Year:	1961		1965	1969		1972			1976			1980			1982	1983	
Month:[2]	6	9	9	10	9	9	10	12	5	8	11	6	9	11	11	2	3
Type[3]	%	%	%	%	%	%	%	%	%	%	%	%	%	%	%	%	%
C-S-F	22.6	15.3	22.6	32.5	37.2	28.0	25.8	17.3	18.5	16.7	11.2	14.7	17.1	11.2	19.6	16.4	12.4
C-F-S	32.2	37.7	30.7	15.9	11.0	14.2	14.3	18.7	28.1	28.1	34.4	22.4	21.3	30.3	24.3	29.7	35.2
F-C-S	3.6	5.6	3.9	2.9	0.6	2.4	1.2	1.3	2.1	2.0	1.4	2.4	2.3	3.4	1.4	1.5	1.7
F-S-C	2.0	2.7	1.7	3.9	1.8	4.3	4.3	5.8	5.7	5.7	5.9	5.8	6.1	11.0	1.2	1.0	1.2
S-F-C	17.7	21.4	12.3	13.6	23.9	32.9	39.0	50.2	37.7	40.8	42.4	44.6	45.2	38.4	16.8	15.6	16.9
S-C-F	21.9	17.3	28.8	31.2	25.5	18.2	15.4	6.4	7.9	6.7	4.7	10.2	8.0	5.8	36.6	35.8	32.6
	100	100	100	100	100	100	100	100	100	100	100	100	100	100	100	100	100

Notes: 1. The preference rankings for 1961 (Zentralarchiv-Nos. 55, 56) and 1965 (ZA-No. 556) were inferred from a question on voting intention and a question on the least preferred party. In the panel study of September and October 1969 (ZA-Nos. 426, 427) a paired comparison question was asked. In the other surveys the respondents were asked to rank order the parties (survey of August 1969: ZA-No. 525, and panel studies of 1972: ZA-Nos. 635–7, of 1976: ZA-No. 823, of 1983: ZA-No. 1276, and trend studies of 1980: ZA-Nos. 1059, 1061, 1063). When CDU and CSU were treated as separate parties, the rank of the CDU was disregarded in Bavaria and the rank of the CSU ignored outside Bavaria. The ranking of the Greens in 1980 and 1983 is also disregarded in this table.

2. Month of the post-election study underlined.

3. Most preferred party is the first party, second most preferred the second and least preferred party the third. C = CDU/CSU, S = SPD, F = FDP.

CDU sympathisers had expected a coalition with the FDP, which was finally formed in October 1982.

The only direct information about the second postulated latent-voter type stems from the supporters of a coalition party whose second choice is the opposition party and not the coalition partner of their party. If the supporters of each party adjusted their preferences completely to the coalition behaviour of the party elites, these deviating preference types would not exist. That they do exist at each point in time since 1961 for which we have data is clear evidence of the triangular party system.

We have an additional piece of information in support of the interpretation of a party triangle. If a one-dimensional party system existed, only four of the six preference rankings should occur. Let us for a moment assume a left–right dimension on which the parties are ranked from left to right in the order SPD–FDP–CDU/CSU. When we ask for preference rankings, the existence of preference types with a third rank for the FDP would not correspond with the left–right interpretation, because it would be impossible to unfold this joint scale out of the individual preference rankings. As can be seen from Table 2, the C–S–F and S–C–F type have been quite frequent at each point in time.

Until now I have interpreted the party system only in political and ideological terms. The empirical evidence supporting the interpretation was plausible, but not very strong. Now I shall analyse the social cleavages underlying the party system and try to show that they exerted a strong influence on the stability of the system.

IV. THE SOCIAL CLEAVAGES UNDERLYING THE PARTY SYSTEM

The dominant interpretation of the social cleavages underlying European party systems is that of a decline of traditional cleavage politics. Thus we have to analyse the stability of traditional cleavages. One result of this analysis will be that one major social group has changed its political alignment. But it will be shown or at least demonstrated as plausible that this change was fully compatible with the logic of the traditional cleavage system.

A social cleavage can be defined as an enduring coalition between a population group and a political party. A set of cleavages becomes a system when the coalitions have consequences not only for the relationship between group and party but also for the different outgroups. The coalition between group and party narrows down also the alignment of the different outgroups. This property of a cleavage system was the crucial insight of Lipset and Rokkan in their famous article on 'Cleavage Structures, Party Systems and Voter Alignments'.[9]

The major coalitions underlying the German party system are the alliance of the working class with the SPD and the coalition between the Catholics and the CDU/CSU. The problem is to delineate the cleavage system in the sense of identifying the opposing groups on the religious and the class dimensions.

The religious cleavage is more interesting in this respect because it had already been transformed immediately after the Second World War. With the founding of the Christian Democratic Union and Christian Social Union an alliance was formed between the religious traditionalists of the two major churches in Germany, the Catholics and the Lutherans. The fault line of the religious conflict thus does not run between Catholics and Protestants but between the religiously oriented and the secularised parts of the population. If we can still use the difference in the CDU vote between Catholics and Protestants as a cleavage indicator, then this is due to the fact that religious traditionalists are over-represented among Catholics and under-represented among Protestants.

In contrast to the religious cleavage, the class cleavage has had from the outset more the character of a zero-sum game between the population groups in question. It is important merely to understand that the main opponents are not status groups but social classes as aggregates of people with a common market capacity.[10] Thus, the widely used Alford index[11] as the percentage difference in vote for leftist parties between manual workers and the middle class is merely a measure of a surrogate conflict, and not the operationalisation of the main class conflict. I prefer the contrast in voting behaviour between manual workers and the self-employed as an index of the class vote, whereas the vote difference between manual and white-collar employees is supposed to be the index of a status group vote.

The empirical evidence for the stability of the traditional cleavage system underlying the German three-party system is presented in Table 3. Instead of percentage differences, the β-effects of a log-linear model were computed as cleavage indicators.[12]

The first important result of the table is the rather steady effect of religion on party preference. Catholics have had a much stronger tendency to vote for the CDU than for the two secular parties of the Liberals and Social Democrats in all election years since the 1950s. No special trend is visible in these figures and therefore the hypothesis of a decline of the religious cleavage can be rejected. The fault line in this dimension separates the religiously conservative CDU and the two secular parties of the Liberals and Social Democrats.

With regard to occupation, the main contrast of the vote for the two major parties is between manual workers and the self-employed. Contrary to much social science folklore, even the class cleavage in this sense has remained stable over time. It is interesting to know that compared with the CDU, the FDP has been the more bourgeois party, a trend which was weakened when the FDP formed a coalition government with the SPD. But after the change of coalition partner in October 1982, the self-employed came back to the FDP, and the small group of liberal workers was further diminished. The small liberal party always was firmly rooted on the secular side of the religious conflict, but it had to adjust somewhat to the clientele of the SPD during the period of the social–liberal government.

The only major change in the traditional cleavages occurred with the white-collar employees. They were originally more in favour of the CDU than of the SPD, but since the Grand Coalition of the late 1960s they have moved closer to the Social Democrats and, at least in the first years of the social–liberal government, also closer to the FDP.

TABLE 3

RELIGION AND OCCUPATION AS DETERMINANTS OF VOTING BEHAVIOUR IN
FEDERAL ELECTIONS SINCE 1953[1]

Contrasts [1] :	u	A	B_a	B_b	B_s	Model without three-way interaction x^2
1953						
SPD/CDU	−.61	−.55	.97	−.07	−.90	2.50
CDU/FDP	1.46	.66	.63	−.14	−.50	
1961						
SPD/CDU	−.58	−.58	.99	−.07	−.92	1.11
CDU/FDP	1.38	.48	.69	−.25	−.44	
1965						
SPD/CDU	−.52	−.60	.74	−.05	−.69	1.28
CDU/FDP	1.89	.55	.82	−.08	−.74	
1969						
SPD/CDU	−.32	−.42	.79	.31	−1.10	.95
CDU/FDP	2.72	1.00	.89	−.58	−.32	
1972						
SPD/CDU	.11	−.50	.84	.30	−1.14	10.51
CDU/FDP	1.24	.56	.18	−.53	.35	
1976						
SPD/CDU	−.37	−.63	.78	.23	−1.01	5.06
CDU/FDP	1.50	.62	.27	−.27	−.00	
1980						
SPD/CDU	−.34	−.58	.76	.37	−1.14	4.85
CDU/FDP	.98	.44	.20	−.37	.16	
1983						
SPD/CDU	−.61	−.43	.65	.31	−.96	10.11
CDU/FDP	2.07	.60	1.35	−.25	−1.10	

Note: 1. The determinants and their categories are as follows: (A) Catholics vs. Protestants;
(B) Occupation of head of household: (a) manual workers vs. (b) non-manual
employees vs. (s) self-employed (non-farm).

Sources: 1953 and 1983 pre-election surveys, in other years post-election surveys. For the data
from 1953 to 1972, see Franz Urban Pappi, 'Parteiensystem und Sozialstruktur in der
BundesRepublik', *Politische Vierteljahrestschrift*, Vol. 14, June 1973, pp. 191–213;
1976 and 1980, ZUMA–Bus, 1983 election study conducted by Werner Kaltefleiter,
Kiel University. Models computed by ECTA.

How can we interpret this movement? It is not sufficient to analyse only
the vote differences of the respective population groups. A second indicator
of the cleavage system is necessary which takes into account the political
meaning or main motivation of the average group member for a vote in
favour of the group's party. One can use political attitudes as intervening
variables between social structural determinants and party preference. I am
arguing that the membership in a population group will lead to a specific
attitude profile, either through socialisation or through common stimuli of

interest aggregation, and that these political attitudes will have a decisive influence on voting.

For the change in party alignment of white-collar employees two inter-pretations are possible. The first one is a class interpretation. One might argue with some Marxist sociologists that white-collar employees are part of the proletariat broadly defined. When this group changed its alignment from the 'bourgeois' CDU to the Social Democrats, this can be interpreted as the developing class-consciousness of that part of the proletariat which had had a false consciousness and political alignment before the change. An alternative interpretation would be that white-collared employees moved away from the CDU on the religious dimension into the direction of both SPD and FDP. Although the Christian Democrats became a little bit more liberal in the late 1960s and early 1970s, this was insufficient for the new middle class, which became the forerunner of a general secularisation. This is why a majority of this status group was attracted by the reform programme of the social–liberal government. Issues relevant for this programme were the influence of the churches in school politics, divorce laws and the regula-tion of abortion. These issues fitted quite nicely into the religious cleavage dimension. It was the prerogative of the social–liberal government in its early years to stress these issues even more than former governments led by the CDU, because many of the promised reforms were concerned with this issue area.

It is difficult to test these rival hypotheses, the class and the value change hypotheses, because we lack good survey evidence for the early years of the Federal Republic. One has to use proxy measures of the subjective meaning of both the class and religious conflict dimensions which are available for two elections far enough apart: the federal elections of 1953 and 1976. The class dimension is indicated by a favourable or unfavourable attitude towards the politics of the unions and the religious dimension by an attitude towards the legal regulation of divorce. The question wordings were the same for both surveys.

To test these rival hypotheses the following design was used:[13] it was first established which attitude has changed more over time, towards divorce or towards the unions, and whether the change caused a homogenisation of manual and white-collar workers; second, a test was used to discover whether the predictive power of these two attitudes for party preference remained stable. Stability in this respect would be a second argument for a stable cleavage system, evaluated this time from the perspective of the political meaning of the old cleavages. If we are able to accept this stability of predictors in the past, we may argue in the third place that the political reorientation of the new middle class can best be explained by that specific attitude variable which has changed most in this population group.

The most impressive result of this analysis was the massive change of the indicator of the religious dimension, whereas attitudes towards the unions did not change much. Manual and white-collar workers came only slightly closer to each other with regard to their 'class consciousness', whereas they drifted apart on the religious dimension. Manual workers were always more conservative in their attitude towards divorce than the new middle class, but this gap was larger in 1976 than in 1953. In addition, the predictive power of the attitudes for the two-party vote remained rather stable, at least for the new middle class. One can conclude, therefore, that the value change hypothesis is corroborated. The class hypothesis can be rejected.

Generally, the old cleavage system remained quite stable even with regard to the stronger, second criterion. My interpretation of the partial reorientation of the new middle class is more parsimonious than the far-reaching assumption of a 'new politics' dimension.[14] The value change, which without doubt was taking place over the past two decades, fitted the already existing religious dimension of German politics. The old party system was a perfect mechanism for transmitting the demands of the increasing numbers of secular voters.

V. THE NEW PARTY OF THE GREENS

With the federal election of 1983, the German three-party system came to an end. For the first time since the 1950s, a fourth party was able to cross the five per cent threshold. The Greens, a new party which had started five years earlier as an environmentalist movement, gained 5.6 per cent of the vote and are now represented in the Bundestag.

The voters for this new party belong mainly to the better-educated groups of the young generation. University towns, for instance, are major strongholds of the Greens. This clear social structural basis cannot be interpreted directly as a new social cleavage. The younger generation is generally more accessible to new movements and it has yet to be seen whether a new coalition can be formed between the Greens and a population group whose composition is changing all the time due to normal changes in the life cycle. On the other hand, the Greens do not stress an interest policy in favour of their clientele. They are interested in public goods such as environmental protection which have been sadly neglected by the established parties.

The best explanatory strategy for new parties such as the Greens is to look for political causes and not social structural ones. A new political agenda was developing in the late 1970s, with issues such as the protection of the natural environment, nuclear power stations and disagreements with the defence policy of NATO. A vigorous West German peace movement, for example, fought the official policy which favoured the deployment of new medium-range missiles. Members of the Green party are among the leaders of this movement as they were at the forefront of the demonstrations against new nuclear power stations. At least up to October 1982, when the federal government was led by an SPD Chancellor, not one of the established parties was able to aggregate votes from the diverse protest movements.

To study the mass basis of these new political conflicts, the political attitudes of the general public and of the voters for the different parties have to be analysed directly. In Table 4, data on some political attitudes are presented for post-election studies of 1980 and 1983. The SPD as the party of traditional class politics advocated egalitarian old age pensions in its campaign platform 1980 and argued strongly in favour of a legal prohibition of

TABLE 4

SELECTED ISSUE POSITIONS[1] OF THE GERMAN VOTER IN 1980 AND 1983

	Party preference				Total
Issues 1980/81	CDU/CSU	FDP	SPD	Greens	
1. For egalitarian old age pension	2.9	3.2	3.3	5.0	3.1
2. For legal inhibition of lock-outs	3.4	3.3	4.1	5.8	3.8
3. For liberal abortion law	2.8	4.3	4.5	5.3	3.8
4. For medium range missile deployment	5.0	3.9	3.8	1.7	4.3
5. For nuclear power plants	4.7	3.7	3.9	1.3	4.2
Issues October 1983	CDU/CSU	FDP	SPD	Greens	
3. For liberal abortion law	2.5	3.5	3.8	5.3	3.3
4. For medium range missile deployment	4.0	4.0	2.8	1.5	3.3

Note: 1. 7-point scales with labelled end-points. All table entries are means. The higher the mean, the more in favour of the mentioned issue position.

Sources: ZUMA–Bus 1980/81 and EMNID survey of October 1983. Both surveys are representative of the population eligible to vote in federal elections.

lock-outs. The abortion issue is related to the religious dimension and was emphasised most by the FDP in 1980.

As one would have expected, voters for the Green party have extreme attitudes with respect to the two new issues 4 and 5, whereas the voters of the old parties were closer together and opposed to the positions of the Greens. More interesting, however, are the attitudes of the Greens towards issues covering the traditional cleavages, especially class-politics issues. Here, voters for the Greens are more in agreement with the official party politics of the SPD than are Social Democratic voters. The Greens, therefore, not only represent an anti-establishment protest of the young generation in the policy area of the new issues, but they are also strongly pushed in a socialist direction, either by their voters or by party activists. For this reason the new conflict dimension is not orthogonal to the traditional political cleavages. This will help the SPD as a party no longer in government to win at least part of the clientele of the Greens, although the SPD will have to change some of its policies to become more attractive to former Green voters. That the party elite is willing to pay attention to policy options first outlined by the new political movements became clear during the last party convention when a huge majority voted against the deployment of new nuclear missiles, thus rejecting the politics of their former Chancellor.

The data on sympathy rankings of the parties show, too, that the Greens were not able to establish a completely new policy dimension. In section III above, the existence of all six preference types which are logically possible with three parties was taken as evidence for a fully-fledged three-party system. We can use the same strategy to study the independence of the fourth party at mass level.

In Table 5, the preference rankings of the three established parties are broken down further according to the rank of the Greens. Whereas in 1980 the Greens could make major inroads among both SPD and FDP supporters, in 1983 they still ranked highest among SPD sympathisers. The FDP and CDU/CSU camp remained now quite resistant to the appeals of the Greens: 92 per cent of voters who sympathised most with the Greens took the SPD as second choice. In 1980, this percentage had already been a quite substantial 71 per cent. One can surmise that the conservative environmentalists are no longer of importance for the Green party, whose voters are overwhelmingly former leftist Social Democrats.

The movement from the SPD to the Greens was caused by the compromise politics of the SPD while in government. This policy alienated the more radical wing of the party, especially when it had no roots in the labour movement. The environmentalist movement functioned as a crystallisation device for the unrest on the left. Today, as an opposition party, the SPD is in a good position to reintegrate a substantial part of its former more radical clientele. If the SPD is able to channel the Green protest vote back to mainstream politics, the fourth party of the Greens will have been just a short episode in the life of the German party system.

VI. CONCLUSION

In this article, I have stressed the stabilising factors of the German three-party system. An important argument has been that this party system is firmly rooted in the historical circumstances of the period immediately after the Second World War and in the social structure of German society. These factors are, of course, no guarantee of everlasting stability; the success of the Greens at the 1983 election showed that political realignments can occur outside the established party system and not only within it, as in earlier years.

It is a great challenge to predict the development of the German party system in the near future. Since every system has a certain structural inertia, the stabilising factors are working in favour of the three established parties. The party leaders should be able to exploit these factors without losing track of new political conflicts. But if they lose their responsiveness to new political movements, those movements will get the chance to stabilise their following and become a part of the established structures themselves.

It is possible to comprehend this whole process only when one takes three levels of analyses into consideration. I dealt with the party elites and their

TABLE 5

THE RANK OF THE GREEN PARTY RELATIVE TO THE RANKINGS OF THE THREE ESTABLISHED PARTIES IN SEPTEMBER 1980 AND IN FEBRUARY 1983

Rank of the Greens	Rank Order of the Three Established Parties													% total	
	C-S-F		C-F-S		F-C-S		F-S-C		S-F-C		S-C-F				
	1980	1983	1980	1983	1980	1983	1980	1983	1980	1983	1980	1983		1980	1983
4th rank	85	80	72	92	61	81	70	80	59	40	76	47		68.5	65.7
3rd rank	9	13	18	6	22	13	20	20	28	8	10	24		20.4	14.1
2nd rank	5	4	10	2	4	6	3	–	8	37	11	22		7.8	15.2
1st rank	1	2	0	–	13	–	7	–	5	14	3	6		3.4	4.9
Total %	100	100	100	100	100	100	100	100	100	100	100	100		100	100
% of total 1980	17.1		21.3		2.3		6.1		45.2		8.0				
% of total 1983		16.4		29.7		1.5		1.0		15.6		35.8			
% 1st rank of row total in 1980	6		3		9		12		65		6			100	
in 1983		8		–		–		–		45		47			100

Note: 1. C = CDU/CSU, S = SPD, F = FDP.

mass following in this article, but skipped over the level of the party activists. These people, being active in the local organisations of the parties, may well be most responsive to new political trends. They enter and leave the organisations and can change the character of a party more than becomes visible at mass or elite levels. To get a complete picture of the German party system, one should consult the literature on party members and the factions within parties. The SPD and the Greens are especially interesting in this respect. The SPD is gradually losing its character as a working-class party owing to the strong influence of young party activists with university degrees who are generally employed in the public sector.[15] The party activists of the Greens come from the same stratum. It is estimated that one half of the inner circle of activists of the Green party are former members of unorthodox communist splinter groups which flourished among the student generation of the 1970s.[16]

In general interpretations of the German party system, some authors argue that traditional cleavages are of declining importance and that the voters, therefore, are becoming more volatile and responsive to new political conflicts.[17] Aggregate measures of volatility are not very helpful in this respect because the individual voter may be volatile within a stable aggregate system.[18] But when the party system is rather stable and traditional social cleavages are still vigorous, it is more fascinating to explain the forces of stability than the subtleties of change. These forces of stability may help the SPD to reintegrate the leftist protest vote, even if the Social Democrats become less attractive to the median voter for a certain period of time.

NOTES

1. Cf. M. McCauley, 'The Rebirth of Democracy: Political Parties in Germany', in H. Döring and G. Smith (eds.), *Party Government and Political Culture in Western Germany* (London and Basingstoke: Macmillan, 1982), p.54.
2. Cf. H. Rattinger, 'Measuring Power in Voting Bodies: Linear Constraints, Spatial Analysis, and a Computer Programme', in M.J. Holler (ed.), *Power, Voting, and Voting Power* (Würzburg and Wien: Physica–Verlag, 1982), p.223.
3. Cf. E. Bonsdorf, 'The Distribution of Power in Specific Decision-Making Bodies', in M.J. Holler (ed.), op. cit., p.285 for the power indices.
4. Cf. W. Kaltefleiter, *Zwischen Konsens und Krise: Eine Analyse der Bundestagswahl 1972* (Cologne: Carl Heymanns Verlag, 1973); and B. Vogel and R.–O. Schultze, 'Deutschland', in D. Sternberger and B. Vogel (eds.), *Die Wahl der Parlamente und anderer Staatsorgane, Band 1: Europa*, erster Halbband (Berlin: Walter de Gruyter, 1969), pp.189–411.
5. Cf. H.–D. Klingemann, 'Testing the Left–Right Continuum on a Sample of German Voters', *Comparative Political Studies*, Vol.5 (April 1972), pp.93–106.
6. Cf. R. Axelrod, *Conflict of Interest* (Chicago: Markham, 1970).
7. Cf. C. Offe, 'The Attribution of Public Status to Interest Groups: Observations on the West German Case', in S. Berger (ed.), *Organizing Interests in Western Europe* (Cambridge: Cambridge University Press, 1981), pp.123–58.
8. Cf. P. Pulzer, 'Responsible Party Government in the German Political System', in H. Döring and G. Smith (eds.), op. cit., pp.9–37.
9. Cf. S.M. Lipset and S. Rokkan (eds.), *Party Systems and Voter Alignments: Cross-National Perspectives* (New York: Free Press, 1967).

10. Cf. A. Giddens, *The Class Structure of Advanced Societies* (London: Hutchinson University Library, 1973).
11. Cf. R.R. Alford, *Party and Society: The Anglo-American Democracies* (Chicago: Rand McNally, 1963).
12. Cf. L.A. Goodman, 'A Modified Multiple Regression Approach to the Analysis of Dichotomous Variables', *American Sociological Review*, Vol. 37 (February 1972), pp. 28–45.
13. Cf. F.U. Pappi and M. Terwey, 'The German Electorate: Old Cleavages and New Political Conflicts', in H. Döring and G. Smith (eds.), op. cit., pp. 174–96.
14. Cf. K. Hildebrandt and R.J. Dalton, 'Die neue Politik: Politischer Wandel oder Schönwetterpolitik?', in M. Kaase (ed.), *Wahlsoziologie heute, Politische Vierteljahresschrift*, Vol. 18 (November 1977), pp. 230–56.
15. Cf. U. Feist and K. Liepelt, 'Neue Eliten in alten Parteien. Anmerkungen zu einer Nebenfolge der Bildungsreform', in M. Kaase and H.–D. Klingemann (eds.), *Wahlen und politisches System* (Opladen: Westdeutscher Verlag, 1983), pp. 81–100.
16. Cf. W. Kaltefleiter, 'The Greens, Alternatives and the Peace Movement: A Challenge to the German Party System', in R.L. Pfaltzgraff, Jr, *et al.*, *The Greens of West Germany: Origins, Strategies, and Transatlantic Implications* (Cambridge, MA, and Washington, DC: Institute for Foreign Policy Analysis, 1983), pp. 86–105.
17. Cf. K.L. Baker, R.J. Dalton and K. Hildebrandt, *Germany Transformed: Political Culture and the New Politics* (Cambridge, MA, and London: Harvard University Press, 1981).
18. M.N. Pedersen, 'Changing Patterns of Electoral Volatility in European Party Systems, 1948–1977: Explorations in Explanation', in H. Daalder and P. Mair (eds.), *West European Party Systems: Continuity and Change* (Beverley Hills and London: Sage Publications, 1983), pp. 29–66.

Britain: Still a Two-Party System?

Philip Norton

In categorisations of party systems, the two-party system is, as Sartori noted, by far the best-known category.[1] Yet, as the same author went on to observe, few countries have such a system. Of those that do, Britain is presented as a 'perfect' two-party system in that it enjoys both the format and the properties of two-partism. Two parties are in a position to compete for the absolute majority of seats. One of the two parties actually succeeds in winning a parliamentary majority; that party is then willing to govern alone. And alternation or rotation in power remains a credible expectation.[2] Britain, in short, has been the very model of a modern two-party system.

To what extent does this remain the case? The purpose of this article is to address that question. It does so through a consideration of (a) the degree of support for the two largest parties, the Conservative and Labour Parties, in Britain; (b) the decline in that support over the past two decades; (c) explanations of that decline; and (d) the extent to which Britain retains a two-party system.[3] Does Britain retain the format and properties of a two-party system? Or is a new categorisation necessary?

(A) STRENGTH OF PARTY SUPPORT 1950–66

During the 1950s and the first half of the 1960s, the Conservative and Labour Parties were dominant at both the mass (electoral) and the elite (parliamentary) levels. Indeed, five generalisations can be drawn pertinent to party support in this period:

1. there was a high turnout of electors in general elections;
2. of those who voted, virtually all voted for either the Conservative or Labour Parties;
3. independent of their behaviour in the polling booths, most electors identified with one or other of the two main parties;
4. each party had a large membership, as well as a developed organisation;
5. at the parliamentary level, the two parties faced one another in disciplined, highly cohesive ranks.

The first and second generalisations are borne out by the data in Table 1. Turnout reached a peak in the 1950 general election, when 84 per cent of those on the electoral register cast a ballot.[4] At each of the five subsequent elections, more than three-quarters of electors turned out to vote. The proportion of voters casting their ballots for one or other of the two main parties reached a peak in the 1951 general election when nearly 97 per cent voted Conservative or Labour. In each of the subsequent four elections, approximately nine out of ten electors going to the polls voted for a Conservative or Labour candidate. The proportion slipped slightly in the 1964 election but showed an increase in the subsequent election held seventeen months later.

TABLE 1

TURNOUT AND TWO-PARTY VOTING: GENERAL ELECTIONS 1950–66

General election	Turnout %	Of those voting, percentage voting Conservative or Labour
1950	84.0	87.6
1951	82.5	96.8
1955	76.7	96.1
1959	78.8	93.2
1964	77.1	87.5
1966	75.8	89.8

Since the 1960s, surveys have asked respondents whether they thought of themselves as being 'Conservative, Labour, Liberal, or what?' The extent of this party identification, or what Butler and Stokes referred to as 'partisan self-image', is shown in Table 2. In the three years covered, 80 per cent or more of respondents identified with the Conservative or Labour Parties. Of those expressing an identification, three quarters or more (and 90 per cent in 1966) expressed a 'strong' or 'fairly strong' identification. There was a strong positive correlation between party identification and voting preference, though with the former proving somewhat more enduring than the latter.[5]

Though a majority of electors voted for and identified with one of the two main parties, only a minority took the positive step of becoming party members. The minority nonetheless was a significant one. Accurate figures for party memberships are not readily available. The recruitment of members is undertaken usually by local party associations and poor record-keeping coupled with some status-seeking can produce suspect figures for local party memberships.[6] Some generalisations are nonetheless possible. In terms of direct membership (individuals taking the positive step of seeking membership and paying a membership subscription) the Conservative Party was the larger of the two parties and in the early 1950s had a membership which was well in excess of two million: in 1953 it claimed a membership of 2,805,832.[7] The Labour Party achieved a peak membership figure around the same time, claiming a membership of just over one million in 1951 and 1952.[8] As with the Conservative Party, this was an exceptional figure. Nonetheless, at no time between 1950 and 1966 did it claim a membership of less than 750,000. It enjoyed also the advantage of a large affiliated membership. Members of trade unions which were affiliated to the Labour Party

TABLE 2

PARTY IDENTIFICATION 1963–66

'Generally speaking, do you usually think of yourself as Conservative, Labour or Liberal (or what)? How strongly (chosen party) do you generally feel – very strongly, fairly strongly, or not very strongly?'

| | Year | | |
Party	1963 %	1964 %	1966 %
Conservative	36	39	35
Labour	44	42	46
Liberal	10	12	10
None	8	5	7
Don't Know/Other	2	2	2
Very strongly	36	47	48
Fairly strongly	43	41	42
Not very strongly	21	12	10

Source: D. Butler and D. Stokes, *Political Change in Britain*, 2nd ed., (London: Macmillan, 1974), Appendix B, question 36, p. 470.

automatically became members of the party (unless they took the positive action of formally 'opting out') and paid a political levy. This provided the party with an extra membership of more than five million and a substantial, and welcome, income.[9] By contrast, the third party in Britain, the Liberal Party, had a membership of under 250,000.[10]

The activity of the more committed party members provided both major parties with the manpower resources necessary to sustain election campaigns, to recruit new members and to raise funds. (Given strict statutory limitations on campaign financing, election campaigns in Britain are as labour-intensive as they are capital-intensive.) Income from members was supplemented by more significant contributions from outside bodies: nearly two thirds of the Conservative Party's income nationally came from institutions such as companies, banks and partnerships; about 90 per cent of the Labour Party's income nationally came from trade unions.[11] In non-election years, the Conservative income nationally varied between half a million and one million pounds; Labour's national income varied between £170,000 and £380,000. During the same period, the Liberal Party income nationally never reached six figures.[12]

This income helped sustain a professional organisation, especially so in the case of the Conservative Party. Both main parties maintained headquarters in Smith Square, Westminister (close to Parliament) with full-time staff, and both had regional offices. Well over 50 per cent of Conservative local associations employed full-time agents (in essence, professional executive officers), with part-time or shared agents being employed by about one half of the remaining associations. Of local Labour parties, about one quarter had full- or part-time agents. As for the Liberal Party, it appears throughout the 1950s to have had fewer than 50 agents in total: in 1955 the number was 27.[13]

The dominance of the two main parties was even more marked at the parliamentary than at the electoral level. The first-past-the-post electoral system worked to the disadvantage of third parties that had support which was fairly evenly spread throughout the country. This was notably so in the case of the Liberal Party: though it achieved between 2.5 per cent and 11.2 per cent of the total vote in the six general elections in this period, it never gained as many as two per cent of the seats in the House of Commons. With the exception of the 1966 general election, the two main parties won 98 per cent or more of the seats in the Commons; in 1966, the proportion was 97.8 per cent.

Within Parliament, the Conservative and Labour Parties were notable for their degree of internal cohesion. Cross-voting in the House of Commons was unusual and rarely serious. Indeed, there were actually two parliamentary sessions in the 1950s in which not one Conservative Member cast a vote dissenting from the line of the party leadership.[14] The number of divisions (parliamentary votes) in which one or more Conservative or Labour Members voted against their own side in the parliaments of 1945 to 1966 is provided in Table 3. There was an increase in the number in the 1959 and 1966 parliaments, but both were parliaments in which the government of the day had a three-figure majority. The government was thus more able to sustain cross-voting than was the case in the preceding parliaments when the government's overall majority was smaller. On no occasion during this period was a government defeated in the division lobbies as a result of its own supporters entering the opposition lobby. The degree of cohesion was such that a noted academic observer, Samuel H. Beer, could write in the 1960s that there was no longer any point in measuring it.[15] The voting behaviour of MPs was predictable. The two parties faced one another in highly cohesive ranks. The handful of Liberal MPs had little impact, leading generally an isolated existence.[16] The House of Commons operated on the basis of two large opposing parties. Those parties, in practice, were the Conservative and Labour Parties.

(B) DECLINE IN SUPPORT 1966–1983

In the latter half of the 1960s and, more especially, during the 1970s and early 1980s the Conservative and Labour Parties witnessed a decline in their strength at the electoral, organisational and parliamentary levels. All five generalisations listed above remained valid but in need of serious qualification.

In the 1970 general election turnout dropped to 72 per cent and in two of the next four elections did not reach 73 per cent. Of those turning out to vote, a smaller percentage than before voted for the Conservative and

TABLE 3

DISSENTING VOTES IN THE HOUSE OF COMMONS 1945–70

Parliament (Number of sessions in parenthesis)	Number of divisions witnessing dissenting votes			Number of divisions witnessing dissenting votes expressed as % of all divisions
	TOTAL	LAB.	CON.	
1945–50 (4)	87	79 [1]	27 [1]	7
1950–51 (2)	6	5	2	2.5
1951–55 (4)	25	17	11	3
1955–59 (4)	19	10	12	2
1959–64 (5)	137	26	120	13.5
1964–66 (2)	2	1	1	0.5
1966–70 (4)	124	109	41	9.5

Note: 1. As one division may involve dissenting votes cast by members of both parties, Labour and Conservative figures do not necessarily add up to the total on the left.

Source: P. Norton, *Dissension in the House of Commons 1945–74* (London: Macmillan, 1975), p. 609.

Labour candidates (Table 4). The biggest slump in support for the two parties occurred in the 1983 general election (Table 5). Though the two parties retained their parliamentary hegemony, their electoral dominance was challenged by the new Social Democratic/Liberal Alliance (formed in 1981) which attracted more than one quarter of the votes cast. Thirty per cent of those who went to the polls voted for a party other than the Conservative or Labour Parties. (In the 1951 general election, the proportion had been 3.2 per cent.) Of all citizens on the electoral register, approximately half of them actually went to the polls to vote Conservative or Labour: the rest either stayed away or voted for another party.

TABLE 4

TURNOUT AND TWO-PARTY VOTING: GENERAL ELECTIONS 1970–83

General election	Turnout %	Of those voting, percentage voting Conservative or Labour
1970	72.0	89.4
1974 (Feb.)	78.7	75.0
1974 (Oct.)	72.8	75.0
1979	76.0	80.8
1983	72.7	70.0

TABLE 5

GENERAL ELECTION RESULT 1983[1]

Party	Votes Won		Number of seats won	
Conservative	13,012,602	(42.4%)	397	(61.1%)
Labour	8,457,124	(27.6%)	209	(32.1%)
SDP/Liberal Alliance	7,780,577	(25.4%)	23	(3.5%)
Scottish National	331,975	(1.1%)	2	(0.3%)
Plaid Cymru	125,309	(0.4%)	2	(0.3%)
Others (Great Britain)	198,834	(0.6%)	0	(0.0%)
Others (Northern Ireland)	764,474	(2.5%)	17	(2.6%)
Total	30,670,895	(100.0%)	650	(99.9%)[2]

Notes: 1. Turnout: 72.7%.
2. Does not add up to 100% because of rounding.

There was also a decline in party identification. In 1964 somewhat over 90 per cent of electors identified with the Conservative, Labour or Liberal Parties. In 1979 the proportion was down to 85 per cent (Table 6). Much more significant was the decline in the number of 'very strong' identifiers. In 1964, 40 per cent of electors thought of themselves as 'very strong' identifiers. By 1979 the proportion was down to 21 per cent. 'Almost all of this decline reflects a diminution of strongly committed support for the two main parties ... both of the major parties must now face the fact that their hard core of supporters, with a firm sense of party allegiance, has shrunk to a tenth of the electorate.'[17]

Both parties also witnessed a decline in organisational support. The membership figures achieved in the early 1950s were exceptional and showed a decline in the rest of the decade. By the mid 1970s, the Conservative Party is believed to have had a membership of approximately 1½ million, roughly half its peak membership figure of 1953. The decline in membership of its youth wing, the Young Conservatives, was more dramatic. After reaching a peak membership of 157,000 in 1949, it declined to 50,000 in 1968 and was put at 27,500 in 1978.[18] Whereas Conservative membership appears to have levelled off at the 1–1½ million level, Labour Party membership has been subject to a constant and dramatic decline since the early 1950s.[19] By the late 1960s, the party claimed a membership of approximately 700,000, though a survey carried out for the Nuffield election studies suggested the real figure was a little over 300,000.[20] By 1978 it was estimated that the party had a membership of about 250,000.[21] Of these, only about a quarter were believed to be active members.

The finances of both parties also came under strain with detrimental consequences for party organisation. The Conservative Party suffered a decline in contributions from business sources, and heavy campaign spending in election campaigns resulted in it incurring considerable financial

TABLE 6

PARTY IDENTIFICATION 1964–79

Generally speaking, respondents who thought of themselves as:				General election		
	1964	1966	1970	1974 Feb.	1974 Oct.	1979
	%	%	%	%	%	%
Conservative	39	35	39	35	34	38
Labour	42	45	42	40	40	36
Liberal	11	10	8	13	14	11
TOTAL:	92	90	89	88	88	85
Strength of party identification:	%	%	%	%	%	%
Very strong	43	43	41	29	26	21
Fairly strong	38	38	36	42	45	45
Not very strong	11	9	11	17	17	7

Source: B. Sarlvik and I. Crewe, *Decade of Dealignment* (Cambridge: Cambridge University Press, 1983), pp. 334–6.

losses in 1964, 1974 and 1979. By 1980 it was estimated that the party's Central Office had exhausted its reserves and was resorting to bank loans to cover its day-to-day operations.[22] The consequence was a number of economy measures. The party closed a college it ran in North Yorkshire, Central Office was rationalised with the loss of a proportion of the staff, and regional offices were slimmed down. Constituency associations found it increasingly difficult to employ agents, and between 1966 and 1980 the number of agents declined by nearly 100. The Labour Party encountered similar difficulties. Though its income increased, so too did its expenditure. It remained heavily dependent upon union support and the unions proved cautious in making funds available for election campaign use.[23] At the 1982 party conference, the party treasurer reported that a deficit of more than £1 million had been carried forward from 1981 to 1982. Constituency parties have encountered severe problems in raising sufficient funds to retain the services of full-time agents. The number of agents showed a marked decline from 1959 onwards and by 1974 there were only 120; the number has declined even further since. In the mid-1970s, in response to the Houghton Committee survey, most constituency associations reported that they were in 'serious or moderate financial difficulties'. Local Labour parties were more likely to report being in difficulty than Conservative ones.[24]

The increase in electoral support had an effect, albeit a relatively marginal one, on the number of MPs representing minor parties sitting in the House of Commons. More significant changes took place in the behaviour of the two largest parliamentary parties. Conservative and Labour MPs proved willing to vote against their party leaders more often than before and with much greater effect. There was an upsurge in intra-party dissent on the Conservative benches during the 1970–74 Parliament. Conservative Members cross-voted in far more divisions (see Table 7) and with greater effect than ever before. The government suffered six defeats in the division lobbies, three of them on three-line whips, and all because Conservative MPs voted with the Labour opposition.[25] In the 1974–79 parliament, Labour MPs proved to be notably dissident. In the period from 1974 to 1979, government was vulnerable to defeat through backbenchers voting with the opposition and (in 1974 and from April 1976 to March 1979) through the opposition parties combining against a minority government. Prior to 1970, no post-war government had been vulnerable to such defeats. In the short 1974 Parliament, the minority Labour government suffered 17 defeats, the product of opposition parties combining against it. In the 1974–79 Parliament, the government was defeated 42 times: 23 of these defeats were the product of Labour MPs voting with the Conservatives, the remaining 19 the result of opposition parties combining in the lobby against the government.[26] In the last session of the parliament, almost half of all divisions witnessed one or more Labour Members going in to the opposite lobby to that of the government. What Beer had termed the 'Prussian discipline' of MPs seemed to be no more. Intra-party dissent remained a feature of the 1979–83 parliament: despite an overall majority in the House, the Conservative government suffered one defeat and retreated on a number of occasions under threat of defeat.[27] In the first session of the new 1983 parliament, the government witnessed a string of embarrassing cross-votes in the division lobbies.[28] Members of Parliament, as Beer noted, appeared to be jettisoning a deferential attitude to government in favour of a more participant one.

TABLE 7

DISSENTING VOTES IN THE HOUSE OF COMMONS 1970–79

Parliament: (Number of sessions in parenthesis)	Number of divisions witnessing dissenting votes:			Number of divisions witnessing dissenting votes expressed as % of all divisions
	TOTAL	LAB.	CON.	
1970–74 (4)	221	34[1]	204[1]	20
1974 (1)	25	8	21	23
1974–79 (5)	423	309	240	28

Note: 1. As one division may witness dissenting votes by Conservative and Labour Members, the Labour and Conservative figures do not necessarily add up to the total on the left.

Source: P. Norton, *Dissension in the House of Commons 1974–1979* (Oxford: Oxford University Press, 1980), p. 428.

By 1984 the Conservative and Labour Parties were clearly not the bodies that they were in the 1950s and 1960s. Both had experienced a loss of electoral support: the 1983 general election result was the worst result for the

Labour Party since the general election of 1918. Both had witnessed 'strong' identifiers drifting away from their attachment to party. Organisationally and financially, both were much weakened and unable to sustain the level of full-time workers that they had enjoyed in the heyday of the 1950s. Within Parliament, both were having difficulty in ensuring that their MPs gave their unstinting support to the party line. With justice, one could thus talk of a 'decline' of the two parties from the decades of the 1950s and 1960s.

(C) EXPLANATIONS OF DECLINE

What might explain the loss of support experienced by the Conservative and Labour Parties over the past two decades? Various explanations have been offered. Those that have sought to explain why electors are now less likely to vote for, identify with or join either of the two main parties can be subsumed under four headings: class, issues, consensus, and the two-party system.

Class

In post-war years, the most significant predictor of party voting has been class. Taking occupation as the basic criterion for determining class, it is usual for analysts to distinguish between the middle class (comprising managerial, professional, skilled or supervisory non-manual and lower non-manual occupations) and the working class (comprising skilled and unskilled manual workers, pensioners and residual categories). In their 1970 survey, Butler and Stokes found that 'virtually everyone accepted the conventional class dichotomy between middle and working class'.[29] In terms of self-ascription, 77 per cent spontaneously described themselves as middle or working class, with a further five per cent adding a slight qualification such as 'upper-middle' class. All but one per cent of the remainder were willing, when prompted, to assign themselves a middle- or working-class label.

The relationship between class and party has been a close one. In the general elections held in the 1950s, 70 per cent or more of middle-class voters voted for the Conservative Party. In the 1960s, 60 per cent or more of working-class voters cast their votes for the Labour Party.[30] Party support was most marked at the two extremes of the social scale. In 1951, 90 per cent of the upper-middle class voted Conservative. In 1966, 72 per cent of the 'very poor' voted Labour.[31] Class was not an exclusive predictor of voting behaviour, nor was the relationship between class and party symmetrical: the middle class was more Conservative than the working class was Labour. One third of working-class voters regularly voted Conservative. Nonetheless, class remained the most important predictor of how an elector might vote. So much so that one writer, Peter Pulzer, was to write in 1967 that 'class is the basis of British party politics: all else is embellishment and detail'.[32]

The 1970s provided a somewhat different picture. The class-party nexus waned. The middle class, especially in the mid-1970s, was less Conservative than it had previously been. More significantly, Labour support declined among the working class. Whereas in pre-1970 general elections more than 60 per cent of working-class voters had supported the Labour Party, in the general elections of the 1970s the proportion was less than 60 per cent (see

Table 8). In the 1979 general election only one in two of working-class voters cast their ballots for Labour candidates. In the 1983 election the proportion was less than one in two. The gap between Labour's share of the manual and non-manual votes, 40 per cent in 1959 and 27 per cent in 1979, was only 21 per cent in 1983.[33] The Conservatives made no significant inroads among their traditional class supporters, though they did attract the support of almost one in three of trade unionists. The 1983 general election was significant also not only for the size but also for the composition of the vote accruing to the SDP/Liberal Alliance. In previous elections, the Liberal Party had drawn its support from across the social spectrum, though marginally more so from the middle than the working class. In 1983, the Alliance drew its support more or less evenly from all social groups (Table 9). As a predictor of party choice, class was significantly less reliable than before.

TABLE 9

VOTE BY SOCIAL CLASS: GENERAL ELECTION 1983 (PERCENTAGES)

Party	Professional and managerial	Office and clerical	Skilled manual	Semi-skilled and unskilled manual	Trade unionists	Unemployed
	%	%	%	%	%	%
Conservative	62	55	39	29	32	30
Labour	12	21	35	44	39	45
SDP/Liberal	27	24	27	28	28	26

Source: Gallup Poll, undertaken for the BBC, on 8 and 9 June 1983. Published in *Guardian*, 13 June 1983.

The importance of the decline in the class–party nexus, however, should not be over-stated.[34] The decline is relative. Social class continues to structure party choice, more so than any other variables such as age, sex or religion, which continue to have no significant predictive value (except, in the case of religion, in Northern Ireland). As the central variable of class – occupation – has declined in importance in structuring party voting (along with another central variable identified by Franklin: parents' class),[35] class-supportive variables have become more important, notably housing tenure (whether owning or renting) and trade union membership. Given the pattern of home ownership in Britain and the concentration of trade union members in particular areas, the effect would appear to have been to increase the power of class to structure partisanship at the constituency level.[36] Furthermore, to identify a decline in the class–party nexus is not to provide an explanation for the *decline* in support for the two main parties. The loosening of the relationship may have facilitated changes in party support but in itself does provide a causal explanation.

TABLE 8
CLASS VOTING 1959–79

Election	1959		1964		1966		1970		February 1974		October 1974		1979	
Class	Non-Manual	Manual	Non-Manual	Manual	Non-Manual	Manual	Non-Manual	Manual	Non-Manual	Manual	Non-Manual	Manual	Non-Manual	Manual
Party Support	%	%	%	%	%	%	%	%	%	%	%	%	%	%
Conservative	69	34	62	28	60	25	64	33	53	24	51	24	60	35
Liberal or minor party	8	4	16	8	14	6	11	9	25	19	24	20	17	15
Labour	22	62	22	64	26	69	25	58	22	57	25	57	23	50
Total	100	100	100	100	100	100	100	100	100	100	100	100	100	100
(N)	(526)	(792)	(595)	(914)	(595)	(945)	(392)	(577)	(893)	(1,060)	(834)	(1,010)	(650)	(779)
Class index of Labour voting (i.e. gap between manual and non-manual)	40		42		43		33		35		32		27	
Non-manual Conservative + manual Labour voters as % of all voters	65		63		66		60		55		54		55	

Source: B. Särlvik and I. Crewe, *Decade of Dealignment* (Cambridge: Cambridge University Press, 1983), p. 87.

Issues

Given the decline in the class–party nexus, a number of analyses have emphasised the importance of issues: 'An electorate which saw politics less in class terms could respond to other issues and events.'[37] One hypothesis was that the decline in support for the two main parties was attributable to new issues coming on to the agenda of political debate to which the established parties could not provide a structured and cohesive response.[38] Notable examples of such issues were Britain's membership of the European Communities and a prices-and-incomes policy.[39] A separate hypothesis was that the decline in support for the Labour Party was the result of a widening gulf between the party's traditional stance on a number of issues and the views of Labour supporters. Labour supporters, it was argued, were moving further away from the stance taken by the party. 'What was already an ideological split in the 1960s', writes Crewe, 'had turned into an ideological chasm by 1979.'[40]

There is little empirical evidence to support the first hypothesis. The two parties were unable to provide an internally unified response to important new issues on the political agenda, and the emergence of these issues may provide a partial explanation for the increase in intra-party dissent in the parliamentary parties.[41] However, there is little evidence that the parties' stances on these issues generated a loss of electoral support, at least not directly. Electors were confused as to the position of the parties on these issues, but Särlvik and Crewe found that in 1979 the issue of the European Communities was among those that made the least difference to individual voting decisions.[42] The balance of opinions on an incomes policy was one that favoured the Conservatives.[43] Furthermore, dissatisfaction with the two main parties because of their stance on new issues such as EC membership would not explain an increase in support for the Liberals or, subsequently, the SDP/Liberal Alliance. Even among its stable supporters, the Liberal Party in 1979 appeared to obtain no more than limited support for its position on the EC and incomes policy.[44]

The second hypothesis has somewhat more empirical evidence to support it. The analysis of Ivor Crewe and his associates found that on certain issues such as nationalisation, Labour voters were moving away from the position taken by the Labour Party. Indeed, on issues which electors considered important, there was a perceptible shift between 1974 and 1979 in favour of the Conservative position.[45] A sophisticated analysis by Mark Franklin suggests the plausibility of the rise in issue voting.[46] Yet, as these analysts concede, a rise in issue voting provides only a partial explanation for changes in voting behaviour in recent years. Though voters may be behaving in a more rational manner, the fit between voting for a party and agreeing with it on a range of issues is far from perfect.[47] The rise of issue voting does not necessarily provide an explanation for the decline in Conservative support in 1983. Though the Conservatives won a landslide in terms of seats, their voting support was down on 1979. In 1983, 50 per cent of electors thought that the Conservatives had the 'best policies'.[48] Only 42 per cent of electors voted Conservative. Nor does issue voting provide a convincing explanation for the support garnered by the SDP/Liberal Alliance in 1983. Its appeal, as Särlvik and Crewe noted, appeared to be negative and diffuse, based on leadership, style and sheer novelty rather than on policies and ideology.[49] For an explanation of two-party *decline*, and a rise of third parties, one has to consider additional hypotheses.

Consensus

A more political explanation is to be found in the performance of the two parties in office. Critics within the parties themselves have argued that the decline in party support was attributable to the consensus politics of the 1950s and 1960s, when the two parties appeared to converge and pursue similar policies. This was an era of the social-democratic consensus, or what Beer termed the 'collectivist' era.[50] After the general election defeat of 1970, those on the left wing within the Labour Party began to push for a greater commitment to more overtly socialist measures. They contended that the period of Labour government from 1964 to 1970 had been characterised by failure and drift, the party having failed to adopt and then pursue a coherent and alternative socialist programme.[51] What was needed, they argued, was an extension of public ownership, greater control of the national economy, and import controls. Working through the party organisation, the left achieved acceptance of a more radical party programme. However, in office from 1974 to 1979, the Labour government found itself hampered by a small and, for most of the time, a non-existent parliamentary majority; by a deteriorating economy; and by international pressures. Instead of implementing the party programme, its internal critics claimed, it reverted to the traditional post-war policies of economic management by deflation. The loss of the 1979 general election gave a further boost to the left wing within the party and in subsequent years it achieved not only a more radical party programme, committing the party to taking a significant public stake in various industries (as well as re-nationalising those industries denationalised by the Conservatives), to a non-nuclear defence policy and to withdrawal from the European Communities, it also achieved various constitutional changes within the party, including the election of the party leader by a wider electorate than that of the Parliamentary Labour Party.[52]

A sophisticated theory of voting developed by Paul Whiteley gives some credence to the thesis developed by the left wing. Voting, he hypothesised, was determined by social attributes and by prospective and retrospective evaluations of Labour performance. Prospective evaluations were derived from assessments of the party's likely future performance in office and retrospective evaluations derived from assessments of past performance in office (or assessments of how the party might have performed in office). Utilising data drawn from the 1979 Election Survey, he concluded that subjective judgements were better predictors of voting behaviour than objective factors, and for that of retrospective and prospective evaluations, the former were much more significant than the latter for explaining support for the Labour Party. 'This is consistent with the performance hypothesis in which voters are passing judgement on Labour's record in office, rather than on its future policy proposals. The dealignment is explained by the failure of the party to represent adequately the objective and subjective interests of its supporters.'[53] If Labour could achieve electoral success, he argued, it could implement a successful economic strategy and reverse the decline in its support base.

A roughly parallel debate has been taking place within the Conservative Party. Neo-liberals within the party have contended that post-war Conservative governments were part of the collectivist consensus, contributing to what Sir Keith Joseph termed the 'ratchet effect of socialism'. In the wake of the 1974 general election defeats, the party found itself in the political wilderness and confused. It sought to generate a new approach. The parliamentary party turned to Mrs Margaret Thatcher to lead the party and she began to blaze a new trail of neo-liberalism. The emphasis was placed on a market economy and on the need for individual self-help; government was limited and could only do so much. Choice and individual responsibility were at the heart of Mrs Thatcher's political morality.[54] By 1979, the party could offer a clear alternative to that of a tired Labour government. It was, ironically, the Conservative Party which now offered itself as a radical choice, competing against a conservative Labour government. Success at the 1979 general election and the landslide victory in 1983 appeared to bear out the new approach adopted by the party.

There are various problems associated with these analyses. Opponents would contend that it is the pursuit of more radical policies by the two main parties that has been responsible for the decline in their support. By deserting the centre ground of politics, the parties were perceived to have left a vacuum to be filled by the Social Democratic and Liberal Parties. Survey data have shown the unpopularity of Labour policies put forward in both the 1979 and 1983 general elections.[55] As for the Conservative neo-liberal argument, the Conservative government was trailing in the opinion polls in 1981 and recovered to establish a clear lead (which it retained up to and including the 1983 general election) as a consequence of the government's response to the Argentine invasion of the Falklands Islands in 1982. Furthermore, though the party won the 1983 election, it suffered a decline in electoral support and was the beneficiary of negative rather than positive voting – that is, more voters were voting against the Labour Party than were voting for the Conservative Party.[56]

The Two-Party System

The final analysis is that which contends that the decline in support for the two main parties is the product of the two-party *system* in Britain. The two parties dominate the national political agenda, taking positions that are not congruent with the wishes of most electors. Aided by the first-past-the-post electoral system, they compete for the all-or-nothing spoils of a general election victory and in so doing compete vigorously with one another in an adversary relationship. Once in office, a party reverses the policies of its predecessors and pursues wildly different policies which it often subsequently has to modify or abandon when other pressures are brought to bear (economic resources not being sufficient to match extravagant election promises). Policy discontinuity makes for uncertainty, industrialists and investors being unable to plan with certainty for the future. Britain, in short, has a dysfunctional party system. This party system cannot be divorced from the workings of the electoral system, and thus it is not surprising that the prescription advanced by critics of the electoral and the two-party system is the same: reform of the electoral system. Indeed, the critics are usually the same people, notably academics such as S.E. Finer and S.A. Walkland, and politicians such as the leaders of the Social Democratic and (more especially) the Liberal Parties.[57] Reform of the electoral system, they argue, would allow for political change. Under a system of proportional representation, no one party would be able to achieve an overall majority in the House of Commons. This would necessitate some form of centre-coalition government, allowing for a return to the consensus politics that electors seek.

The problem with this argument, as Nevil Johnson has observed, is that a decline in support for one or both of the two main parties does not of itself demonstrate a decline in support for the two-party system.[58] Britain may be witnessing a transitional stage in which the Social Democratic Party displaces the Labour Party as the second of the two major parties. There are no objective data to suggest that electors wish to dispense with what supporters view as the fruits of a two-party system – that is, a clear choice between parties, and a party government with an overall majority. In the 1983 general election, only one in four of electors who voted cast a ballot for a party (or alliance of parties) that advocated consensus politics and a reform of the electoral system.

Where, then, does this leave us? The 'decline' in support for the two parties is clearly a complex phenomenon, operating at different levels of votes, identification, membership and parliamentary cohesion. There is no one theory or hypothesis which appears to explain comprehensively, certainly not exclusively, that decline. The increase in intra-party dissent in the House of Commons would appear to be explained partially by the rise of new issues on the political agenda, but this by itself is not a sufficient explanation. For that, one has to look further: one analysis, by this writer, identifies the leadership style of Edward Heath in the 1970–74 parliament as being the most significant motivator of Conservative dissent.[59] Explanations of electoral decline are not necessarily sufficient to explain a decline in party membership. In the 1950s, both parties witnessed a decline in membership, a significant decline which preceded rather than followed a significant decline in electoral support. The two-party thesis does not help explain a differential decline in support for the two main parties. The 1970s witnessed a shrinkage of the Labour Party's electoral base, one more significant and continuous than that of the Conservatives' electoral base. None of this is to suggest that the various analyses offered are not useful in helping understand particular aspects of the 'decline'. But none by itself is a sufficient explanation. What Britain has witnessed has been a decline in two-party support which would appear to be the product of analytically distinct developments.

(D) A TWO-PARTY SYSTEM?

How, then, is the British party system to be characterised in the 1980s? At the parliamentary level, the Conservative and Labour Parties remain dominant. The format of a two-party system is maintained. Coalition government has not been necessary. There was a pact between the Labour government and the Parliamentary Liberal Party from 1977 to 1978, but no incorporation of Liberal MPs in the government.[60] The properties of a two-party system have been maintained. There has been the alternation of parties in office (Conservative 1970–74, Labour 1974–79, and Conservative 1979 to date); a future Labour government is not impossible. With the partial exception of the Lib–Lab Pact, the party in government has governed alone.

However, domination at the parliamentary level (seats won) is no longer based on domination at the electoral level (votes won). In 1983, multi-party competition was a feature of the general election (see Table 5). The electoral system and the spread of party support ensured that multi-partism at the electoral level was not translated into multi-partism at the parliamentary level. The SDP/Liberal Alliance failed to achieve the 30 per cent of votes generally believed to be necessary for it to achieve the number of seats commensurate with its electoral support. The number of votes cast for the Alliance was nonetheless sufficient to throw in doubt the continued alternation in power of the Conservative and Labour Parties. The Alliance emerged as a challenger to Labour's position as the second largest party.

To characterise Britain as retaining a two-party system would thus appear to be inapt in the 1980s. Two questions follow. How is it to be characterised? And what for the future? Given that Britain can witness two- or multi-party competition at the electoral level and similar but not coterminous competition at the parliamentary level, a four-box matrix can be constructed (Figure 1).[61]

FIGURE 1

PARTY COMPETITION IN BRITAIN

Parliamentary

		Two-party	Multi-party
	Two-party	TWO-PARTY	MIXED (coalition/ minority govt.)
Electoral	Multi-party	MIXED (majority govt.)	MULTI-PARTY

The two-party system, with the two parties dominating at both electoral and parliamentary levels, was a feature of the period from 1945 to 1970. This, though, was the only period in modern British history to have witnessed two-partism over a period encompassing several general elections. Prior to 1945, the country experienced examples of both mixed (coalition/minority government) and multi-partism. The mixed system, with two-party competition at the electoral level but multi-partism at the parliamentary level, was seen early in the twentieth century, the product of concentrated support for Irish Nationalist MPs (support that produced a significant number of Nationalist MPs but made no major dent on the proportion of votes cast for the main parties). Multi-partism was witnessed sporadically as the Labour Party came to rival and then overtake the Liberal Party as the second largest party. The 1970s and early 1980s have witnessed primarily a mixed (majority government) system of competition, though bordering on multi-partism in the 1974–79 period.

What, then, for the future? The simple answer is that no one knows for sure. As both Crewe and Whiteley have stressed, a dealignment does not constitute a re-alignment. Britain is not necessarily in a transitional stage between two-partism and multi-partism. Indeed, there are three possibilities. One is the re-emergence of a two-party system. Studies sympathetic to the Conservative and Labour Parties have stressed that the developments of the 1970s provide no insuperable bar to the parties regaining their former strength.[62] Despite its relative decline in support, the Conservative Party remains strong in terms of votes, identification, membership and parliamentary support. Subsequent to the 1983 general election, the Labour Party improved its position in the opinion polls, initially more at the expense of the SDP/Liberal Alliance than (as might be expected) of the Conservative Party. Two-partism might be less stable than in the period from 1945 to 1970, but it is possible.

Another possibility is multi-partism, multi-party competition in electoral terms being translated into multi-party competition at the parliamentary level. Despite the Conservative landslide in seats at the 1983 general election, the underlying electoral trends point to the distinct possibility of future 'hung' parliaments, that is, parliaments in which no one party has an overall majority.[63] Increased support for the SDP/Liberal Alliance at the next general election would make this possible. It could be the product of a sudden collapse of the class–party nexus, a possibility considered by Franklin in drawing on catastrophe theory.[64]

The third distinct possibility is the continuation of a mixed system. One could envisage the next general election producing the return of a Conservative government with a reduced but nonetheless absolute majority of seats. Whether or not competition was moving (if at all) towards a multi-party or a two-party system would depend on whether Labour improved its electoral position at the expense of the Alliance parties or vice versa.

Britain, in short, no longer provides a perfect fit for the two-party model. In historical terms, it did so only for a short period. Since that period, the party system has been not so much in transition as in a state of perplexing flux.

NOTES

1. G. Sartori, *Parties and Party Systems: A Framework for Analysis* (Cambridge: Cambridge University Press, 1976), p. 185.
2. Ibid., pp. 188–9.
3. This categorisation and subsequent analysis derives in part from P. Norton, *The British Polity* (New York: Longman, 1984), Chs. 5 and 6.
4. As a proportion of those actually able to vote, the figure is somewhat higher. A survey of the electoral register in 1966 found that it was only 93 per cent accurate on publication day and only 85 per cent accurate on its last day of validity. G. Alderman, *British Elections: Myth and Reality* (London: Batsford, 1978), p. 45.
5. D. Butler and D. Stokes, *Political Change in Britain*, 2nd ed. (London: Macmillan, 1974), pp. 45–7.
6. *Report of the Committee on Financial Aid to Political Parties* under the Chairmanship of The Rt. Hon. Lord Houghton, Cmnd. 6601 (London: Her Majesty's Stationery Office, 1976), p. 31, para 5.9.
7. D. Butler and A. Sloman, *British Political Facts 1900–1979*, 5th ed. (London: Macmillan, 1980), p. 133.
8. Ibid., p. 143.
9. M. Pinto-Duschinsky, *British Political Finance 1830–1980* (Washington, DC: American Enterprise Institute, 1981), pp. 212–28.
10. *Report of the Committee on Financial Aid*, op. cit., p. 31, which refers to the Liberal membership reaching a peak of 250,000 in 1964–65.
11. Pinto-Duschinsky, op. cit., Chs. 5 and 6.
12. Ibid., Ch. 7. As Pinto-Duschinsky emphasises, the figures need to be treated with caution.
13. Ibid., p. 203.
14. P. Norton, *The Commons in Perspective* (Oxford: Martin Robertson, 1981), p. 27.
15. S.H. Beer, *Modern British Politics* (London: Faber & Faber, 1969), p. 350.
16. See P. Norton, 'The Liberal Party in Parliament', in V. Bogdanor (ed.), *Liberal Party Politics* (Oxford: Oxford University Press, 1983), p. 143.
17. B. Särlvik and I. Crewe, *Decade of Dealignment* (Cambridge: Cambridge University Press, 1983), pp. 333–4.
18. P. Norton and A. Aughey, *Conservatives and Conservatism* (London: Temple Smith, 1981), p. 213.
19. See Pinto-Duschinsky, op. cit., p. 158, figure 1.
20. D. Butler and M. Pinto-Duschinsky, *The British General Election of 1970* (London: Macmillan, 1971), p. 265.
21. P. Whiteley, *The Labour Party in Crisis* (London: Methuen, 1983), p. 55.
22. Pinto-Duschinsky, op. cit., p. 153.
23. Ibid., pp. 165–8.
24. *Report of the Committee on Financial Aid*, op. cit., pp. 38–9, para. 5.53.
25. P. Norton, *Conservative Dissidents* (London: Temple Smith, 1978).
26. P. Norton, *Dissension in the House of Commons 1974–1979* (Oxford: Oxford University Press, 1980).
27. P. Norton, 'The Norton View', in D. Judge (ed.), *The Politics of Parliamentary Reform* (London: Heinemann, 1983), p. 68; M. Shah, 'Revolts and Retreats: Division Lobby Dissent within the Parliamentary Conservative Party, Nov. 1979–March 1983', unpublished undergraduate dissertation, Essex University Department of Government, 1983.
28. In one week in January 1984, approximately 20 Conservatives voted against the government, and a further 40 to 50 abstained from voting, in four separate divisions: on a bill to de-nationalise the Royal Ordinance Factories, on the Second Reading of the Rates Bill (the most significant incident), on housing benefits, and on the rate-support grant.
29. Butler and Stokes, op. cit., p. 69.
30. Särlvik and Crewe, op. cit., p. 87.
31. The Gallup Poll, 'Voting Behaviour in Britain, 1945–1974', in R. Rose (ed.), *Studies in British Politics*, 3rd ed. (London: Macmillan, 1976), p. 206.
32. P. Pulzer, *Political Representation and Elections in Britain* (London: Macmillan, 1967), p. 98.

33. I. Crewe, 'The Disturbing Truth Behind Labour's Rout', *The Guardian*, 13 June 1983.
34. See M.N. Franklin and A. Mughan, 'The Decline of Class Voting in Britain: Problems of Analysis and Interpretation', *American Political Science Review*, Vol. 72, No. 2 (1978), pp. 523–4.
35. M.N. Franklin, 'Is Class Still the Basis of British Politics?' *Strathclyde Papers on Government and Politics No. 2* (Glasgow: Strathclyde University Politics Department, 1983), pp. 12–18.
36. See ibid., pp. 18–24.
37. Butler and Stokes, op. cit., p. 414.
38. A hypothesis which had been tested earlier, with some effect, in relation to the United States. See R.E. Dawson, *Public Opinion and Contemporary Disarray* (New York: Harper & Row, 1973).
39. P. Dunleavy, 'Voting and the Electorate', in H. Drucker *et al.* (eds.), *Developments in British Politics* (London: Macmillan, 1983), p. 43.
40. I. Crewe, B. Särlvik and J. Alt, 'Partisan Dealignment in Britain, 1964–1974', *British Journal of Political Science*, Vol. 7, No. 2 (1977), p. 187.
41. See Norton, *Conservative Dissidents*, op. cit., Ch. 9.
42. Sarlvik and Crewe, op. cit., pp. 203–5 and 278.
43. Ibid., p. 280.
44. Ibid., p. 255.
45. Ibid., p. 280.
46. M.N. Franklin, 'The Rise of Issue Voting in British Elections', *Strathclyde Papers on Government and Politics No. 3*, 2nd ed. (Glasgow: Strathclyde University Politics Department, 1983).
47. See Särlvik and Crewe, op. cit., Ch. 11.
48. *The Guardian*, 14 June 1983.
49. Särlvik and Crewe, op. cit., p. 343.
50. Beer, *Modern British Politics*, op. cit.
51. See M. Hatfield, *The House the Left Built* (London: Gollancz, 1978).
52. See, for example, D. Kogan and M. Kogan, *The Battle for the Labour Party* (London: Fontana, 1982).
53. Whiteley, op. cit., p. 106.
54. Norton and Aughey, op. cit., p. 162.
55. I. Crewe, 'The Labour Party and the Electorate', in D. Kavanagh (ed.), *The Politics of the Labour Party* (London: George Allen & Unwin, 1982); I. Crewe, 'How Labour was Trounced All Round', *The Guardian*, 14 June 1983.
56. I. Crewe, 'The Disturbing Truth Behind Labour's Rout', *The Guardian*, 13 June 1983.
57. See especially S.E. Finer, *Adversary Politics and Electoral Reform* (London: Wigram, 1975); S.A. Walkland, 'Whither the Commons?', in S.A. Walkland and M. Ryle (eds.), *The Commons Today* (London: Fontana, 1981); and D. Owen, *Face The Future* (Oxford: Oxford University Press, 1981).
58. N. Johnson, book review, *The Times Higher Education Supplement*, 22 July 1983.
59. Norton, *Conservative Dissidents*, op. cit., Ch. 9.
60. See A. Michie and S. Hoggart, *The Pact* (London: Quartet, 1978).
61. Constructed on the basis of categories identified in R. Rose, 'Class Does Not Equal Party', *CSPP Studies in Public Policy No. 74* (Glasgow: Centre for the Study of Public Policy, 1980), pp. 11–12.
62. Norton and Aughey on the Conservative side and Whiteley on the Labour side.
63. J. Curtice and M. Steed, 'Electoral Choice and the Production of Government', *British Journal of Political Science*, Vol. 12, No. 2 (1982), pp. 249–98.
64. Franklin, 'Is Class Still the Basis of British Politics?' op. cit., pp. 24–8.

The Changing Relationship Between Parties and Society in Italy

Leonardo Morlino

POLITICAL PARTIES AND ITALIAN SOCIETY

The time span considered in this paper covers the last decade, from the election of May 1972 to that of June 1983. It is a period which is striking in terms of the degree of change not only at the level of the parties, but also at that of the democratic regime itself, the economy, the society, and also the structures of intermediation other than the parties themselves.

At the level of civil society at large, for instance, the past ten years have witnessed the birth, growth, and either total or partial decline of two phenomena of great salience: the mobilisation of collective movements on the one hand, and left- and right-wing terrorism on the other. At the level of intermediate structures other than political parties, the beginning of this ten-year period witnessed a growth in the role of the labour unions, which at a certain moment appeared to become structures for the articulation of general interests. Thereafter, their role began to diminish, eventually leading to a profound and apparently irremediable crisis in the relations between the Socialist and Communist currents within the CGIL and to the breakdown of unity within the labour movement at the end of the decade.

At regime level, the most important changes concern the lowering of the voting age to 18, the recourse to referenda in 1974, 1978 and 1981, and then the (probably long-term) abandonment of the referendum as an effective instrument of political participation. At the governmental level, the latter half of the 1970s witnessed a major change in the role of the Communist Party. The PCI first abstained and later directly supported – although without direct participation – a government headed by the Christian Democratic leader Andreotti. For the first time since 1945, there have been also three different governments led by non-Christian Democrats: the two governments of the Republican leader Spadolini, and, after the elections of June 1983, that led by the Socialist leader Craxi.

At the level of policies, following the approval of the Workers' Statute and the institutionalisation of the regions (probably the single most important reform of the entire post-war period) at the beginning of the 1970s, there have been a series of provisions of far-reaching importance which include the law regarding state financing of political parties; university reform; health reform; provision for divorce; the abortion law; military reform; and rent control. Finally, and not least as a result of these and other provisions, there has been a dramatic increase in the size of the budget deficit.

This brief overview of the important changes which have occurred in Italy at the non-party level[1] might lead one to expect similarly profound changes at the level of the parties. Yet it is often maintained that in contrast to these profound and radical changes affecting all the other aspects of the Italian system, the political parties did not change significantly during the decade, and that this in turn has led to a growing detachment between them and the civil society.[2] Is this hypothesis a correct reading of the present Italian political situation or does it lay too much stress on the crisis of the political parties? Does it correspond at least in part to reality?

In order to answer these questions, it would be necessary to assess the parties' role and performance in at least six different domains. First, one would need to examine the organisational structures of at least the three major parties – the Christian Democrats (DC), the Communists (PCI) and the Socialists (PSI) – throughout the entire decade, looking for example at the methods for electing the party secretary and the delegates to party conventions, the currents or factions within the parties, the increase or decrease in party membership, the changing social composition of party membership and changes in the methods of recruitment.[3] Secondly, it would be necessary to take into consideration changes in party strategy. For example, in the case of the PCI, it would be necessary to trace the shift from the 'historic compromise', proposed in late 1973, through the period of 'national solidarity', to the next strategy of the 'democratic alternative'.[4] Thirdly, and linked with this, it would be necessary to assess whether there had been any real change at the level of the party system. More precisely, one would need to look at changes in the type and direction of party competition, at the spatial position on the left–right spectrum, and at the ideological distance and transformation of the anti-system parties.[5] Fourthly, it would be particularly important to analyse the role of the parties with respect to the other structures of intermediation, and principally to the labour unions, business associations, and other pressure groups within a democratic system where parties have always played a decisive role.[6] A fifth direction of analysis should concern what is called *lottizzazione*, that is, party expansion in the state. This refers to the presence and influence of the parties not only in the candidacies for all elective offices, but also in the appointments to a large number of non-elective positions. For example, this occurs in both local and central bureaucracy, in the army, in the state-owned broadcasting company, in the health-care system, in state-run industries, the banking system and so on.[7] Finally, the sixth direction of research would have to focus on the relationship between party and civil society.[8] As will be seen, the main problem here is that of empirically demonstrating the transformations which have taken place in this relationship. It is this latter aspect which will be the central concern of this paper, the other potential directions of research being considered only when they can usefully clarify changes in that relationship during the past decade.

More specifically, it will be argued that the entire decade has been characterised by an increasing gap between civil society and the parties as structures of intermediation. This gap has manifested itself differently during the period, the first phase being marked by mobilisation and participation and the second by apathy and political indifference. The final problem that will be raised concerns the explanation for this gap between civil society and party, in the process of which a number of alternative suggestions and hypotheses will be proposed.

Traditionally, the first level at which one can assess civil society–party relationships is at that of the electoral arena. First of all, therefore, the fluctuations in the vote should be considered. This means examining the degree of electoral volatility which, in the Italian case, is not affected by the nature of the basically proportional electoral system. Increasing volatility would suggest a decline in the vote of *appartenenza*, that is, in the type of vote which demonstrates a subjective identification with a political force organically connected to the social group to which the voter belongs. Such a decline would be compounded, of course, by a corresponding decline in party identification which, in turn, should also be apparent in a declining party membership. Another important indicator will be provided by changes in voter turnout and in the proportion of blank and invalid ballots. The possible success of minor parties and collective movements would provide an additional indirect indicator of the entire phenomenon. Outside the electoral arena, one would also need to look to data concerning the affective attitudes of the citizens towards parties, and also, more generally, towards other political actors and/or towards the democratic regime as a whole.

As regards empirically based explanations, once again changes in the electoral arena, and particularly a greater degree of volatility in areas characterised by specific subcultures, might act to sustain the hypothesis of the disaggregation of such subcultures. The end of the so-called *collateralismo*, that is, the support of particular organisations for the parties, is another factor which needs to be examined. However, these are aspects which will be discussed at a later stage.

ELECTORAL VOLATILITY

Despite the problems and limits inherent in the analysis of aggregate electoral volatility as a measure of the real level of vote fluctuation, it remains a useful index of electoral change[9] which, moreover, can be considered as a sort of abridged indicator of what is going on in the relationship between parties and civil society. As Table 1 shows,[10] average total volatility (ATV) in the last three elections is clearly higher than that in the previous decade. In particular, it was only the election of 1963 which reached a similar degree of volatility to those of 1976 and 1983, though it should be emphasised that the low level in 1968 is the result of a calculus that correctly glosses over the unification of the two Socialist parties, PSI and PSDI (Social Democrats), and the formation of the new Party of Socialist Proletarian Unity (PSIUP), a splinter party resulting from that unification.

Table 1 also reports the level of *area volatility* (AV), which is an index of the fluctuation between the centre area on the one hand and the leftist area on the other. In this case, the centre area is considered as only one 'party' and its electoral strength is the result of the addition of the percentage of votes cast for the DC, PRI (Republicans), PLI (Liberals) and the PSDI, while the left represents the sum of the leftist parties – PCI, PSI, Radicals

TABLE 1

MEASURES OF ELECTORAL CHANGE IN ITALY, 1963–83

	1963	1968	1972	1976	1979	1983
TV	8.5	3.5	5.3	9.1	5.3	8.8
ATV		5.8			7.7	
AV	1.3	1.4	1.1	5.4	0.7	0.3
LV	3.0	10.4	3.7	10.8	7.2	5.5
CV	9.2	3.9	3.4	4.5	1.6	8.8
MPV	1.7	2.4	0	7.2	4.4	6.0

Notes:

Total Volatility (TV) = the sum of every difference (variation in comparison with the previous elections) in the percentages of votes cast for each party participating in the elections, divided by two.

Average Volatility (ATV) = the average of TV for the first three elections and the other three elections.

Area Volatility (AV) = the volatility between the centre area, formed by all centre–centre/right–centre/left parties, and the leftist area, formed by Socialists, Communists and other leftist parties.

Leftist Area Volatility (LV) = the volatility only within the leftist area.

Centre Area Volatility (CV) = the volatility only within the centre area.

Major Parties Volatility (MPV) = the sum of differences in the percentages of votes cast for the two largest parties (Christian Democrats and Communist Party).

and extreme left. The index of AV is the sum of the absolute differences in percentage between the strength of the two areas, divided by two. As Table 1 shows, the only election in which this volatility is numerically relevant is that of 1976. In other elections, in spite of similar levels of total volatility – for example, those of 1963 or those of 1983 – AV remains very low. As such, and as has been stated by several authors, the election of 1976 was characterised by a major party realignment, which altered the relative strength of the two main electoral areas in the Italian political spectrum.[11]

Table 1 also reports measures of *left volatility* (LV), and *centre volatility* (CV), which are calculated by adding the percentage differences (in comparison with the previous elections) of the parties belonging respectively to the two areas. Given that the figure for LV in 1968 may be artificially high as a result of Socialist unification and the foundation of PSIUP, then it can be noted that only in the elections of 1976, 1979 and 1983 has there been a significant fluctuation within the left.[12] In addition, there has been an appreciable degree of fluctuation within the centre only in the elections of 1963 and 1983.

The final measure in Table 1 (MPV) shows the fluctuation in the total of the major parties vote (DC and PCI), here artificially treated as only one party. It is evident that MPV is much higher in the last three elections than in the previous decade: the mean for the period 1976–83 is 5.9, while that for the period 1963–72 is just 1.4.

These data confirm at least two of the hypotheses which were already put forward by Parisi and Pasquino in 1979 and which suggested that electoral change in Italy involved 'a reduction in the weight of the vote of *appartenenza* both with respect to its relevance for the electorate as a whole and for each political area, and a concomitant expansion of the vote of opinion ...'[13] The overall result of the election of 1983 (Table 2) also confirms these hypotheses. First of all, there has been a substantial drop in the vote for the DC, from 38.3 per cent in 1979 (38.7 per cent in 1976) to 32.9 per cent in 1983, that is, a 5.4 per cent fall; in order to find a similar decline in the vote of the DC one has to go back to the very particular election of 1953. Secondly, these elections confirm a reverse in the trend of the Communist vote, which had been growing between 1946 and 1976. After the surge of 1976, when the PCI won 34.4 per cent (an increase of 7.2 per cent compared with 1972), the change is very clear: 29.9 per cent in 1983 and 30.4 per cent in 1979. Moreover, if one analyses the left area in general, it can be seen that the left as a whole won 31.4 per cent in 1983, as against 32.6 per cent in 1979.

Thirdly, there is a growth in the centre/centre-left parties, with the Social-

TABLE 2

ELECTION RESULTS, 1979 AND 1983 (LOWER CHAMBER)

PARTIES	1979			1983			difference 1983–1979	
	votes	%	seats	votes	%	seats	%	seats
DC	14,046,290	38.3	262	12,145,800	32.9	225	−5.4	−37
PCI	11,139,231	30.4	201	11,028,158	29.9	198	−0.5	− 3
PSI	3,596,802	9.8	62	4,222,487	11.4	73	+1.6	+11
MSI–DN	1,930,639	5.3	30	2,511,722	6.8	42	+1.5	+12
DN–CD	229,205	0.6	–	–	–	–	−0.6	–
PSDI	1,407,535	3.8	20	1,507,431	4.1	23	+0.3	+ 3
PRI	1,110,209	3.0	16	1,872,536	5.1	29	+2.1	+13
PLI	712,646	1.9	9	1,065,833	2.9	16	+1.0	+ 7
PDUP	502,247	1.4	6	–	–	–	−1.4	− 6
DP–NSU	294,462	0.8	–	541,493	1.5	7	+0.7	+ 7
Part. Radicale	1,264,870	3.5	18	809,672	2.2	11	−1.3	− 7
P. Naz. Pens.	–	–	–	502,841	1.4	–	+1.4	–
Lista Trieste	65,505	0.2	1	91,985	0.25	–	+0.05	–
PPST	204,899	0.6	4	184,892	0.5	3	−0.1	− 1
Liga Veneta	–	–	–	125,347	0.3	1	+0.3	+ 1
P.S. d'Az.	17,673	–	–	91,868	0.25	1	+0.25	+ 1
Others	149,095	0.4	1	188,224	0.5	1	+0.1	=
Total	36,671,308	100.0	630	36,890,289	100.0	630		

Source: Official data.

ists (PSI) gaining 1.6 per cent (11.4 per cent in 1983, 9.8 per cent in 1979, and 9.6 per cent in 1976), the Social Democrats (PSDI) gaining 0.3 per cent (4.1 per cent in 1983, 3.8 per cent in 1979, and 3.4 per cent in 1976), the Republicans (PRI) gaining 2.1 per cent (5.1 per cent in 1983, 3.0 per cent in 1979, 3.1 per cent in 1976), and the Liberals (PLI) gaining 1.0 per cent (2.9 per cent in 1983, 1.9 per cent in 1979, and 1.3 per cent in 1976, when it seemed as if they were about to disappear). On the whole, the centre/ centre-left parties, typically representing the area of the opinion vote, gained a very important 5.0 per cent. The voting trend away from the two major parties, which had already begun in 1979, was therefore accentuated: in 1976 the total of the vote for the two major parties (DC and PCI) was 73.1 per cent, dropping in 1979 to 68.7 per cent, and in 1983 to 62.8 per cent. Moreover two parties, even if very small, the PLI and the PRI, increased their vote by over half.[14] The results for the Radical Party, the success of local lists and other aspects concerning the 1983 elections will be discussed later. At this stage, however, the major additional change to note is the growth of the extreme right with the MSI increasing its vote by 1.5 per cent. More precisely, since the other rightist formation (DN–CD) did not contest in 1983, the real growth is 0.9 per cent (see Table 2).

On the whole this brief analysis of most recent elections shows a decline in *appartenenza* among the electorate and a growth of the opinion vote. If so, there is also likely to be a clear decline in party identification and, from this point of view, a deeper gap between a larger part of population and the parties. The next question is, therefore, whether this change is also mirrored by a corresponding decline in party membership.

CHANGES IN PARTY MEMBERSHIP

The tendency for certain parties artificially to inflate their membership figures is certainly familiar,[15] and it is clear that such data must be treated with caution. On the other hand, to the extent that it is only *variations* in membership which are of interest, even if over a period of two decades, then the data are likely to be more reliable, particularly if they evidence a declining trend. Such certainly seems to be the case; Cazzola has noted that while 11 per cent of Italians were members of either the DC, PCI or PSI in 1970, this figure had dropped to nine per cent by the beginning of the 1980s. Moreover, the decline was reasonably even across the country, although more accentuated in the South (15 per cent in 1970 to 10 per cent in 1980) than in the North (nine per cent to seven per cent).[16]

The more detailed picture evident in Table 3 shows the actual collapse of membership between 1974 and 1977; this is followed by a gradual recovery, and is then followed by another decline of minor proportions after 1980. In the Socialist Party there is an essential continuity, with small highs and lows. (While the Socialist Party has never been organised efficiently, in the last years it has enjoyed greater visibility under the leadership of Craxi.) There is a continual, steady erosion in Communist membership after 1976, with a notable decline of new membership being coupled with the evident problem of a lack of renewal of lapsed membership.

TABLE 3

MEMBERSHIP OF THE THREE LARGEST ITALIAN PARTIES, 1963–83

	DC		PSI		PCI	
	total	new	total	new	total	new
year						
1963	1,612,730	189,729			1,615,571	129,782
1964	1,676,222				1,641,214	136,649
1965	1,613,314				1,615,296	121,771
1966	1,641,615				,ɔ75,935	107,607
1967	1,624,687				1,534,705	103,405
1968	1,696,402				1,502,862	102,340
1969	1,743,651				1,503,816	107,515
1970	1,738,996		506,533		1,507,047	108,622
1971	1,814,580		592,586		1,521,642	112,818
1972	1,827,925		560,187		1,584,659	134,926
1973	1,879,429		465,189		1,623,082	136,334
1974	1,843,515		511,714		1,657,825	144,630
1975	1,732,501		539,339		1,730,453	157,934
1976	1,365,187		509,388	64,181	1,814,262	170,671
1977	1,201,707	145,255	482,916	47,550	1,814,154	127,166
1978	1,355,423	189,884	479,769	53,884	1,790,450	100,458
1979	1,384,148	195,323	472,544	44,255	1,761,297	91,836
1980	1,395,584		502,211	57,471	1,751,323	91,149
1981	1,385,141	180,212	508,898	69,052	1,714,052	
1982	1,361,064	163,901	541,526		1,673,751	
1983	1,303,148		554,398		1,636,314	

Sources:

M. Rossi, 'Un partito di "anime morte"? Il tesseramento democristiano tra mito e realtà', in A. Parisi (ed.), *Democristiani* (Bologna: Il Mulino, 1979); M. Caciagli, 'Il resistibile declino della Democrazia Cristiana', in G. Pasquino (ed.), *Il sistema politico italiano* (forthcoming); F. Cazzola, 'Il PSI negli anni settanta', *Schema*, Vol. 5 (1982); F. C. Ghini, 'Gli iscritti al partito e alla FGCI', in M. Ilardi and A. Accornero (eds.), *Il Partito Comunista Italiano. Struttura e storia dell 'oranizzazione 1921–1979* (Milano: Feltrinelli, 1982). For 1983, published party data.

There are certain arguments which state that a degree of turnover of membership can be a positive attribute, in that it provides evidence of organisational vitality and demonstrates the existence of a continual flow of communication between society and party.[17] At the same time, however, the fact remains that a high or even a growing turnover in membership is evidence of at least the partial existence of unstable party identification. Such is the case when a large number of new enrolments is not accompanied by a similarly large increase in total membership. The second, fourth and sixth columns of Table 3 do not provide clear evidence on this point, however. The data are incomplete and there is no evident trend in any direction, except for the Communists. First, figures for new members in the PCI show a steady decline since 1976 that parallels the decreasing total membership. Furthermore, other data about the PCI allow us to reach some cautious conclusions. In 1982, 52 per cent of members had 12 to 14 years of membership seniority, while 25 per cent had joined since 1976. Of the one and a half million members at the end of the 1960s, some 50 per cent had left by the end of the 1970s. Therefore, turnover – a sort of membership volatility – existed precisely in that party in which it would have been least expected. Moreover, it existed in considerable proportions.[18]

The analysis of party membership in Italy can be further defined by reference to geographic distribution, social origins, the vote:membership ratio, as well as to several other aspects. But for the purposes of this article, it is sufficient to note a final additional point concerning the case of the PCI, which is that its success among young people in the mid-1970s had already become a memory by 1982: the proportion of members under 30 years old fell from 29 per cent in 1975 to 18 per cent in 1982,[19] a change which acts to complicate but at the same time to define better the contemporary situation of the party.

NEW PARTIES AND COLLECTIVE MOVEMENTS

The existence of an electoral law which does not impose high thresholds on winning a parliamentary seat enables us to look to the eventual success – although not the creation – of new parties as evidence of the presence in the electorate of groups less readily identified with the established parties. To the extent that the previous identification patterns had remained strong enough and that the traditional mechanisms of political socialisation continued to work efficiently, then new parties should not be expected to succeed. Obviously, if the trend towards a decline in party identification is to be maintained, and, therefore, if the civil society–party gap is to persist, the 'newcomers' parties must not create new patterns of identification. Moreover, they must remain poorly organised and, in the last analysis, be flash-in-the-pan parties. In Italy, the first condition regarding the electoral law does exist. In fact, the threshold for winning a parliamentary seat is rather low, in that it involves winning an electoral quota in a multi-member constituency and at least 300,000 votes at the national level. Have there then been such parties which are electorally successful but which nevertheless have not led to the establishment of new identifications?

The most interesting and significant case in this respect is that of the Radical Party, followed by that of the extreme left. Following the 1953 election and the period of party system consolidation it can be said that no really new party emerged before the 1970s. The birth and disappearance of the PSIUP between the mid-1960s and the beginning of the 1970s is not an exception in this regard. As already mentioned, the PSIUP was born following Socialist unification and as a result of a reaction in the leadership. It achieved a notable electoral success in 1968, gaining 4.5 per cent of the vote and 23 seats, and disappeared in 1972 when, with 648,000 votes, it failed to win a single seat. The success of the Radicals in the 1970s (from 1976 on, with 1.1 per cent) is, therefore, a significant change.[20] If one also considers the electoral fluctuation and the shaping and reshaping of the extreme left around various small parties (Table 2), then it must be said that we have witnessed the emergence of new parties as expressions of civil society which at the same time do not appear to have managed to establish new patterns of identification. Moreover, it should also be noted that the 1983 election resulted in a party of retired citizens (the PNP) winning half a million votes (though no seats), and also in substantial levels of support for local lists as, for example, in the case of the Liga Veneta (Table 2).

The same pattern holds true for collective movements,[21] even if their presence and effective political influence is contained within a more limited time span, in that they were all in evident decline by the mid-1970s. The workers' movement, for instance, reached its peak between the end of the 1960s and the beginning of the 1970s, and then it lost much of its momentum and was constrained by the economic crisis; the youth and student movement was also in decline after the beginning of the 1970s, as was the case with the movements grouping themselves around the problems of divorce and abortion. The relationship between these and the parties, above all the traditional left parties (Socialists and Communists), betrays a complex dynamic in which, on the one hand, the parties react with caution and diffidence and, on the other, the movements manifest anti-party positions. Nor can it be shown that a large part of the youth movement and of the extremist movement combine in a more or less stable way in the PCI,[22] or even in other parties such as Radicals or extreme left. Rather, the birth and success of the collective movements indicate the existence of a new type of political space and forms of participation which are no longer restricted exclusively to the parties at either the level of the militants or that of the electors.

THE GROWTH OF APATHY

The phenomenon of abstention, including both non-voting and the casting of blank and/or invalid ballots, was effectively non-existent until the two referenda of 1978, when electoral participation registered seven per cent less than that of the previous referendum on divorce in 1974 (Table 4). Indeed, until 1979, and as a result of several factors (legislative, cultural, and political in the strict sense), electoral turnout in Italy was higher than in most other Western democracies.[23]

The first real indication of non-participation appeared to come with the 1979 election, albeit not to a very pronounced degree. In fact, however, analyses of the 1979 vote underline, first of all, that this change gives a misleading impression, insofar as a law of February 1979 had increased the electorate by about 750,000 persons – Italian citizens living abroad who were officially registered as eligible voters.[24] As such, the effective increase in non-voting was only 1.7 per cent (to which can be added an increase of 1.4 per cent in the number of invalid votes, and of 0.6 per cent of blank ballot papers).

Other analyses[25] show that there is no clear difference in the patterns of abstention in the vote for the Lower House and the Senate, which means that since only people over 25 years of age are eligible to vote for the Senate, abstention amongst the young is not particularly in evidence. Other, more sophisticated research concerning the 1979 elections, and which analysed

TABLE 4
PERCENTAGE OF NON-VOTERS, 1948-83

	1948	1953	1958	1963	1968	1970	1972	1974	1975	1976	1978	1979	1980	1981	1983
National elections	7.9	6.2	6.1	7.1	7.2		6.8			6.6		9.4			11.0
Regional elections						7.5			8.2				11.5		
Referendum								11.9			18.8			20.4	

Source: Official data.

non-voting in terms of partisanship, age, social status and level of education, has shown that abstention has only 'minor social and political connotations', and that 'the diffusion of the phenomenon suggests a situation of general apathy rather than one of explicit protest, and therefore suggests a rather marginal event of limited political significance'. The conclusion is that there has been simply 'a diffuse ... growth of political apathy which lacks, however, any consequence for the balance of the parties'.[26] More specifically, there is a rejection of the hypothesis which claims a relationship between abstentionism and specific parties: all the parties are affected by abstention, even if the major parties (DC and PCI), and the extremist parties, including the Radicals, are clearly affected to a greater extent.[27]

Following the growth of abstentionism in the regional elections of 1980, in the referendum of 1981, but above all at the 1983 election, the problem has to be seen in different tems. As Table 5 shows, total abstention now runs at 16 per cent of the electorate. Moreover, in the absence of new enfranchising laws, the increase from 13.1 per cent in 1979 to 16 per cent in 1983 is a real increase. In absolute figures, non-voters now number more than 7,000,000 persons. The greatest increase in abstentionism has taken place neither in the South of Italy, nor in the Islands (where the phenomenon was traditionally more accentuated), but in Northern and Central Italy. Moreover, an additional element is the growth of abstentionism in the urban and industrial zones, particularly in the cities of the so-called industrial triangle of the north-west. Though many other patterns can be observed,[28] it suffices to note at this stage that the phenomenon of abstentionism has become an important factor in Italian politics, and is no longer limited to occasional elections of minor importance. On the contrary, it shows an increasing trend particularly in those zones and sectors that traditionally record the greatest proportion of electoral participation.

ATTITUDES TOWARDS PARTIES

In order to give a more complete picture of the relationship between civil society and party it is necessary to refer to survey data concerning attitudes towards the parties and, more generally, towards the political system as a whole.

The first point to note is that there is no clear evidence of a growth in the perceived 'illegitimacy' of the parties, even if negative attitudes towards them are both consistent and significant and, as such, give evidence of a wide gap between society and the parties. For example, a survey of 1972 showed that 63.3 per cent of those interviewed agreed with the view that 'political parties only help to create discord', while 81.5 per cent agreed that politicians 'talk very much, but accomplish very little'. In the same survey, in response to the question, 'Whom do you rely on the most to defend your interests?', electors of the left stated that they regarded the trade unions as much more important than the parties, while those of the centre/centre-right replied that they mainly trusted elected officials, or else they trusted nobody.[29]

The survey research conducted by Sartori and Marradi in 1975 found that

TABLE 5
ELECTORAL ABSTENSION IN 1979 AND 1983 (LOWER CHAMBER)

	Non voters			Blank Ballots			Void Ballots			Total invalid votes			Total abstension		
	1979	1983	diff.	1979	1983	diff.	1979	1983	diff.	1979	1983	diff.	1979	1983	diff.
	%	%	%	%	%	%	%	%	%	%	%	%	%	%	%
North West	5.8	8.3	+2.5	2.5	2.5	0.0	1.8	3.3	+1.5	4.3	5.8	+1.5	10.1	14.1	+4.0
North East	5.4	7.2	+1.8	2.0	2.2	+0.2	1.3	2.5	+1.2	3.3	4.7	+1.4	8.7	11.9	+3.2
Centre	6.4	8.5	+2.1	1.8	1.8	0.0	1.7	2.9	+1.2	3.5	4.7	+1.2	9.9	13.2	+3.3
South	15.4	15.6	+0.2	1.6	1.8	+0.2	1.9	2.8	+0.9	3.5	4.6	+1.1	18.9	20.2	+1.3
Isles	17.9	18.4	+0.5	1.6	1.9	+0.3	2.5	3.4	+0.9	4.1	5.3	+1.2	22.0	23.7	+1.7
Italy	9.4	11.0	+1.6	2.0	2.1	+0.1	1.7	2.9	+1.2	3.7	5.0	+1.3	13.1	16.0	+2.9

Source: 'Postfazione', in M. Caciagli and P. Scaramozzino (eds.), *Il voto di chi non vota* (Milano: Comunità, 1983), p. 324.

77.3 per cent agreed that 'the parties are interested only in getting votes from the people and not in their opinions'; 85.6 per cent agreed that 'usually, the persons we elect to parliament very quickly lose contact with the electors', and 76.4 per cent agreed that 'the politicians are not very interested in what persons like myself think'.[30] A large survey of the following year showed that 40.4 per cent agreed that 'no matter who wins the election, things will remain the same', while 53.4 per cent agreed that 'in all the parties there are a few at the top who command, and all the others have no voice in the matter', and 61.2 per cent agreed that 'whoever gains power always tries to serve his personal interests'.[31] In 1978, to the question, 'Is there any cleavage between common people and the political class?', 74.8 per cent answered in the affirmative, either in part or in entirety.[32] On the whole, therefore, and for our purposes, a relevant steady *growth* of lack of confidence in the parties as institutions is not clearly demonstrated, even if there is evidence of a substantial lack of confidence over time. Moreover, data for the most recent years are unavailable, and the gap cannot be filled except by reference to questions of a larger scope that involve the parties only indirectly.

Before passing to this theme, however, it is useful to refer to a more recent survey conducted by Calvi which again basically concerns the relationship between party and citizens. Using multivariate analysis, Calvi shows that, with the exception of the extreme left, 'all the political choices expressed by respondents are related to a set of values consistent with those of the chosen "party" to a degree of 50 per cent or less'. In other words, 'the data concerning the three major parties, which are chosen by 80 per cent of voters, show clearly that there is no consistency between the social values in which the respondents believe and the preferences they give to a party'.[33]

Yet such a conclusion seems inevitable when analysing the relationship between modern mass parties and their electorates. The ambiguity of the values of the parties themselves, and the likelihood that voting choice emanates from motives other than perceived consistency between the values of the voters and those of the parties, are not unexpected findings. As has been found in similar studies in France, it is evident that, with respect to modern mass parties, there exists a distance between the citizen and the parties which might be defined as 'structural' and almost inevitable.

ATTITUDES TOWARDS THE POLITICAL SYSTEM

Eurobarometer data[34] show that the degree of satisfaction with respect to the functioning of democracy in Italy has not changed significantly over the last decade: in 1973, 27 per cent were very satisfied or rather satisfied, with 72 per cent being not very satisfied or at all not satisfied; in 1982, the figures were 21 per cent and 75 per cent respectively. Nevertheless, these data do show that the index of satisfaction in Italy is the lowest in Europe, registering 1.91 as against a Community average of 2.38 in 1980. In addition, one can note an increase in dissatisfaction between 1963 and 1976 and a partial recovery towards the end of the decade (Table 6).

The picture for Italy can be completed by reference to other survey questions which tap essential aspects of attitudes towards politics. Thus,

TABLE 6

EVALUATION OF THE CONDUCT OF THE GOVERNMENT

	1963	1965	1966	1968	1972	1976	1978
	%	%	%	%	%	%	%
Satisfied or fairly satisfied	38	16.3	22.5	30.8	16.7	3.3	12.8
Neither satisfied, nor dissatisfied	32	32.0	36.6	35.7	22.4	16.9	31.0
Dissatisfied or very dissatisfied	14	26.5	16.0	22.5	35.7	74.1	52.7
Don't know	16	25.2	24.9	11.0	25.2	5.7	3.5

Sources: Published in G. Guidorossi, *Gli italiani e la politica* (Milano: Angeli, 1984), p.55.

while interest in politics appeared to be growing among the population until 1976, as is shown by research by Fabris,[35] and while there was evidence of a willingness to participate not only in elections but also in other forms of political action, the situation has now reversed. Between 1976 and 1982, for example, there was a decline in the percentage of persons who agreed that 'all citizens should be involved in some political undertaking' – from 61.3 per cent in 1976 to 58.3 per cent in 1982.[36] Between 1977 and 1982 there was also a decline in the percentage of those who stated that they discussed politics with friends, and conversely, an increase in the percentage of persons who never discussed politics (from 46.5 per cent to 52.1 per cent).[37]

Bearing in mind the fact that the questions are often not formulated in the same way, and/or that the answers themselves may be different, the results of other inquiries concerning political interest and participation show a similar trend, with a post-1977/78 decline, more or less accentuated, in general interest and disposition towards participation. What is of particular interest here is that while it had been young people who were more clearly responsible for the increase in the index of interest and participation in the first half of the 1970s, it is also the young people who are most evident in the later decline of participation and interest.[38]

EXPLANATIONS

The hypothesis which we were most concerned to test empirically stated that the relationship between parties and civil society had changed significantly in the last decade. More precisely, the period in question has witnessed an increase in the distance between the party institutions and the citizenry, an increase characterised in the first half of the decade by greater participation and involvement outwith the traditional party forms, and at the end of the 1970s and the beginning of the 1980s by a decline in participation. The empirical indicators which have been used have shown the hypothesis to be correct at both the general and the specific level. The analysis of electoral volatility, of changes in the size of party membership, of the level of abstentionism, and also of the attitudes towards the parties and, more generally, towards the political system have also provided useful indicators for measuring the depth of this process. The next problem is, therefore, to look for explanations.

Before coming to this, however, two points should be noted. First, the gap between civil society and the parties has been clearly perceived by the political class and has been the centre of a major discussion and debate which has been widely covered by the mass media. For some time now, Italy has been concerned about 'the crisis of the parties'. Secondly, and more significantly, that phenomenon has probably been one of the most typical and recurring feature of Western democracies, not just Italy, during the last decades and is a phenomenon of relevance to the United States as well as to Europe. As Lipset and Schneider have recently shown on the basis of an analysis of hundreds of surveys conducted in the United States during the past 40 years, the lack of confidence towards political (as well as economic) institutions has grown substantially over the last 15 years.[39] Here also, manifest discontent towards the behaviour of government, increased electoral abstentionism, and a decline in party and labour union membership are central elements which, as in Italy, provide a picture of declining confidence. Lipset and Schneider offer two hypotheses in order to explain this change. The first is primarily cultural, and can be defined as a sort of basic and particularly American aversion towards the concentration of public and private power. The second hypothesis maintains that declining confidence was due to failures in domestic and foreign policy, as well as in the economy as a result of the oil crisis, recession and inflation.

TABLE 7

ELECTORAL RESULTS FOR CHRISTIAN DEMOCRACY (LOWER CHAMBER), BY GEOGRAPHICAL AREAS, 1963–83

	1963	1968	1972	1976	1979	1983
	%	%	%	%	%	%
Italy	38.3	39.1	38.7	38.8	38.3	32.9
North	38.4	39.4	39.3	39	37.3	31.5
Centre	32.8	33.5	33.7	34.2	33	29
South	41.5	42.2	41.2	41.3	42.9	37.4
'White area'[1]	52.3	52.4	52.5	50.4	48.5	42.2

Note: 1. The so called 'white' area is formed by the following provinces: Asti, Cuneo, Como, Sondrio, Bergamo, Brescia, Trento, Bolzano, Verona, Padova, Vicenza, Treviso, Belluno, Udine, Pordenone and Lucca.

Source: Adapted from Tables 1 and 2 and M. Caciagli, 'Il resistibile declino della Democrazia Cristiana', in G. Pasquino (ed.), *Il sistema politico italiano* (forthcoming).

While the second hypothesis is not completely irrelevant to explanations of the Italian experience,[40] nevertheless there are also other aspects which are empirically controllable and which can suggest another basic explanation. If one looks at the electoral record of the Christian Democrats in the various geographic areas and, above all, at its constant electoral decline since 1972 in the so-called 'white provinces' – where Catholic subculture has traditionally been strong – and in the large Italian cities (Table 7); if one then considers the decline in DC membership in the same zones; if one also notes that the organic connection between religious associations and the Catholic party has ended; and finally, if one looks to the overall decline in religious practice,[41] then one is drawn to the inevitable conclusion that there has been a substantial process of secularisation, a process which has involved young people and the inhabitants of the cities and the more industrialised zones. In effect, the DC 'finds itself confronted with a progressive demobilisation of organisation in the Catholic world ... the old "collateralism" is waning throughout the national territory'.[42] There is, in short, an evident disaggregation of the 'white' Catholic subculture which for decades had sustained the vote for the Christian Democrats.

On the basis of electoral data alone it is not possible to reach similar conclusions for the so-called 'red belt' and the Communist Party (see Table 2). Nevertheless, in this case, too, the decline in PCI recruitment since the end of the 1970s (see Table 3), particularly in the large cities; the growth of abstentionism in these zones (this can be seen indirectly in Table 5); and above all what has already been noted regarding new parties (both the Radicals and the extreme left) and the collective movements during the 1970s, all offer a picture which is anything but stable.

All of this suggests a general explanatory hypothesis which is also of theoretical interest. In general terms, Italy has experienced substantial socio-economic change in the 1960s as a result of increased urbanisation, industrialisation, growth in eduction, and so on. It is a country which has been characterised by phenomena which, on the one hand, can be labelled as socio-economic modernisation and, on the other hand, as social mobilisation.[43] The existence, diffusion and depth of these processes are brought out in the mass of statistical data and research that has been carried out since the end of the 1960s. Moreover, it is a social mobilisation which has been 'translated', with profound effects, at the political level, serving to initiate the process by which a gap has grown between party and civil society.

The political 'manifestation' of mobilisation is obviously incomplete due to some counter-reactions on the one hand and the force of institutional inertia on the other. In particular, one may note the tendency towards an 'electoral freezing', at least until the mid-1970s, which is typical of a party system which remains polarised and where resistance is offered by the political subcultures and by the clientelistic control of civil society, particularly in certain areas. On this last point, it is possible to suggest some sort of sub-hypothesis concerning the way in which the parties have reacted to the increasing gap between their own organisations and civil society. Partly as a result also of the economic crisis, the parties have increased their influence and their level of intervention in the various governmental and para-governmental structures by means of an increasing penetration of the state itself (*lottizzazione*). In other words, in the face of a declining representative role, the parties have reacted by trying to acquire a greater consensus-control of civil society, becoming more evidently a sort of 'gatekeeper', both nationally and locally, in the recruitment to the various agencies of the government (and outside the government) of allied personnel. They also determine, to some extent, the allocation of resources in economic activity, both industrial and non-industrial. Thus they try to gain consensus-control of large strata of dependent workers and employees, and of other social groups whose incomes are bound to the indirect presence of the parties in the economy.[44] It is clearly difficult to test this hypothesis empirically; but what presents even greater difficulty to the analyst is its diachronic nature, in that it would be necessary to demonstrate a growth of *lottizzazione* over time, comparing the situation now with that pertaining some 15 or 20 years ago. The hypothesis does, however, remain plausible.[45] It can even be argued that *lottizzazione* has always existed in Italy, but that 20 years ago it was less visible insofar as it worked to the advantage only of the Christian Democrats, while now it involves all the parties in the political spectrum, including the Communists at local level. This change in itself, however, has brought about several conflicts between the parties, thus inevitably giving the whole phenomenon more visibility.

In addition to this, there are also two relatively new phenomena that can be seen as means through which party elites have attempted to counter the growing gap between society and party, and to avoid a greater detachment from the democratic regime. These are the various proposals for institutional reform and for a renewed role for the top party leadership, both proposals ultimately stressing the need for improved decisional efficacy. The debate on institutional reforms or, more specifically, on changes of the electoral law, changes in the relationship between cabinet and parliament, the transformation of a bicameral parliament into a unicameral institution, and other proposals of the different actors, basically stress the relevance of a transformation towards improved 'governability'. In other words, they are seeking to transform the image of immobilism and inefficiency attaching to the democratic institutions and the party system. The debate has heated up following the 1983 election, and the formation of a parliamentary committee, composed of both Senators and Deputies, is a clear and at least external sign of the parties' intentions. Whether this will actually result in a tangible reform is, of course, another question.

The second phenomenon that has to be mentioned here is less easily defined, in that it involves a new, more visible role for the top party leaders, a change which has also been magnified by the increased political role of the mass media in Italy during the last few years. The profile accorded to the Socialist leader, Craxi – who became Prime Minister after the 1983 elections – as well as that of the Republican Party leader, Spadolini – Prime Minister of the two previous governments – the Christian Democrat De Mita, and even more so in the case of the Radical leader Pannella, have exemplified this trend. Again in this case, stress is laid on the capacity of such leaders to make effective decisions without the various constraints imposed by party and organised interests. The results of this phenomenon seem mixed and ambiguous. While it has undermined the role of fractions within the parties, an emphasis on the appeal of the party leader is immediately and directly addressed to electors and citize'ns, and leapfrogs over the more traditional party channels. To the extent that it represents an attempt to create new identifications or even maintain the older ones, it is likely that the object of identification will change from party to leader. And insofar as there develops a personalisation of politics,'then the older identifications, rooted in subcultures, ancillary organisations, party structures and so on, will wane. In this sense, the paradoxical result of an effort to close the growing gap between party and society could be a reaction which involves at least the marginalisation of the institution of party.

In conclusion, and reverting to the central explanatory hypothesis concerning the 'translation' of social mobilisation, it is necessary to explain how the growth of participation (a manifestation typical of political mobilisation) during the first part of the 1970s was followed by the apathy of more recent years. Herein lies the specificity and theoretical relevance of the traditional theories of mobilisation. According to Deutsch, Germani and other scholars who have analysed this process, mobilisation – both social and political – usually completes its cycle with a new form of integration or assimilation. The Italian case appears to suggest that such an end-phase is not necessary, however, in that at the political level (but also, arguably, at the social level), there is no evidence of a new integration. On the contrary; precisely because of its own inherent characteristics, mobilisation and the subsequent growth of participation through channels and forms that are not institutionalised cannot endure. Rather than being succeeded by a new integration, there is a stage of demobilisation, in the sense of a decrease in political participation and the absence of support for new values.[46] From one perspective, such a stage can persist and develop into a normal state characterised by apathy and indifference towards political institutions (and, in the first place, towards the parties themselves). As mentioned above, this phenomenon may also be relevant to Western political development in general and to the institutionalisation of mass democracies. Nevertheless, there is no doubt that it is of particular importance in Italy, where mass democracy since the Second World War has been characterised by the centrality and increased role of the parties with respect to civil society.

NOTES

1. For the best general surveys of the Italian political system published during the last decade, see: P. Farneti (ed.), *Il sistema politico italiano* (Bologna: Il Mulino, 1973); F.L. Cavazza and S.R. Graubard (eds.), *Il caso italiano* (Milan: Garzanti, 1974); V. Castronovo (ed.), *L'Italia contemporanea, 1945–1975* (Turin: Einaudi, 1976); A. Martinelli and G. Pasquino, *La politica nell'Italia che cambia* (Milan: Feltrinelli, 1978); L. Graziano and S. Tarrow (eds.), *La crisi italiana*, 2 vols. (Turin: Einaudi, 1979).
2. The crisis of parties has been a recurring theme of debate in Italy. See G. Pasquino, *Crisi dei partiti e governabilità* (Bologna: Il Mulino, 1980); R. Ruffilli, 'Crisi dei partiti e culture politiche in Italia', *Il Politico*, Vol. 46 (1981), pp.675–90; and P. Farneti, 'Elementi per un'analisi della crisi del partito di massa', *Democrazia e diritto*, Vol. 18, No.3 (1978),

pp. 713–25. But to understand how this is a debated topic also within the political class see the collective work edited by Senator (Independent Left) G. Gozzini, *I partiti e lo stato* (Bari: De Donato, 1982).

3. On the DC, see A. Parisi (ed.), *Democristiani* (Bologna: Il Mulino, 1979); on the PCI, M. Ilardi and A. Accornero, *Il Partito Comunista Italiano. Struttura e storia dell'organizzazione* (Milan: Feltrinelli, 1982); on the PSI, V. Spini and S. Mattana (eds.), *I quadri del PSI* (Florence: Nuova Guaraldi, 1981); and F. Cazzola, 'Il PSI negli anni settanta', *Schema*, Vol. 5 (1982), pp. 19–47. See also G. Poggi (ed.), *L'organizzazione del PCI e della DC* (Bologna: Il Mulino, 1968); and F. Cazzola, *Il partito come organizzazione. Studio di un caso: il PSI* (Rome: Edizioni del Tritone, 1970). The largest amount of research on a party has been that carried out on the PCI. For example, in the last year three valuable works have been published: S. Belligni (ed.), *La giraffa e il liocorno. Il PCI dagli anni '70 al nuovo decennio* (Milano: Angeli, 1983); A. Accornero, R. Mannheimer and C. Sebastiani (eds.), *L'identità comunista. I militanti, le strutture, la cultura del PCI* (Roma: Editori Riuniti, 1983); and R. Mieli (ed.), *Il PCI allo specchio* (Milan: Rizzoli, 1983).

4. See G. Pasquino, 'Sources of Stability and Instability in the Italian Party System', *West European Politics*, Vol. 6 (1983), pp. 93–110; and also P. Lange, 'La teoria degli incentivi e l'analisi dei partiti politici', *Rassegna italiana di sociologia*, Vol. 18 (1977), pp. 501–26.

5. A recent review article on the Italian party system is S. Belligni, 'Sul sistema partitico dell'Italia contemporanea', *Stato e mercato*, Vol. 3 (1983), pp. 317–41. But see also G. Sartori, *Teoria dei partiti e caso italiano* (Milan: Sugarco, 1982), esp. Chs. I and XI; S. Tarrow, 'The Italian Party System Between Crisis and Transition', *American Journal of Political Science*, Vol. 21 (1977), pp. 193–224; G. Sani, 'Notas sobre el sistema italiano de partidos', *Revista de estudios politicos*, No. 27 (May–June 1982), pp. 29–63; P. Farneti, *Il sistema dei partiti in Italia, 1946–1979* (Bologna: Il Mulino, 1983). There are also several essays devoted to more specific features of the Italian party system. Among these, at least two deserve to be cited: R.D. Putnam, R. Leonardi and R.Y. Nanetti, 'Polarization and Depolarization in Italian Politics, 1968–1981', paper delivered at the APSA Annual Meeting, New York, September 1981; and I.H. Daalder, 'The Italian Party System in Transition: The End of Polarized Pluralism?', *West European Politics*, Vol. 6 (1983), pp. 216–36.

6. There has been little work published on the role of the different structures of intermediation from a comparative perspective. On party government, however, see G. Pasquino, 'Party Government in Italy: Achievements and Prospects', in R. Katz (ed.), *The Future of Party Government* (Florence: European University Institute, forthcoming).

7. In spite of the salience of the topic, the '*occupazione dello stato*' is not a well-researched area; however, see F. Cazzola (ed.), *Anatomia del potere DC. Enti pubblici e 'centralita democristiana*' (Bari: De Donato, 1979). This problem is also related to the various scandals and corruption that have affected the Italian Republic. A good, basically journalistic account of this history is G. Galli, *L'Italia sotterranea. Storia, politica e scandali* (Bari: Laterza, 1983).

8. This is also, for example, the focus of M. Fedele, *Classi e partiti negli anni '70* (Rome: Editori Riuniti, 1979); or more recently G. Pasquino, 'Partiti, società civile, istituzioni e il caso italiano', *Stato e mercato*, Vol. 3 (1983), pp. 169–205.

9. For example, M.N. Pedersen, 'Changing Patterns of Electoral Volatility in European Party Systems, 1948–1977', in H. Daalder and P. Mair (eds.) *Western European Party Systems, Continuity and Change* (London: Sage Publications, 1983), pp. 29–36. More sophisticated techniques to analyse electoral fluidity or volatility were formulated by M. Barbagli, P. Corbetta, A. Parisi and H.M.A. Schadee, *Fluidità elettorale e classi sociali in Italia* (Bologna: Il Mulino, 1979).

10. I would like to thank Stefano Bartolini, who provided me with the data set on which I calculated the different types of volatility shown in Table 1.

11. On these elections, see A. Parisi and G. Pasquino (eds.) *Continuità e mutamento elettorale in Italia* (Bologna: Il Mulino, 1977); and H.R. Penniman (ed.), *Italy at the Polls. The Parliamentary Elections of 1976* (Washington: American Enterprise Institute, 1977).

12. See A. Parisi (ed.), *Mobilità senza movimento. Le elezioni del 3 giugno 1979* (Bologna: Il Mulino, 1980); and H.R. Penniman (ed.), *Italy at the Polls, 1979. A Study of the Parliamentary Elections* (Washington: American Enterprise Institute, 1981).

13. A. Parisi and G. Pasquino, 'Changes in Italian Electoral Behaviour: The Relationships Between Parties and Voters', in P. Lange and S. Tarrow (eds.), *Italy in Transition. Conflict and Consensus* (London: Frank Cass, 1980), p. 20. In their previous work of 1977 (see note 11), Parisi and Pasquino had developed an important typology of voting in which the third type is the *exchange vote*, that is, the clientelistic vote.
14. Up to now no analysis of the last elections has been published. For a first overview of the data see A. Agosta, 'Le elezioni in Italia', in *Quaderni dell'Osservatorio Elettorale*, No. 11 (1983), pp. 119–55.
15. See M. Rossi, 'Un partito d'anime morte? Il tesseramento democristiano tra mito e realtà', in A. Parisi (ed.), *Democristiani*, op. cit., pp. 13–59.
16. F. Cazzola, 'Le difficili identità dei partiti di massa', *Laboratorio politico*, Vol. 2 (1982), pp. 20–21.
17. On this point see G. Poggi (ed.), *L'organizzazione del PCI e della DC*, op. cit., p. 341.
18. Here I am following the data and the analysis proposed by F. Cazzola, 'Le difficili identità dei partiti di massa', op. cit.
19. See ibid., p. 24.
20. On the Radical Party, see M. Teodori and A. Panebianco, *I nuovi radicali. Storia e sociologia di un movimento politico* (Milano: Mondadori, 1977); and M. Gusso, *Il Partito Radicale. Organizzazione e leadership* (Padua: Cleup, 1982).
21. On this topic, see F. Alberoni, *Movimento e istituzione* (Bologna: Il Mulino, 1981); A. Melucci, *L'invenzione del presente. Movimenti, identità, bisogni individuali* (Bologna: Il Mulino, 1982); A. Melucci, *Sistema politico, partiti e movimenti sociali* (Milan: Feltrinelli, 1977); G.E. Rusconi, 'I partiti italiani di fronte ai movimenti collettivi', *Rivista di storia contemporanea*, Vol. 6 (1977), pp. 552–67; and S. Tarrow, 'Protest and Institutional Reforms in Italy: Movements, Events and Political Cycles', paper delivered at Centro di Scienza Politica, Fondazione Feltrinelli, Milano, May 1983.
22. See M. Barbagli and P. Corbetta, 'L'elettorato, l'organizzazione del PCI e i movimenti', *Il Mulino*, Vol. 29, No. 269 (1980), pp. 467–90.
23. For a recent assessment, see G. Bingham Powell, 'Voting Turnout in Thirty Democracies: Partisan, Legal, and Socio-Economic Influences', in R. Rose (ed.), *Electoral Participation. A Comparative Analysis* (London and Beverly Hills: Sage Publications, 1980); and K. Dittrich and L.N. Johansen 'Voting Turnout in Europe, 1945–1978', in H. Daalder and P. Mair (eds.), *Western European Party Systems*, op. cit.
24. V. La Mesa, 'Considerazioni utili ai fini della quantificazione del fenomeno', in M. Caciagli and P. Scaramozzino (eds.), *Il voto di chi non vota. L'astensionismo elettorale in Italia e in Europa* (Milan: Comunità, 1983), p. 196.
25. See A. Bucciarelli and M. Tinacci Mossello, 'I connotati territoriali dell'astensionismo in Italia in rapporto ad alcuni fenomeni economici e politici', in M. Caciagli and P. Scaramozzino (eds.), *Il voto di chi non vota*, op. cit.; but also P. Giovannini, 'Astensionismo elettorale e questione giovanile', *Rivista italiana di scienza politica*, Vol. 12 (1982), pp. 457–77.
26. P.G. Corbetta and H.M.A. Schadee, 'L'astensionsimo elettorale in Italia dal 1968 al 1980', in M. Caciagli and P. Scaramozzino (eds.), *Il voto di chi non vota*, op. cit., pp. 272 and 274.
27. Ibid., p. 263.
28. All these data can be found in the official publication, *Risultati delle elezioni della Camera dei Deputati del 26 giugno 1983*, Camera dei Deputati – IX Legislatura, Prerogative e Immunità, Roma, 1 August 1983 (and in a similar official source for the Senate).
29. G. Sani, 'L'immagine dei partiti nell'elettorato', in M. Caciagli and A. Spreafico (eds.), *Un sistema politico alla prova* (Bologna: Il Mulino, 1975), pp. 94 and 117.
30. These data come from the Sartori–Marradi Survey, Institute of Political Science, University of Florence, 1975.
31. G. Fabris, *Il comportamento politico degli italiani* (Milan: Angeli, 1977), p. 30.
32. Doxa Survey, Bulletin 8–9, 1979. This figure is also quoted by G. Guidorossi, *Gli italiani e la politica. Valori, opinioni, atteggiamenti dal dopoguerra a oggi* (Milano: Angeli, 1984), pp. 64–5. As suggested by the title, Guidorossi made a very accurate and thorough analysis of the survey research conducted in Italy over the last 30 years, focusing her attention on the changes in attitudes towards the political system, the parties, political interests and

participation. Here I will not deal with some of the features concerning the parties. For their image at mass level see, recently, M.G. Favara and L. Giuliano, *Immagine dei partiti or partiti dell'immagine?* (Milano: Angeli, 1983).

33. G. Calvi, *La classe fortezza. Scelte degli elettori e responsabilità della classe politica in Italia* (Milano: Angeli, 1980), p. 121. See also his previous, *Valori e stili di vita degli italiani* (Milano: Isedi, 1977).

34. See the various issues of *Eurobarometer. Public opinion in the European Community*, Commission of the European Community, Brussels. The surveys for Italy are conducted by the Doxa Institute.

35. G. Fabris, *Il comportamento politico degli italiani*, op. cit., p. 18.

36. G. Guidórissi, *Gli italiani e la politica*, op. cit., p. 251.

37. Ibid., p. 140.

38. Among the research carried out on youth attitudes, one should also note C. Tullio-Altan and A. Marradi, *Valori, classi sociali, scelte politiche. Indagine sulla gioventù degli anni settanta* (Milano: Bompiani, 1976). For workers' attitudes, G. Urbani and M. Weber, *Cosa pensano gli operai. Lavoro, economia e politica negli oreintamenti degli operai agli inizi degli anni ottanta* (Milano: Angeli, 1984).

39. See S.M. Lipset and W. Schneider, *The Confidence Gap: Business, Labor, and Government in the Public Mind* (New York: The Free Press, 1983).

40. I developed a similar hypothesis for Italy in an earlier paper, 'Which Crisis of Democracy in Italy?', delivered at ISPP Sixth Annual Scientific Meeting, St Catherine's College, Oxford, 19–22 July 1983.

41. G. Guidorissi, *Gli italiani e la politica*, op. cit., p. 242.

42. M. Caciagli, 'Il resistible declino della Democrazia Cristiana', in G. Pasquino (ed.), *Il sistema politico italiano*, forthcoming.

43. See the seminal essay by K.W. Deutsch, 'Social Mobilization and Political Development', *American Political Science Review*, Vol. 55 (1961), pp. 493–514.

44. A similar hypothesis is briefly put forward by A. Panebianco, 'Tendenze carismatiche nelle società contemporanee', *Il Mulino*, Vol. 22 (1983), p. 523.

45. I have not dealt with the growing role of the mass media, particularly television, in Italian politics, all of which is also part of the phenomenon analysed in this article. For a recent assessment, see G. Pasquino, 'Mass media, partito di massa e trasformazione della politica', and C. Marletti, 'Il "potere dei media": sulla crescente interazione fra comunicazioni e politica', both in *Il Mulino*, Vol. 32, No. 288 (1983), pp. 559–79 and 580–98; and G. Grossi (ed.), *Comunicare politica* (Milano: Angeli, 1983).

46. Germani does consider the possibility of apathy instead of a new integration. See his 'Nuovi elementi per una teoria della mobilitazione sociale', in G. Germani, *Autoritarismo, fascismo e classi sociali* (Bologna: Il Mulino, 1975), p. 37.

Scandinavian Party Politics Re-examined: Social Democracy in Decline?

Diane Sainsbury

In two important respects, developments in the 1970s appear to challenge the classic textbook presentation of Scandinavian party politics. First, standard treatments have underlined stability as a hallmark of Scandinavian politics,[1] and Denmark, Norway and Sweden seemed to provide prime examples of party systems based on frozen alignments. The 1973 elections in Denmark and Norway did much to shatter this image of Scandinavian party politics. In both countries, but especially in Denmark, unprecedented numbers of voters switched parties in 1973. New parties also competed successfully with the established parties, and their success was phenomenal in Denmark where they polled one third of the vote. Virtually overnight the number of parties represented in the Danish parliament doubled, increasing from five to ten.[2] These elections, in fact, led to speculations about the de-freezing of party systems. Writing in the wake of the elections, Giovanni Sartori declared that the frozen party systems were under serious challenge, and that the Scandinavian countries were presumably only the forerunners of a more general trend.[3]

A second hallmark of Scandinavian party politics has been the dominant role of the Social Democratic parties since the inter-war period. In the 1970s the electoral fortunes of the Scandinavian Social Democrats waned, and the three parties experienced serious erosion or stagnation at the polls. The most conspicuous election losses during the decade were the devastating defeats of the Danish and Norwegian Social Democrats in 1973 – the worst in their histories – and the 1976 Swedish election which ended the 44-year reign of the Social Democrats. The fading fortunes of the Social Democrats have caused observers to question the future of a predominant party system in the Scandinavian countries. Thus the electoral politics of the past decade indicate that a re-examination of what have been regarded as the distinctive characteristics of the Scandinavian party systems is warranted.

This re-examination of Scandinavian party politics focuses on the three Social Democratic parties. By way of introduction, it discusses the nature of Social Democratic predominance and several of its major contributing factors. This part of the discussion also looks more closely at the difficulties of the parties during the 1970s and changes in the bases of Social Democratic predominance.

The central part of the analysis addresses simultaneously two issues related to the distinctive features of Scandinavian party politics. The first issue is the nature of the difficulties of the Social Democrats – and whether the difficulties are so grave as to undermine the pre-eminence of the Scandinavian Social Democrats. The analysis concentrates on enduring sources of partisan attachment, and it attempts to discover whether serious erosion in these dimensions of party support occurred during the past decade. Secondly, this analysis is also relevant to the discussion on the de-freezing of party systems. By concentrating on the enduring sources of party support, the analysis adds to our knowledge of stabilising influences in Scandinavian party politics – influences which assumedly counteract or slow down the de-freezing process. Drawing on this analysis, the concluding section speculates on the future prospects of the Scandinavian Social Democrats.

I. THE PREDOMINANCE OF THE SOCIAL DEMOCRATS

The dominant position of the Social Democrats in Scandinavian party politics has been clearly reflected in their control of the executive. Table 1 shows the party composition of governments in the three countries during the post-war period, and at first glance the Social Democrats' long periods in government stand out. During the 35 years between 1945 and 1980 the Danish Social Democrats (SD) were in office for roughly 25 years, the Norwegian Social Democrats (DNA) for 28 years, and the Swedish Social Democrats (SAP) for 31 years. In all three cases this is an impressive record.

The number of years in government, however, is only one measure of party dominance of the executive, and in multi-party systems it must be complemented. Equally important is the nature of the government: firstly, whether it is a coalition government or a single-party government and, secondly, whether it is a minority or a majority government.

During the post-war decades coalition governments involving the Social Democrats have not been as prominent a feature of Scandinavian party politics as, for example, in West Germany and Austria.[4] It should also be noted that the Scandinavian Social Democrats have always been the dominant partner in such governments. As can be seen in Table 1, coalition governments consisting of the Social Democrats and one or more non-socialist parties have been most numerous in Denmark. The heyday of this type of government was from the late 1950s through the mid-1960s, but as recently as 1978–79 a coalition government was formed by the Social Democrats and the Agrarian Liberals. In Sweden only one Social Democratic/non-socialist coalition has existed during the post-war period when a red–green coalition was resurrected for six years in the 1950s. Coalition governments between the Social Democrats and the non-socialists have not figured at all in Norwegian party politics.

Minority Social Democratic governments have been commonplace in all three countries – but most common in Denmark. In fact, a Social Democratic government with a Social Democratic parliamentary majority has never occurred in Denmark. Furthermore, as is evident from Table 1, purely Social Democratic governments in Denmark have had a narrower parliamentary base than those in Norway and Sweden. An inspection of Table 1 discloses that the parliamentary strength of the SD (percentage of seats) has been consistently less than that of the DNA and SAP. Indeed, the highest percentages of the SD barely match the poorest percentage of the SAP after its defeat in 1976. Alternation of parties in government has also occurred

TABLE 1

SOCIALIST ELECTORAL PERFORMANCE, PARLIAMENTARY STRENGTH AND THE COMPOSITION OF GOVERNMENT IN DENMARK, NORWAY AND SWEDEN

DENMARK

Year	Social Democrats (SD)		Other Socialist Parties		Socialist Bloc		Government Party/Parties
	Vote %	Seats %	Vote %	Seats %	Vote %	Seats %	
1945	32.8	32.4	12.5	12.1	45.3	44.5	Agrarian Liberals
1947	40.0	38.5	6.8	6.1	46.8	44.6	SD
1950	39.6	39.6	4.6	4.7	44.2	44.3	Agrarian Liberals-Conservatives
1953	40.4	40.9	4.8	4.7	45.2	45.6	SD
1953	41.3	42.3	4.3	4.6	45.6	46.9	
1957	39.4	40.0	3.1	3.4	42.5	43.4	SD-Radicals-Single Tax (M)
1960	42.1	43.4	7.2	6.3	49.3	49.7	SD-Radicals (M)
1964	41.2	43.4	7.0	5.7	48.9	49.1	SD
1966	38.2	39.4	11.7	11.4	49.9	50.9	SD
1968	34.2	35.4	9.1	8.6	43.3	44.0	Radicals-Conservatives-Agrarian Liberals (M)
1971	37.3	40.0	12.1	9.7	49.4	49.7	SD
1973	25.6	26.3	11.1	9.7	36.7	36.0	Agrarian Liberals
1975	29.9	30.3	11.3	11.4	41.2	41.7	SD
1977	37.0	37.1	10.3	10.9	47.3	48.0	SD-Agrarian Liberals (1978–79)
1979	38.3	38.9	11.9	9.7	50.2	48.6	SD (1981–82)
1981	32.9	33.7	15.3	14.9	48.2	48.6	Non-socialist coalition (1982 –)

Note: M = government with parliamentary majority.

Sources: Statistisk årbog, 1982, pp. 368–9; Mogens N. Pedersen, 'Denmark: The Breakdown of a "Working Multiparty System"?', Odense University Working Papers, No.11, 1981, pp. 8, 16–17, 40–41.

TABLE 1 (continued)

Year	Social Democrats (DNA)		Other Socialist Parties		Socialist Bloc		Government Party/Parties
	Vote %	Seats %	Vote %	Seats %	Vote %	Seats %	
1945	41.0	50.7	11.9	7.3	52.9	58.	DNA (M)
1949	45.7	56.7	5.8	0	51.5	56.7	DNA (M)
1953	46.7	51.3	5.1	2.0	51.8	53.3	DNA (M)
1957	48.3	52.0	3.4	0.7	51.7	52.7	DNA (M)
1961	46.8	49.3	5.3	1.3	52.1	50.6	DNA
1965	43.1	45.3	7.4	1.3	50.5	46.6	Non-Socialist Four-Party Coalition (M)
1969	46.5	49.3	4.5	0	51.0	49.3	Non-socialists (M) / DNA (1971–72) / Non-Socialist – Centre & Christian People's Party (1972–73)
1973	35.3	40.0	11.6	10.3	46.9	50.3	DNA
1977	42.3	49.0	5.2	1.3	47.5	50.3	DNA
1981	37.2	42.6	5.9	2.6	43.1	45.2	Conservatives (1981–83) / Non-socialist Three-Party Coalition (1983 –) (M)

NORWAY

Notes: M = government with parliamentary majority. A non-socialist government existed for four weeks in 1963.

Sources: Henry Valen, *Valg og politikk* (Oslo: NKS-Forlaget, 1981), pp. 24, 27; *Statistisk årbok*, 1983, pp. 381–3.

TABLE 1 (continued)

Year	Social Democrats (SAP)		Other Socialist Parties		Socialist Bloc		Government Party/Parties
	Vote %	Seats %	Vote %	Seats %	Vote %	Seats %	
1948	46.1	48.7	6.3	3.5	52.4	52.2	SAP
1952	46.1	47.8	4.3	2.2	50.4	50.0	SAP-Agrarians (1951–57) (M)
1956	44.6	45.9	5.0	2.6	49.6	48.5	SAP
1958	46.2	48.1	3.4	2.2	49.6	50.3	SAP
1960	47.8	49.1	4.5	2.2	52.3	51.3	SAP
1964	47.3	48.5	5.2	3.4	52.5	51.9	SAP
1968	50.1	53.6	3.0	1.3	53.1	54.9	SAP (M)
1970	45.3	46.6	5.2	4.9	50.5	51.4	SAP
1973	43.6	44.6	5.7	5.4	49.3	50.0	SAP
1976	42.7	43.6	5.1	4.9	47.8	48.4	Non-Socialists(1976–78) (M) Liberals (1978–79)
1979	43.2	44.1	6.0	5.7	49.2	49.9	Non-Socialists (1979–81) (M) Centre-Liberals (1981–82) (M) SAP
1982	45.6	47.6	5.7	6.0	51.3	53.6	

SWEDEN

Notes: M = government with parliamentary majority. The percentages of seats through 1968 pertain to the Lower Chamber. The vote of other socialist parties includes the Communists and such parties as KFML, SKP and APK.

Source: SOS, 'Allmänna Valen 1982', Del. 1, pp.8, 15.

more often in Denmark, and the Danish Social Democrats have been 'in' and 'out' of office more frequently. Nonetheless, the SD has enjoyed long periods in power. The party's longest period of consecutive government was from 1953 until early 1968, and its second longest period was from 1975 to 1982.

Another crucial difference between the Social Democratic minority governments in Denmark and those in Sweden and Norway is that there has been a left majority (the Social Democrats and the parties to their left) on only one occasion in the Danish parliament, which was after the 1966 election to the Folketing. Thus the non-socialist parties, as a rule, have possessed a parliamentary majority in Denmark. The obvious importance of this constellation of party strength in parliament is that a majority decision could only be achieved through negotiations and compromises with the non-socialist parties.[5]

The Swedish Social Democrats' continuity in power during the post-war period stretched from 1945 to 1976. However, only once (1968–70) has the SAP formed a government based on an absolute majority of its own in parliament. Otherwise purely Social Democratic governments have been essentially minority governments – and this has clearly been the case since the introduction of the unicameral Riksdag in 1970. Even during the years of bicameralism Social Democratic governments were not fully-fledged majority administrations. Although the party had a majority in the upper chamber, it lacked a majority in the lower chamber. The lack of a Social Democratic majority in the lower chamber was a serious handicap, and the passage of legislation required the support or abstention of at least one additional party. As distinct from the Danish situation, however, the SAP minority governments have generally had the advantage of a left majority in parliament (see Table 1) which in theory has meant an option of compromising either to the left or the right. In this sense, the centre of political gravity in parliamentary party politics has been further to the left in Sweden than in Denmark.

The Norwegian Social Democrats – in contrast to the Danish and Swedish parties – enjoyed a lengthy period of continuous majority government from 1945 to 1961. From the early 1960s onwards, however, Social Democratic administrations have been minority governments – which, as in the Swedish case, usually had a left majority in parliament. As can be seen in Table 1, a key factor behind the DNA's period of majority rule was that the party was considerably overrepresented in parliament in relation to its share of the vote. Since 1961 the Social Democrats have failed to secure a majority in the Storting, although the party only missed the mark by one seat in 1961 and 1969. Social Democratic dominance of the executive was broken a decade earlier than in Sweden when a majority coalition government consisting of the four non-socialist parties took office in 1965. However, the DNA was in government during most of the 1970s.

Determinants of Social Democratic Predominance: Continuity and Change

Several circumstances have contributed to the predominance of the Scandinavian Social Democrats. This discussion examines a number of these factors in terms of continuity and change. It deals with persistent aspects which have helped to sustain the strong positions of the parties. It subsequently turns to the critical matter of changes in these determinants of Social Democratic strength.

Electoral strength. One major factor contributing to Social Democratic predominance has been the parties' ability to command the loyalties of large sections of their respective electorates. Table 1 shows that through the 1970s the Social Democrats frequently polled nearly 40 per cent or more of the vote. The main exceptions were the débâcles of the Danish and Norwegian parties in 1973, and the SD also did poorly in the 1968 and 1975 elections. The electoral performance of the Social Democrats appears even more impressive when it is compared with that of their competitors. In all three countries the Social Democrats have been and continue to be the largest party, and generally the only party possessing the possibility of gaining a majority of the vote, albeit an increasingly remote possibility in Denmark. Furthermore, in winning votes the Social Democrats have generally far outdistanced the next largest party. The gap in electoral strength between the Social Democrats and their largest rival can be assessed by comparing the Social Democrats' share of the vote with that of the next largest party.

TABLE 2

AVERAGE PERCENTAGE MARGIN OF ADVANTAGE OF THE SOCIAL DEMOCRATS
OVER THE NEXT LARGEST PARTY 1940–84

	1940s	1950s	1960s	1970s		1980s	
						(1981)	(1984)
SD	+15	+17	+19	+19		+18	+8
						(1981)	
DNA	+27	+30	+26	+18		+6	
						(1982)	
SAP	+30	+23	+32	+22		+22	

Note: For the 1980s the percentage differences are based on individual elections. The remaining figures are decade averages.

Sources: F.G. Castles, *The Social Democratic Image of Society* (London: Routledge & Kegan Paul, 1978), p. 11 and same as Table 1; *Politiken*, 12 January 1984, p. 6.

This gap in electoral strength is vividly illustrated by Table 2, which contains the average percentage margin of advantage for the Social Democratic parties per decade through the 1970s (and their percentage margins for the individual elections of the 1980s). Although the Danish party's relative weakness again shows up in a long-term perspective, the SD has generally enjoyed an average margin of advantage in the neighbourhood of 15 to 20 percentage points over the next largest party during most of the post-war period. The margin of advantage for the DNA and SAP has been as high as 30 percentage points during certain post-war decades. Throughout the 1970s the three parties, on the whole, managed to retain a substantial electoral lead over the next largest party, polling between 18 and 22 percentage points more than the nearest competitor.

The electoral performance of the Social Democrats in the 1970s and early 1980s, however, raises serious question marks about their continuing ability to command the allegiances of as large sections of the electorate as earlier. A weakening of their electoral strength is evidenced in their average share of the vote per decade, and the parties' margins of advantage suggest problems for the SD and DNA. In the case of the DNA the figures in Table 2 indicate an erosion in the 1970s and a drastic narrowing of its margins of advantage over the next largest party in the first election of the 1980s. The SD's percentage margin was also substantially reduced in the 1984 election. Although caution is in order here since it is not an advisable procedure to compare the results of single elections with decade averages, the figures for the 1981 Norwegian election and the 1984 Danish election reflect a recent important trend in Scandinavian party politics – a conservative surge.[6]

The average share of the parties' vote per decade reveals a decline for all three parties in the 1970s (Table 3). Looking at the SD's average for the 1970s, as well as its share of the vote in the 1981 and 1984 elections, it is necessary to ask whether the 'normal' vote of the Danish Social Democrats has not fallen from around 40 per cent to a little over 30 per cent. In light of the decade averages and the outcome of the 1981 Norwegian election, a similar question is justified with respect to the normal vote of the DNA: has it declined from substantially over 40 per cent to a little under this mark? The decline for the SAP is less than that of the other two parties. Nor is the slippage for the Swedish Social Democrats so serious in relation to their average in the 1950s. As distinct from the SD and DNA, the Swedish party also improved its performance in the first election of the 1980s.[7]

TABLE 3

AVERAGE PERCENTAGE OF SOCIAL DEMOCRATIC VOTE PER DECADE

	1940s	1950s	1960s	1970s
SD	39.1	40.2	39.1	33.6
DNA	43.4	47.5	45.5	38.6
SAP	48.9	46.6	48.4	43.7

Sources: Same as Table 1.

Divided opposition. A second crucial determinant of the Social Democrats' hegemonic position has been the fragmentation of the non-socialist opposition. Rather than confronting a single, large opposition party the Social

Democrats have been blessed with a situation of facing at least three or more non-socialist parties. This situation has entailed several advantages for the Social Democrats. In the electoral arena, non-socialist competition for votes is keen, and frequently the electoral gains of one non-socialist party have been at the expense of another non-socialist party. In the parliamentary arena, the division of the opposition into separate parties has provided the Social Democrats with considerable tactical manoeuvring room when they have been the party in government. The Social Democrats have often been able to enlist the support of one or more non-socialist parties in the middle of the political spectrum. Thus the division of the non-socialist opposition has allowed an accommodation between the moderate left and the centre, producing policies based on a fairly broad consensus and generally weakening the parliamentary influence of the conservative parties.

The crucial nature of the fragmentation of the non-socialist opposition for the Social Democrats' control of the executive made itself especially evident during the past decade in two quite dissimilar ways. First, the 1973 election in Denmark significantly altered the party system, and one of the effects was a further fragmentation of the non-socialist bloc of parties. Among the new non-socialist parties entering the Folketing was Møgens Glistrup's Progress Party. This party, however, was scorned by the other non-socialist parties and viewed as an unacceptable ally in parliamentary politics. Much of the SD's period in office during the 1970s and early 1980s, despite its weakened position, was facilitated by the increased fractionalisation of the Danish party system caused by the 1973 protest election.

By contrast, party politics in Sweden (and also in Norway except for the years of discord over EEC membership) have been characterised by greater coalescence among the non-socialist parties during the past two decades. The SAP's fall from power in 1976 was a historic event. But equally, if not more, historic was the formation of a majority non-socialist coalition government. The Swedish and Norwegian experiences underline that non-socialist cooperation and unity can seriously undermine the pre-eminence of the Social Democrats. Non-socialist cooperation raises the threshold of parliamentary representation required by the Social Democrats to form a government, and it can negate the Social Democratic parties' margin of advantage in the electoral arena. Thus the SAP racked up an impressive average margin of advantage of 22 percentage points over its nearest rival during the 1970s but spent nearly half of the decade out of power. In sum, the advantage of a fragmented and disunited non-socialist opposition cannot be underestimated.

Thus a critical question is whether the non-socialist parties are moving towards greater unity. The answer is inconclusive. On the one hand, coalescent tendencies in the parliamentary arena have been more apparent in recent decades than earlier. The non-socialist parties in all three countries have shown themselves capable of forming majority coalition governments. In Norway and Sweden the parties have repeatedly demonstrated their ability to do so. This has certainly made life more difficult for the Social Democrats – and created a challenge to their dominance over executive leadership. On the other hand, centrifugal tendencies among the non-socialists are also discernible. The non-socialist opposition still consists of several distinct parties, and party mergers remain unlikely. In fact, the opposite has been the case, especially in Denmark but also in Norway during the 1970s. Besides election rivalries, ideological and policy differences among the non-socialists continue to create strains. These differences have produced a hesitancy among some parties to enter a non-socialist coalition government and have even toppled non-socialist governments in all three countries. The conservative surge in popularity may also increase frictions among the non-socialists, mainly in Sweden and Norway.

The left vote. A third circumstance, which has frequently but not always favoured the Social Democrats, has been the size of the left vote (the combined electoral strength of the Social Democrats and parties to their left). In Sweden and Norway, votes cast for parties to the left of the Social Democrats have often deprived the non-socialists of a parliamentary majority and in some instances even prevented them from acquiring a larger number of seats than the Social Democrats. The 1965 and 1969 Norwegian elections constitute exceptions when the distribution of the vote operated to the disadvantage of left representation in the Storting (see Table 1). On the other hand, the DNA minority governments in the 1970s and early 1980s were generally possible because of the parliamentary representation of other left parties. Similarly, the SAP's ability to form a government became heavily – and more visibly – dependent upon the parliamentary representation of the Left Party–Communists from 1970 onwards. Previously, however, the tacit and sometimes unwilling support of the Communists was significant in contributing to the long reign of the Swedish Social Democrats. Since left voting has not been so extensive in Denmark, it has been of less significance. But in the future the implications of left voting for the SD – both positive and negative ones – may increase, as will be brought out in the concluding section.

The electoral support of other left parties, of course, also entails drawbacks for the Social Democrats. Since the early 1960s competition between the Social Democrats and the parties to their left has intensified in the electoral arena. The leftist parties have gained ground especially in Denmark. These parties won impressive victories in the first elections of the 1980s, receiving around 15 per cent of the vote. In comparison, the leftist parties in Norway and Sweden have experienced only modest success, polling roughly five to six per cent of the vote in recent elections (see Table 1).[8]

Mobilising resources. A fourth contributing factor has been the extensive mobilisation of the working class in Scandinavia. In a comparative context, working-class mobilisation in the Scandinavian countries is impressive, and it appears exceptional in the Swedish case. Some indication of its impressive nature is provided by looking at the membership of the two major organisational arms of the Scandinavian labour movements – the Social Democratic parties and the LO unions. Examining the membership of West European socialist parties in the late 1940s, Maurice Duverger found that the membership ratios (the number of party members in relation to party voters) of the Scandinavian parties were surpassed by only two other parties – the British Labour Party and the Austrian Socialist Party.[9] A similar comparison of party membership ratios of socialist parties in the 1970s puts the SAP at the top of the list. The DNA and SD also have comparatively high ratios despite stagnation or decline in party enrolment in recent decades. The trade unions have been even more successful than the parties in recruiting members, and union membership in Scandinavia ranks among the highest in the Western countries.[10] In the latter half of the 1970s the level of unionisation among workers was between 80 and 85 per cent in Sweden and Denmark, and around 60 per cent in Norway.

The organisational bases of Social Democratic strength show signs of erosion in Denmark and Norway, although in different ways. The prime weakness of the Danish Social Democrats has been a steady deterioration in party resources. At the close of the 1970s the organisational resources of the SD – party enrolment, funding and the labour press – were inferior to those of the Norwegian and Swedish Social Democrats. Most notably, party membership has experienced a severe and continuous decline during the post-war period. The labour press has also become a mere shadow of its former self through the decades. Trade union membership has continued to grow, and the LO unions provide important supportive links for the SD. However, frictions between the party and the unions in Denmark appeared greater than in Norway and Sweden during the past decade. Nor have the LO unions in Denmark been as effective in transmitting or reinforcing Social Democratic norms, at least in the case of party choice, as have the Swedish and Norwegian unions.

In Norway party membership underwent a decline in the 1950s but has subsequently more or less stabilised in the long run, although short-term fluctuations have occurred.[11] Instead the major area of organisational weakness of the Norwegian labour movement is the faltering level of unionisation. In particular, the Norwegian unions have been much less successful in recruiting young workers and women than their Swedish and Danish counterparts. Among working-class voters who have recently opted for the non-socialist parties in Norway, non-unionised workers have been a major group. These trends – the faltering level of unionisation and the deterioration of party resources – represent a weakening in the mobilising potential of the Social Democratic parties in Norway and Denmark.

In summary, this brief survey of the predominance of the Scandinavian Social Democrats reveals a number of changes. A general long-range tendency towards weaker Social Democratic governments and, for that matter, weaker governments in general can be observed. This trend of governments with a narrower parliamentary base became prominent during the 1970s in all three countries. An additional long-range tendency has been the lessening of Social Democratic dominance of the executive. These tendencies have also been accompanied by greater instability of governments, as witnessed in cabinets with shorter life spans. The contrast is sharpest in the Swedish case where six years of non-socialist government resulted in four different administrations, in comparison to 31 years of Social Democratic government basically characterised by successive renewal of cabinets – except for the formation of the red–green coalition and its dissolution in the 1950s.

The preceding discussion has also pointed to changes affecting the bases of Social Democratic pre-eminence and to possible problems: coalescent tendencies among the non-socialists, the challenge of the radical socialist parties, and a weakening of mobilising resources. Perhaps most fundamental to the future prospects of the Scandinavian Social Democrats as 'dominant parties' in control of the executive is the size of their electoral support. Admittedly, as we have seen, their control of the executive does not exclusively depend upon the share of the vote they poll. Nonetheless, the importance of the parties' polling strength cannot be denied. Accordingly, the electoral difficulties of the Social Democrats deserve a more detailed examination.

II. DIMENSIONS OF PARTY SUPPORT

The electoral performance of the Scandinavian Social Democrats, measured in terms of their average share of the vote per decade, shows a general decline in the 1970s. An essential question is whether the electoral difficulties of the Social Democrats are of an enduring or a transitory nature. This question is explored through an analysis of basic dimensions of party support which are presumed to constitute enduring sources of party attachments and long-term influences on electoral choice.

Borrowing from Ivor Crewe, I shall distinguish between the following three sources of party attachment: social, psychological and ideological.[12] The *social dimension* of party support refers to the group basis of a party and the voters' sense of identification with social groupings. The *psychological dimension* of party support consists of voters' feelings towards parties, both positive and negative. Most central to this dimension is the intensity of voters' identification with a party. The *ideological dimension* of party support involves a belief in the party's goals and programme. Essentially, this is an attitudinal component, and the focus here is confined to a number of left–right attitudes: voters' attitudes towards equalisation, welfare reforms and state intervention in the economy. If a weakening in these dimensions of party support is found, it suggests grave difficulties for the Social Democratic parties and a stronger likelihood of sustained decline and a permanent erosion of their dominance.

The logic behind this inquiry entails assumptions about the enduring nature of these dimensions of support. However, there are serious question marks about *how* enduring are these dimensions of support, as we shall see. Despite this important reservation it can be argued that these dimensions of party support clearly represent long-term forces shaping electoral choice, and that they are more enduring influences than such factors as the major issues of the election, events during the campaign, the attributes and appeal of candidates, campaign strategies and resources, and party performance between elections.

An examination of these dimensions of party support also casts light on the de-freezing of the Scandinavian party systems. Generally speaking, dealignment is viewed as the product of the weakening of enduring sources of partisan attachment, and in effect entails several distinct processes. One of these is related to the social dimension of party support. A major cleavage line, emphasised by Seymour M. Lipset and Stein Rokkan in their seminal discussion of the freezing of party systems, has been the owner–worker cleavage institutionalised through the establishment of working-class parties. The decline in class voting has been interpreted as a weakening of this cleavage alignment and its importance to electoral choice. A second set of processes centres on the psychological dimension of party support and trends in partisan decline: apathy towards elections as reflected in low turnouts, a lessening of the incidence and strength of party identification, and a growing lack of confidence in parties and party politicians. A third process is value change and concomitant changes in attitudes, which have a bearing on the ideological dimension of party support. Lipset and Rokkan spoke of the freezing of political alternatives, but they noted that these alternatives had been made increasingly irrelevant by structural change and economic growth.[13] In addition, much discussion has been devoted to the possible mounting irrelevancy of the traditional left–right axis or alternatively to its changing content and the possible emergence of a competing ideological axis during the 1970s. The analysis below, although it focuses on the Social Democrats' electoral problems, therefore, also contributes to the discussion on the 'thawing' of frozen party systems.

The Social Dimension of Party Support

A distinctive feature of the Scandinavian party systems has been an unusually strong influence of social class on partisanship. In a comparative perspective the role of class in structuring party preferences has been much stronger in Scandinavia than in many other Western countries. A cross-national comparison of recent trends in class voting indicates that occupational class continued to be a substantially more important factor shaping electoral choice in the Scandinavian countries than in several other nations in the late 1970s and early 1980s. Recent election studies further document that class was the single most important social source of party attachment in Scandinavia.

Class voting. Despite the strong continuing influence of class on partisanship, a decline in class voting has occurred during the past decades in Denmark, Norway and Sweden – as elsewhere. Broad trends in class voting have generally been summarised by employing the Alford index, which measures the difference between the percentage of the working class and the percentage of the middle class voting socialist (here the combined vote for the Social Democrats and the parties to their left). Figure 1 displays the trends in class voting in Denmark, Norway and Sweden – based on the Alford index – from the mid-1950s through the early 1980s.

The actual extent of the decline in class voting and its causes are the topic of much debate, and the Danish scores for the late 1950s and the first half of the 1960s in Figures 1 and 2 are based on data which probably inflate percentages and index values. However, even taking less dramatic estimates

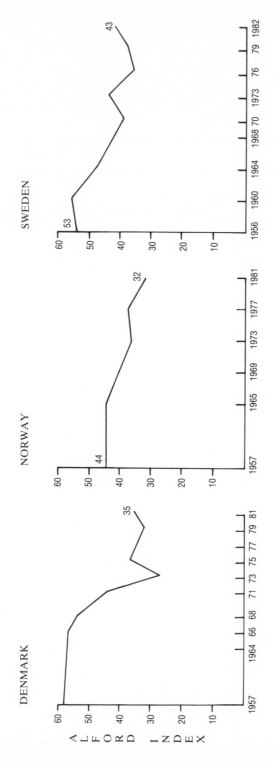

FIGURE 1
TRENDS IN CLASS VOTING IN SCANDINAVIA (ALFORD INDEX)

Sources: Torben Worre, 'Class Parties and Class Voting in the Scandinavian Countries', *Scandinavian Political Studies* (1980), p. 315; Ingemar Glans, 'Valvindar välter teoribyggnader', *Statsvetenskaplig tidskrift* (1983), p. 118; Walter Korpi, *The Democratic Class Struggle* (London: Routledge & Kegan Paul, 1983), p. 88; Henry Valen, *Valg og politikk* (Oslo: NKS–Forlaget, 1981), p. 131 and data from the 1981 Norwegian election survey.

in the Danish case, we can observe a considerable downward trend over the years in all three countries.

Implicit in much of the discussion about the decline in class voting has been the notion that such a development would work to the detriment of socialist parties. As working-class parties, the Social Democrats would witness a dwindling in their core of faithful voters. However, an inspection of the Alford index and the Social Democrats' share of the vote in various elections reveals that something is amiss with these assumptions. There is no consistent relationship between the index scores and the electoral perform-ance of the Social Democrats. Let us take the example of the SAP in the 1968 and 1973 elections. The index score for the 1968 election was 42 and the SAP won its largest victory at the polls during the post-war period. In 1973 the index score was 44 and this was one of the SAP's poorest elections. The main fault seems to be that the index measures similarities or differences between the classes but without indicating the level of socialist voting within each class.

Thus, in examining the social dimension of party support, it is much more insightful to take a separate look at each of the two components of the Alford index. Figure 2 plots, firstly, the percentage of the working class voting socialist and the percentage voting Social Democrat and, secondly, the percentage of the middle class voting socialist during the past two decades. It should be underlined that the class profiles for the three coun-tries in Figure 2 are not entirely comparable. Nevertheless, the profiles present the basic contours of class voting in each country and allow us to make broad comparisons.

Looking first at the pattern of leftist voting among workers, we find that a high proportion of Scandinavian workers vote socialist. On only one occa-sion – the 1973 Danish election – has this fallen below 60 per cent. However, a decline in socialist allegiances among working-class voters in the 1970s, compared to the 1960s, can also be detected in all three countries. Moreover, the decline in Social Democratic voting is more pronounced than the decline in socialist voting, as illustrated by the broken lines in Figure 2. Since the late 1950s the parties to the left of the Social Democrats have increased their share of the working-class vote, and their gains have been largest in Denmark.

Besides these common trends, quite dissimilar patterns for the three countries also emerge. In *Sweden* both socialist and Social Democratic voting have been characterised by the least amount of erosion. In fact, the picture of a long-term decline in socialist voting in Sweden must perhaps be revised in light of the 1982 election as the upswing in socialist voting of the working class continued. Even prior to the 1982 election, the decline was of relatively modest proportions. The stability of the working-class vote for the Social Democrats also stands out, and the SAP's decline is less extensive than that of the DNA and SD. In *Denmark* the Social Democrats have experienced the severest decline in working-class support – decreasing by 20 percentage points or more since the first half of the 1960s. The SD's support among young workers also deteriorated badly in the 1970s. On the other hand, the SD's decline has been largely offset by an impressive increase in

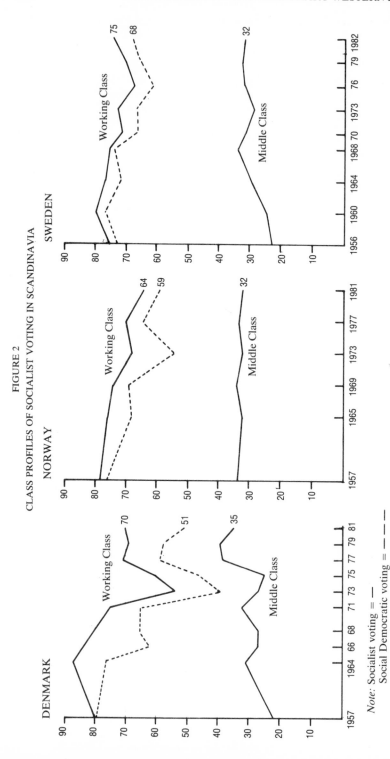

FIGURE 2
CLASS PROFILES OF SOCIALIST VOTING IN SCANDINAVIA

Note: Socialist voting = ——
Social Democratic voting = — — — —

Sources: Same as Figure 1 and also Ingemar Glans, 'Valvindar välter teoribyggnadar', *Statsvetenskaplig tidskrift*, Vol. 86, No. 2 (1983), pp. 137–8; Walter Korpi *The Democratic Class Struggle* (London: Routledge & Kegan Paul, 1983), p. 242; Henry Valen, *Valg og politikk* (Oslo: NKS–Forlaget, 1981). p. 105; Henry Valen and Bernt Aardal, *Et valg i perspektiv* (Oslo: Central Bureau of Statistics of Norway, 1983), p. 68.

the popularity of other leftist parties. In *Norway* the decline in the working-class vote for the Social Democrats has not seemed as serious as in the Danish case. However, in the 1981 election the magnitude of erosion in workers' support for the DNA began to approximate to that of the SD. The long-term decline in the working-class vote for the DNA now amounted to 17 percentage points (compared to 12 percentage points in 1977). Furthermore, in the early 1980s working-class support of both the DNA and other socialist parties ebbed. Socialist voting among Norwegian workers was actually lower in the 1981 election than in the 1973 election, and in recent elections around half of the young workers voted non-socialist. In the early 1980s the level of socialist voting was lower among Norwegian workers than their Swedish and Danish counterparts.

Turning to socialist voting among middle-class electors in Scandinavia, two major points should be brought out. The first is that during the past two decades the Social Democrats and the parties to their left have managed to win a sizeable proportion of the middle-class vote and simultaneously maintain high levels of support among working-class voters. In the first elections of the 1980s the socialist parties polled roughly one third of the middle-class vote. A second and related point is that through the 1970s the Social Democrats, together with the parties to their left, were generally more successful in winning middle-class votes than the non-socialists were in gaining working-class votes. In other words, electoral support for the socialist parties by the middle class – with the exceptions of the 1973 and 1975 Danish elections – counterbalanced and usually outweighed the non-socialist voting of the working class.

The 1970s, however, witnessed a diminishing advantage for the socialist parties as the non-socialists made inroads upon the working-class vote. This difficulty was compounded by a stagnation in the Social Democrats' middle-class support during the decade. Thus, in terms of class support, the electoral problems of the Social Democratic parties in the 1970s can be summed up as an erosion in workers' backing and a failure to make gains among middle-class voters.

Class identification. The social dimension of party support not only consists of occupational class but also voters' perceptions of their location in the class structure. It is well documented that voters' awareness of their class position and a sense of belonging to their class reinforce class voting. Working-class identification among workers increases the proclivity to vote socialist and, conversely, an identification with the middle class encourages non-socialist voting. The decline in class voting has triggered off speculation that this might be the result of an overall weakening of class identification in the electorate or increasing middle-class identification among workers.

These speculations raise a number of interesting questions. To be more precise, what are the patterns of class identification among the voters – and especially the workers – in Denmark, Norway and Sweden? What trends in class identification are observable and what are the relationships between these trends and class voting?

Class identification is quite common in the Scandinavian countries.

TABLE 4
CLASS IDENTIFICATION IN NORWAY, DENMARK AND SWEDEN

Class Identification in the Norwegian Electorate 1969–81

	1969		1973		1977		1981	
Working-Class Identification	%		%		%		%	
Spontaneous	40	60	39	55	30	50	23	45
Solicited	20		16		20		22	
Middle-Class Identification								
Spontaneous	16	32	22	37	17	37	16	41
Solicited	16		15		20		25	
No Class	8		8		13		14	
Total	100		100		100		100	
N	1476		1215		1730		1596	

Class Identification in the Danish Electorate 1971–81

	1971		1973		1979		1981	
Working-Class Identification	%		%		%		%	
Spontaneous	20	35	16	32	26	35	29	39
Solicited	15		16		9		10	
Middle-Class Identification								
Spontaneous	24	50	20	51	31	47	32	46
Solicited	26		31		16		14	
No Class	11		11		15		13	
No Answer, or question not asked	4		6		3		2	
Total	100		100		100		100	
N	1302		533		1989		986	

Class Identification in the Swedish Electorate 1968–76

	1968		1973		1976	
Working-Class Identification	%		%		%	
Spontaneous	42	58	31	55	31	53
Solicited	16		24		22	
Middle-Class Identification						
Spontaneous	22	33	15	30	13	30
Solicited	11		15		17	
No Class	6		14		16	
Miscellaneous	3		1		1	
Total	100		100		100	
N	2866		2421		2681	

Notes: Spontaneous class identification refers to persons who placed themselves in a class without any prompting. Solicited class identification refers to respondents who upon failing to answer the question on class identification were asked to try to place themselves in a class.
The questions tapping class identification are not identical for the three countries, and in Denmark the wording of the questions is not the same for all four elections as indicated by the broken line in the Table. Details about the wording of the questions are available from the author upon request.

Sources: Henry Valen, *Valg og politikk* (Oslo: NKS–Forlaget, 1981), p. 134 and data from the Norwegian Electoral Project; Olof Petersson, 'Klassidentifikation', in K. Asp, *et al.*, *Väljare Partier Massmedia* (Stockholm: Liber Förlag, 1982), pp. 21, 241; Danish Election Surveys, Danish Data Archive file nos. 007, 148, 287 and 529. I am indebted to Prof. Ole Borre, Institute of Political Science, University of Aarhus, for the Danish data.

Between roughly 80 and 90 per cent of the voters placed themselves in either the working class or middle class during the 1970s (see Table 4). But a uniform pattern of class identification for the Scandinavian countries fails to manifest itself. The most striking difference between the three countries is that in Denmark middle-class identification was more prevalent than working-class identification during the 1970s and early 1980s. In Sweden and Norway working-class identification was more prominent. In fact, the general pattern of class identification in the Danish electorate, as displayed in Table 4, is the inverse of the one found in Sweden and Norway during the 1970s. In Norway, however, middle-class identification has gained ground since 1969 at the same time as working-class identification has declined considerably. In this respect, the Norwegian pattern has increasingly come to resemble the Danish one. In Sweden working-class identification had fallen slightly by the mid-1970s but – in contrast to the Norwegian case – so had middle-class identification.[14]

Of special interest here is class identification among workers. At face value, working-class identification among Norwegian workers appears to be remarkably high and subject to only minor erosion. In 1965 the proportion of workers identifying with the working class (both spontaneous and solicited identification) was 85 per cent, and in 1977 it was 80 per cent. Conversely the number of workers identifying with the middle class remained relatively modest (around 20 per cent in 1977). Two trends detract from this impressive picture. First, spontaneous class identification among workers, which reflects greater class awareness than does solicited class identification, slipped from 62 per cent in 1965 to 55 per cent in 1977. Second, a weakening of working-class identification (both spontaneous and solicited) can be detected among younger workers (30 and under), and this has been accompanied by an increase in middle-class identification. In the late 1970s, 65 per cent of the younger workers identified with the working class and 35 per cent with the middle class.

The pattern of working-class identification among Swedish workers bears several resemblances to the Norwegian one. Working-class identification was very high among workers – approximately the same level as in Norway.

During the period 1968–76 there was some slippage in working-class identification among Swedish workers, and the erosion occurred mainly among workers under 40. The main contrast between Norway and Sweden is the absence of an increase in middle-class identification in the Swedish working class.

Working-class identification among Danish workers was not as common as among Norwegian and Swedish workers in the 1970s. In 1971 slightly over one half of the workers stated that they belonged to the working class, a much lower portion compared to roughly three fourths of the Norwegian and Swedish workers. Furthermore, workers identified with the middle class more frequently in Denmark than in Norway and Sweden. In the early 1980s, however, this picture of substantially weaker class attachments may have changed. In any event, spontaneous working-class identification was actually more widespread among Danish voters in 1981 than among Norwegian voters (Table 4). Among workers, middle-class identification had definitely waned and working-class identification seems to have increased.

One aspect of class identification among middle-class voters also deserves comment. In Denmark few middle-class voters reported working-class identification. By contrast, large sections of middle-class voters in Norway and Sweden (approximately 40 and 30 per cent respectively) thought of themselves as working class. Paradoxically, and as distinct from working-class voters, no deterioration in working-class identification among middle-class electors is evident in the Norwegian and Swedish data.

There are a number of *parallels* between the patterns of class identification and the profiles of class voting. Firstly, much sharper fluctuations have characterised class voting in Denmark. This is true for both the working and middle classes – but especially the working class. Greater vacillations in class voting among Danish workers coincide with a weaker working-class identification. It would seem that the larger incidence of working-class identification among Swedish and Norwegian workers has acted as a brake on inclinations to desert leftist parties. In contrast to the Danish case where class voting among workers literally plummeted in 1973, socialist voting among workers underwent a gradual decline in Sweden and Norway throughout the late 1970s, and in Norway the decline continued into the 1980s. Secondly, the decrease in leftist voting among Norwegian workers in the 1977 and 1981 elections was very pronounced among younger workers – precisely the group of workers displaying a serious erosion in working-class identification. Thirdly, a parallel can be observed concerning socialist voting and working-class identification among middle-class electors in Sweden and Norway. Variations in socialist voting of the Swedish and Norwegian middle classes were negligible, at the same time as working-class identification among middle-class voters was more firmly entrenched than among working-class voters in that there is no evidence of decline. Fourthly, the revival of class voting in the 1981 Danish election coincides with a strengthening of working-class identification and spontaneous class identification in the electorate. These parallels suggest that working-class identification is indeed an asset for the Social Democratic parties.

In the discussion of the de-freezing of party politics, class dealignment has been viewed as a major force that is transforming contemporary party systems. In Scandinavia class voting has declined and occupational class has become less influential in determining partisanship. Despite this, major occupational groups still provide fairly solid backing for 'class' parties. In fact, what is interesting in the Scandinavian case is not the decline in class voting but rather the high level of class voting. In these times of crumbling workers' allegiance to working-class parties, the strength of socialist voting among Scandinavian workers assumes added interest.

The intriguing question, then, is why the erosion in class voting among Scandinavian workers has not been more extensive. Obviously, a full explanation of the strength of socialist voting in the working class cannot be offered here. Instead I shall confine my remarks to one plausible explanation. Scandinavian exceptionalism with regard to a persistently high level of class voting among workers seems to be related to Scandinavian exceptionalism in another area: the high level of unionisation among workers. In the early 1980s, roughly 70 and 75 per cent of the Danish and Swedish workers respectively voted socialist, and the unionisation of workers was extremely high. The most serious erosion in socialist voting is currently among Norwegian workers, and this coincides with a lower level of unionisation. Moreover, it is primarily the *unorganised* workers who have deserted the socialist parties and have voted non-socialist. For example, in the 1981 election, socialist allegiances remained steadfast among workers who were union members but fell sharply among non-union workers. The Norwegian and Swedish data also suggest that membership in an LO union is an important factor in shaping and reinforcing working-class identification.

The Psychological Dimension of Party Support

Most Scandinavians are positively oriented to political parties in that they evince some feeling of identification with or leanings towards a party. At the close of the 1970s and the beginning of the 1980s only around 10 per cent of the electorate could be classified as 'independents' who neither thought of themselves as adherents to a party nor felt closer to one party than to the other parties. Among the remaining voters there are, however, cross-national differences in the distribution of the intensity of party identification. Table 5 presents the strength of party identification in the electorates of the three countries. As can be observed in the table, party identification is least widespread in Denmark. During the 1970s the percentage of Danes who considered themselves adherents to a party was consistently lower than in Sweden and Norway, with the percentage of Danish identifiers hovering a little above the 50 per cent mark. By contrast, the proportion of party identifiers in Sweden was roughly 60 per cent during the decade, and in Norway party identifiers ranged from 60 to 70 per cent. However, *strong* identifiers are somewhat more numerous in Sweden and Denmark than in Norway.

A common feature of party identification in the three countries is that both party identifiers and strong identifiers are overrepresented among Social Democratic voters. The SAP has a very high ratio of party identifiers among its voters, and a higher percentage of identifiers in the electorate than

TABLE 5
THE STRENGTH OF PARTY IDENTIFICATION IN THE SCANDINAVIAN ELECTORATES

	Sweden 1979	Norway 1981	Denmark 1979
Party identifiers	%	%	%
Strong adherents	36 ⎫ 58	28 ⎫ 64	32 ⎫ 52
Weak adherents	22 ⎭	36 ⎭	20 ⎭
Leaners	33	25	34
Independents	9	11	11
No answer	-	-	3
Total	100	100	100
N	2669	1170	1981

Sources: Sören Holmberg, *Svenska väljare* (Stockholm: Liber Förlag, 1981), p. 180; Ole Borre *et al.*, *Efter vælgerskredet* (Aarhus: Forlaget Politica, 1983), p. 86. The Norwegian data have been kindly made available by William M. Lafferty and Oddbjørn Knutsen, Institute of Political Science, University of Oslo. Details about the data and survey questions are available from the author upon request.

either the SD or the DNA. In the 1979 election nearly eight out of every ten SAP voters were party identifiers. Moreover, the pattern of party identification in Sweden is characterised by asymmetry. No other Swedish party can match the SAP's ratio of party identifiers– not even among their more stable voters. In fact, the proportion of party identifiers among the stable voters of the other parties generally decreased during the past decade, while the SAP's proportion increased.

The Danish Social Democrats also had a high percentage of party identifiers among their voters in the 1979 election – nearly seven out of ten voters. But the SD was not alone in boasting such a high percentage; nor did the party have the highest ratio. (The Agrarian Liberals did.) The Danish configuration of party identification is marked by fairly sharp differences between the 'old' and 'new' parties. Unsurprisingly, the 'new' parties tend to have fewer identifiers among their voters. The 'old' parties, with the exception of the Radical Liberals, still have sizeable ranks of party identifiers and strong identifiers. This is especially the case for the two parties most clearly based on class interests – the SD and the Agrarian Liberals. Nonetheless, the SD experienced a loss of party identifiers during the 1970s. In 1979 the party's proportion of identifiers was not as high as in 1971.

Of the Norwegian parties, the DNA had the largest percentage of party identifiers among its voters in the 1977 election – around eight out of every ten voters. Like the SAP the Norwegian Social Democrats have had the advantage of a preponderance of party identifiers. However, the asymmetrical pattern may be eroding. In the early 1980s the DNA's advantage seems to have been whittled down. Both the DNA and the Conservatives have large percentages of party identifiers, and the Conservatives appeared to have an edge over the DNA in terms of strong identifiers.

Looking more generally at the de-freezing of the Scandinavian party systems and the question of partisan dealignment through an erosion of party identification during the 1970s, we find mixed trends in the three countries. In Norway party identification rose during the decade, climbing from around 60 per cent in 1969 to approximately 70 per cent in 1977. The DNA and Conservatives generally accounted for the increase in the 1970s. The oscillations in Norwegian party identification seem to be related to the conflict structure of different elections.[15]

Denmark is an especially interesting case, firstly, because of the 1973 protest election when party identification fell among voters and defection rates among party identifiers were unusually high. A natural question is whether the 1973 election resulted in a permanent erosion in party identification among Danish voters. The answer, based on data from the 1979 election survey, is evidently not, since the distribution of strength of party identification in the Danish electorate in 1979 was very similar to that in 1971. Secondly, the Danish case is of major interest because trends in party identification run contrary to the main findings reported in the literature on partisan dealignment. Two recurrent trends in the literature have been a decline in party identification among the younger generation and the well-educated. The Danish data suggest that the development during the past decade was the reverse. At the beginning of the decade the age structure and educational levels of party identifiers exhibited a greater skew than in 1979. In particular, the proportion of strong identifiers in the youngest age group (21–24) and the proportion of identifiers between the ages of 25–39 had increased. Similar increases in identifiers had also occurred among the well-educated.

In Sweden the percentage of voters reporting party identification during the 1970s was fairly stable, and the proportion of strong identifiers in the electorate was actually higher in 1979 than during any other election of the decade. These figures conceal a skewed age structure among party identifiers. The asymmetrical pattern of Swedish party identification, however, is largely replicated among the younger voters. The SAP has a predominant share of identifiers.

In summary, dealignment in the sense of a serious attenuation of partisan attachments is not a very appropriate description of the trends in party identification in Scandinavia during the 1970s. Judging from available data, there has not been any major permanent increase in voters who completely dissociate themselves from parties in recent years. At the end of the decade, the level of party identification in the electorates of the three countries was either roughly the same or higher than at the beginning. This can also be said of strong identifiers in the Danish and Swedish electorates. (Data for Norway are not available.) The most serious signs of erosion are found in the large contrasts in party identification among young and elderly voters. In Denmark, however, disaffection of the young and the well-educated from the political parties appears to have been more prevalent in the early 1970s than in the late 1970s.

The analysis here further indicates that party identification is an important electoral asset of the Social Democrats. In all three countries the Social

Democrats are fortunate in having a disproportionately large share of party identifiers who provide a substantial base of support. Generally, identifiers – and especially strong identifiers – are more likely to vote and attempt to persuade others how to vote, and they are less prone to switch parties in elections. The Danish SD's proportion of party identifiers declined during the past decade. In this respect, the party entered the 1980s with less of an advantage than it had at the start of the 1970s. Yet in comparison to other Danish parties, the SD had one of the highest percentages of party identifiers and strong adherents among its voters at the end of the decade. The DNA's party identifiers increased during the 1970s, but so did the party identifiers of the DNA's chief rival. The SAP's proportion of identifiers remained consistently high during the decade, while the party identifiers of the other parties declined.

The Ideological Dimension of Party Support

Perhaps equally as distinctive as the strong role of class in shaping electoral choice is the prominence of left–right attitudes in structuring partisanship in Scandinavia. Many students of Scandinavian political parties and electoral politics have called attention to the importance of the left–right axis. Its centrality in the Swedish case has led one observer to note that Sweden is probably one of the best examples of a close approximation to a uni-dimensional model.[16] In all three countries no other set of attitudes – or single opinion – correlates so strongly and consistently with electoral choice.

The classic set of issues related to the left–right axis deal with the distribution of production as well as the organisation and control of the economy. In analysing the ideological dimension of party support and the electoral difficulties of the Social Democratic parties, I shall concentrate on voters' opinions on issues of this kind and look at attitudes towards greater equality and equalisation, progressivity in taxation, welfare reforms, greater employee influence, government controls on the economy, and public ownership.

Table 6 summarises Scandinavian voters' attitudes towards a number of issues involving distribution and control of the economy during the latter half of the 1970s. The table presents the balance of opinion on these issues both for the electorate as a whole and for voters of the different parties. The balance of opinion is a measure obtained by subtracting the proportion of negative answers from the proportion of positive answers. In the table the issues have been ranked according to the preponderance of leftist attitudes in the electorate. A plus sign indicates a predominance of leftist views, while a minus sign indicates a predominance of rightist views.

It needs to be stressed that differences in question wording severely limit the possibility of making any reliable comparisons between the countries. Three of the Norwegian and Swedish questions (those marked with a figure 1) are not identical, and none of the Danish survey items has wording identical to the Norwegian and Swedish questions. For example, the more negative responses of Swedish voters towards social welfare, compared to Norwegian and Danish voters, are undoubtedly a reflection of dissimilar wording of the questions. The Swedish question mentions allowances and assistance, thus probably tapping negative attitudes towards welfare in the form of public assistance. The Norwegian and Danish questions refer to social insurance and most likely tap positive attitudes towards national health insurance and pensions. Differences in the Danish responses concerning greater employee influence are also a case in point.

The most striking feature of the table is that the distribution of voter opinions generally follows a left–right pattern: voters for the radical socialist parties were most enthusiastic in endorsing greater equalisation, state intervention in the economy, welfare reforms, expanded employee influence and progressivity in the tax system, while the voters for the conservative parties were the most negative. A second important feature which emerges from the table is that a majority of Social Democratic voters clearly have leftist views on issues of distribution and control of the economy. In all cases but one, the opinion balances of the Social Democrats indicate substantial ideological support among party voters. The one exception consists of the SD voters' attitudes towards state ownership. The party's voters overwhelmingly disapproved of nationalising banks and large corporations. The opinion balances for SAP voters and DNA voters disclose lukewarm support, but nevertheless a majority approving nationalisation.

Explanations of the electoral difficulties of the Social Democratic parties in the 1970s have pointed to problems related to the ideological dimension of party support. One explanation has emphasised a general change in the political climate during the 1970s. It is argued that the radicalism of the late 1960s gave way to a conservative mood characterised by widespread disenchantment with the welfare state and growing opposition to government controls. A rightward shift in opinion has meant an uphill battle for the Social Democrats in winning votes in the 1970s, and welfare backlash is cited as the major cause of the defeats of the SD and DNA in 1973 and the SAP in 1976. What trends are observable with regard to Scandinavian voters' attitudes towards state intervention in the economy and welfare reforms during the past decade? Do the opinion balances in Table 6 represent a shift to the right in attitudes? And did Social Democratic voters' support for government controls and reforms decrease?

Although support for welfare reforms and state intervention did recede during some of the elections of the 1970s, survey data fail to substantiate an overall and continuous deterioration in leftist opinions in the Scandinavian electorates during the decade. Instead the picture is much more complex, and trends are dissimilar in the three countries.

Norwegian voters' attitudes towards welfare reforms and state intervention followed divergent patterns during the past decade. On the one hand, the electorate's support for welfare policies diminished in the 1973 election. By 1977, however, support for the welfare state had returned to a high level (see Table 6). In the 1981 election the general level of support for welfare reforms was roughly the same as in 1977, despite the gains of the Progress Party, which campaigned against the current level of benefits and its costs. It should be noted, however, that the Progress Party's backing came largely from young voters, suggesting a possible schism in the support for welfare policies between generations. Nevertheless, in the early 1980s the electo-

TABLE 6
ATTITUDES TOWARDS DISTRIBUTION AND CONTROL OF
THE ECONOMY AMONG SCANDINAVIAN VOTERS

Balance of Opinion among Norwegian Voters, by Party

Issue	Party Choice 1977						
	SV	DNA	V	KRF	SP	H	Electorate
Further equalization of income and working conditions	+94	+81	+81	+62	+70	+66	+75
Maintain and expand welfare reforms[1]	+60	+62	+60	+53	+43	+40	+54
Greater employee influence	+94	+70	+49	+29	+28	+20	+51
Progessivity in taxes	+75	+38	+42	0	+2	-47	+11
Big business too powerful without government control[1]	+84	+42	-6	-17	-10	-48	+8
Government controls on the economy	+60	+13	-17	-25	-18	-39	-6
Government influence lessens risk of unemployment[1]	+77	+23	-62	-51	-59	-82	-21
Nationalize large corporations	+66	+15	-62	-52	-58	-85	-25

Balance of Opinion among Swedish Voters, by Party

Issue	Party Choice 1976					
	VPK	SAP	C	FP	M	Electorate
Further equalization of income and working conditions	+95	+84	+72	+58	+27	+70
Greater employee influence	+97	+84	+47	+58	+19	+63
Progressivity in taxes	+77	+57	+32	+22	-19	+36

Abbreviations:

SV = Socialist Left Party
V = Liberals
KRF = Christian People's Party
SP = Centre Party
H = Conservatives

Big business too powerful without government control[1]	+89	+63	+11	-3	-41	+28
Government influence lessens risk of unemployment[1]	+69	+42	-41	-46	-73	-4
Government controls on the economy	+44	+4	-38	-50	-59	-19
Welfare reforms[1]	+42	+5	-62	-51	-72	-28
Nationalize large corporations	+72	+2	-66	-78	-90	-34

Abbreviations:

VPK = Communists
C = Centre Party
FP = Liberals
M = Conservatives

Balance of Opinion among Danish Voters, by Party

Issue	Party Choice 1979						Electorate
	VF	SD	MP	FRP	V	K	
Progressivity in taxes[1]	+81	+61	+33	+14	+10	-13	+36
Maintain existing welfare reforms[1]	+71	+54	+13	-37	-7	-6	+24
Equalization of incomes[1]	+79	+44	+2	+4	-16	-41	+18
Economic equality[1]	+71	+28	-9	-4	-21	-33	+10
Greater employee influence[1]	+70	+27	-13	-61	-52	-55	+1
Government controls on the economy[1]	+52	+22	-29	-57	-56	-51	-10
Nationalise banks and large corporations[1]	+42	-54	-77	-84	-90	-94	-51

Abbreviations:

VF = Left socialist parties
MP = Middle parties
FRP = Progress Party
V = Agrarian Liberals
K = Conservatives

Note: 1. indicates that the wording of the question is not identical. Details about the survey questions are available from the author.

Sources: Adapted from Olof Petersson and Henry Valen, 'Political Cleavages in Sweden and Norway', *Scandinavian Political Studies* (1979), pp.316–17, 325; Henry Valen, *Valg og politikk* (Oslo: NKS-Forlaget, 1981), p.254; Ole Borre *et al.*, *Efter vælgerskredet* (Aarhus: Forlaget Politica, 1983), p. 42.

rate's attitudes were more positive than at the time of the 1973 election. On the other hand, the 1970s witnessed a decline in attitudes favouring government controls on the economy. More specifically, in 1969 positive views towards government influence to combat unemployment outweighed negative views, while in 1977 the balance had been reversed. Favourable attitudes towards government controls to check big business also declined significantly. This rightward shift in opinion occurred more or less uniformly in all social strata. Even DNA voters shared less enthusiasm for government controls at the end of the 1970s.[17]

Trends in the attitudes of the Swedish electorate were the exact opposite of those in Norway, according to Swedish election survey data. At the end of the decade Swedish attitudes towards government influence to lessen unemployment and to check big business did not reveal a rightward shift either in the electorate or among SAP voters. In fact, the long-range trends from the mid-1960s to the late 1970s, as measured by these attitudes, were (1) a slight increase in leftist views in the electorate, (2) a strengthening of positive attitudes towards state intervention among Social Democratic (and Communist) voters, and (3) a polarisation in the attitudes of socialist and non-socialist voters. In the case of welfare reforms, the opinion balance for the electorate in Table 6 does not signify a major decline in support. Over the years this question has regularly drawn negative responses with the single exception of 1968. The opinion balance in Table 6 is roughly the same as in 1964. However, in the 1979 election, negative attitudes registered a new high.[18] As noted earlier, the formulation of this survey question leaves much to be desired. Other survey questions have not resulted in such negative responses. Nor do they confirm a substantial erosion in support for the welfare state in the 1970s. Instead opinion polls from the 1960s and late 1970s indicate little change in the willingness to pay the bill for welfare policies in spite of an enormous increase in welfare expenditure since the 1960s. In the late 1970s, according to the polls, it was only among Conservative voters that there was a majority who thought that social welfare was too expensive and should be cut down. Moreover, polls gauging attitudes towards the public sector reveal that the electorate's opposition to the size of the public sector was greater in the early 1970s than at the end of the decade.[19]

The Danish protest election in 1973 has been regarded by many observers as a dramatic case of welfare backlash.[20] It is true that most Danish voters agreed that too many people received social benefits without being in need. Besides, an overwhelming portion of the electorate desired income tax cuts. But the evidence is by no means conclusive. The voters favoured lower government expenditure. But they did not advocate cutbacks in welfare spending, and large numbers of voters wanted welfare programmes to be exempt from budget cuts. The areas singled out for reductions were instead defence, salaries of public employees, grants to students, and highway construction. In any event, as is evident from Table 6, a large majority of Danes supported welfare reforms at the end of the 1970s. The table also shows a massive rejection of nationalisation measures. These opinion balances do not, however, represent a swing to the right in the electorate's or SD voters' views. During the entire decade Danish attitudes towards public ownership were marked by greater scepticism than those in Norway and Sweden. Rather the major trends seem to have been towards an increasing polarisation of attitudes to government controls and equalisation, accompanied by a small shift to the left in the electorate.[21]

To sum up, Scandinavian voters' attitudes towards welfare reforms and state intervention were more positive in several respects at the close of the 1970s than during the first half of the decade. Despite scattered data to the contrary, and the fact that one such item is included in Table 6, much of the survey evidence indicates high levels of support for social welfare among Scandinavian voters in the latter part of the decade. The trends of the 1970s demonstrate, however, the vulnerability of support for the welfare state and thus highlight the possible vulnerability of what has been a major asset of the Social Democrats: voters' esteem of the Social Democrats as the main architects of the welfare state. Danish and Swedish attitudes towards state intervention did not grow increasingly negative during the course of the decade. One main exception appears to be Norwegian attitudes towards state intervention, and erosion seems to have occurred both in the electorate and among DNA voters.

In the discussion of the 'thawing' of frozen party systems, one underlying assumption has concerned the growing irrelevancy of the left–right axis. Much of this speculation is based on a 'structuralist' line of reasoning which views the left–right axis as the product of conflicts generated by industrialisation. The issues related to the left–right axis, it is held, lose their salience and become obsolete as society changes from an industrial to a post-industrial economy. The old issues of the left–right axis are eclipsed by new issues divorced from this cleavage structure.

New issues have, of course, emerged in Scandinavian party politics, and in some instances they have been important for electoral choice, but they have not supplanted the left–right axis. The importance of the left–right axis as a cleavage line and its role in structuring attitudes remain.

The Danish case is instructive concerning the strength and resilience of the left–right axis as a cleavage structure. The 1973 election significantly altered the party system, and it is perhaps best described as a 'restructuring' election. However, the election does not qualify as a 'realigning' election in the sense which would suggest that a new cleavage alignment replaced the left–right axis. Instead the left–right axis was complemented by a new cleavage structure – an 'establishment/non-establishment' axis.[22] The initial emergence of this axis was accompanied by a sharp drop in socialist voting. By the 1977 election, however, socialist voting had returned to its usual level, and in 1979 there was a socialist majority in the electorate (see Table 1). In retrospect, the 1973 and 1975 elections appear to have been deviating elections with respect to socialist voting. Apart from these elections, the importance of the left–right axis in structuring the vote stands out, as does the stability of the socialist–non-socialist cleavage in contrast to the vicissitudes in the electoral strength of individual parties.

Scandinavian party politics suggest that the structuralist line of reasoning has tended to underestimate the durability and salience of the left–right axis.

In any event, it is useful to ask what factors contribute to the centrality of the left–right axis in Scandinavian party politics. First, the axis is still anchored in the class structure and the worker–owner cleavage. In turn, the worker–owner cleavage is reinforced by powerful interest organisations of labour and business, which also have supportive links with the parties. Second, the actions of parties can be a crucial factor in shaping the salience and importance of left–right issues. The SAP's offensive for greater equality in the late 1960s and early 1970s, and its launching proposals to democratise the workplace and to introduce wage-earner funds in the 1970s, obviously increased the relevance of left–right issues to electoral choice. Party actions can also be decisive in determining whether 'new' issues are integrated into the existing left–right dimension or whether the issues produce cross-cleavages. It should also be noted that the Scandinavian parties and their voters array themselves along a left–right axis on a variety of other issues, not just the ones discussed above. Third, the classic issues of the left–right axis centre on the economy, and in recent elections voters have assigned main importance to economic issues. In the light of the revival of economic difficulties, the left–right axis seems far from losing its relevance. Thus 'period' influences can heighten the centrality of the left–right axis. More important factors, frequently neglected by the structuralist line of reasoning, are the pattern of reinforcing organisational affiliations and the strategic responses of political parties.

III. CONCLUSIONS: WHITHER THE SCANDINAVIAN SOCIAL DEMOCRATS?

The dominant position of the Social Democrats has been a characteristic feature of Scandinavian party politics. One central question, in contemplating possible changes in the party systems, concerns the future governmental status of the Social Democratic parties. On the basis of the preceding analysis of the dimensions of party support, this concluding discussion therefore considers the future prospects of the Scandinavian Social Democrats.

An obvious limitation of this analysis, when speculating about the future prospects of the parties, is that these three dimensions of support are not the sole determinants of electoral choice. Nor, as brought out in the discussion of the bases of Social Democratic dominance, does electoral strength exclusively determine governmental status. Nonetheless, an examination of these dimensions provides valuable clues in attempting to assess the likelihood of future gains and losses of the parties in the electoral arena. Serious erosion in these dimensions suggests that the parties' electoral difficulties are not merely transient. Therefore the discussion first sums up the major findings for each party concerning the three dimensions. Subsequently it comments on the implications of voting patterns among generations for the Social Democratic parties.

In the case of the *Danish* party we have generally found weaker partisan attachments with regard to each dimension. The long-term decline in Social Democratic voting among workers has been severest for the SD, and erosion has proceeded furthest among young workers. The desertion of young working-class voters during the 1970s undoubtedly makes it more difficult for the SD to re-establish its former position among workers. Furthermore, working-class identification was less common among Danish workers than among Swedish and Norwegian workers in the 1970s, although currently there are signs of a possible strengthening of class awareness in Denmark.

Party identification among Social Democratic voters declined during the 1970s, but at the end of the decade the SD had one of the largest percentages of party identifiers and strong identifiers among its voters. The experiences of the Danish Social Democrats in the 1970s also underscore the importance of party identification. Widespread Social Democratic identification did not insulate the party's voters from the sway of powerful short-term forces in the 1973 election. Yet sizeable ranks of party identifiers were probably a key factor enabling the SD to recoup its losses only a few years later.

Although there was not a general rightward shift in attitudes of SD voters towards reforms and state intervention during the 1970s, the Danish party faces a number of problems with regard to ideological support. During the entire decade SD voters' attitudes towards state ownership were largely in accord with those of the rest of the electorate, and they could scarcely be characterised as leftist. In addition, on such issues as economic equalisation, employee influence, the size of unemployment benefits, the dangers of abuse of social benefits and wage policy the opinions of SD voters were closer to those of the non-socialist parties than they were to the opinions of voters for other socialist parties in the 1979 election. SD voters thus might be susceptible to the ideological appeals of the centrist parties.

This summary perhaps paints too bleak a picture of the SD's prospects. Looking at a variety of trends related to voting behaviour during the 1970s, we find a basic pattern of critical change or deviation in the mid-1970s followed by partial and, in some instances, complete restoration.[23] Moreover, the outlook for the party is possibly put in an overly disadvantageous light through a comparison with the SAP and DNA. A more relevant focus of comparison is the other Danish parties. The 1973 election dealt a hard blow to the established parties and temporarily weakened voters' attachments to the parties, but during the course of the decade several of the old parties – and in particular the SD – managed to regain much of the terrain they had lost. Furthermore, the new parties have been less successful in establishing enduring partisan attachments among the voters. The bulk of their support has come from marginal and volatile voters influenced by short-term forces. By contrast, the SD's electoral support is made up of an unusually large proportion of regular voters – larger than any other Danish party in the early 1980s.

The electoral difficulties of the *Norwegian* Social Democrats have not seemed as grave as those of the Social Democrats in Denmark. However, with the DNA's losses in the 1981 election the party's predicament took on a stronger resemblance to the quandary of the SD. Working-class support continued to decline and, as in the Danish case, the DNA did poorly in winning the votes of young workers in the 1977 and 1981 elections. Working-class identification appeared impressively high among Norwegian workers in the late 1970s, but substantial erosion had occurred among young workers.

Moreover, the long-term trends in class identification have shown a decrease in working-class identification and a rise in middle-class identification. Ideological attachments also seem to have weakened during the 1970s. Since the late 1960s the electorate's enthusiasm for government intervention has dampened. This rightward shift in opinion even occurred among workers. There are also some indications that the shift has been more pronounced among young voters. Thus, a particularly disturbing development for the DNA has been a lessening of social and, possibly, ideological partisan attachments among the younger generation. Unfortunately, the lack of data on the age structure of party identifiers in Norway precludes any conclusions about the possibility of erosion in all three dimensions of party support among young voters.

On the positive side, party identification increased during the 1970s. Among the DNA's other assets are a much stronger party organisation and larger membership than the SD. The electoral system has also tended to favour the DNA, and frequently the party has been overrepresented in parliament in relation to its votes. The importance of this factor was once again emphasised in the 1983 local elections. The DNA and the parties to its left bettered their share of the vote, receiving approximately 45 per cent. If it had been a parliamentary election, the left would have won a bare majority of the seats in the Storting.[24]

The electoral fortunes of the *Swedish* Social Democrats have not ebbed as low as those of the other two parties. Nor has the weakening in the enduring sources of party attachment for the SAP been as severe as in the cases of the SD and DNA. The decline in the working-class vote for the SAP has not been on the same scale as that of the other two parties. The downward trend in workers' support was also reversed in the 1979 and 1982 elections. Working-class identification among workers appeared to be high, and the erosion which occurred in the mid-1970s was not accompanied by an increase in middle-class identification in either the working class or the electorate. Party identification among the SAP's supporters increased during the past decade, and the Swedish Social Democrats enjoyed a decided advantage in the asymmetrical distribution of party identifiers, even among young voters. At the end of the decade neither the electorate's nor the Social Democratic voters' approval of state intervention had lessened, but survey data from the 1979 election indicate growing negativism towards welfare reforms. Other polls from the late 1970s, however, show little deterioration in the support of social welfare. In sum, this analysis fails to uncover deepening erosion in the three dimensions of party support during the 1970s in the case of the SAP.

At various points the foregoing comments have hinted at possible difficulties for the Social Democrats in gaining the support of young voters. What do recent trends in the voting behaviour of different generations tell us about the parties' future prospects?

Socialist voting among generations has followed divergent trends in the three countries during the past decade. In Norway there has been a successive weakening of socialist allegiances among the youngest generation (voters under 30). Since the mid-1970s a majority of young electors has voted non-socialist, and young voters have increasingly veered towards conservative parties (the Conservatives and the Progressives) in the 1977 and 1981 elections. Furthermore, to the detriment of the DNA there has been a polarisation in the party preferences of young voters. Not only have the conservative parties gained in support, so too have the parties to the left of the DNA. In contrast, older voters have been more prone to vote socialist and to vote Social Democratic. A majority of the middle-aged generation and a near majority of the oldest generation voted socialist until the 1981 election. Only a small segment of these voters supported parties to the left of the DNA.[25]

In Denmark there has been a solid socialist majority in the youngest generation of voters in recent elections (approximately 60 per cent in 1979 and 1981). The parties to the left of the Social Democrats have also been much more successful than their counterparts in Norway and Sweden in winning the votes of young people. Since the mid-1970s the left socialist parties have generally received a larger percentage of the votes of people born after 1949 than has the SD. The socialist voting of young electors assumes added importance when compared to the voting behaviour of older generations. Although a much larger proportion of older electors have voted for the SD than for other socialist parties, seldom has a majority of the older generations voted socialist.

The Swedish pattern differs from those found in Norway and Denmark. First, differences in both socialist and Social Democratic voting among generations have been much smaller in Sweden than in the other two countries during the 1970s and early 1980s. Second, the SAP had much stronger support among voters in the younger generation than either the DNA or the SD. The Swedish Social Democrats received well over 40 per cent of the votes of persons under 30 in the 1979 and 1982 elections, whereas the share of votes for the DNA and SD was under 30 per cent in the 1981 elections.[26]

Predictions based on voting patterns of generations have seldom been borne out. In the Swedish case, moreover, such speculations are more or less meaningless. Generational differences are small and elections have been very close. When the SAP and the socialist bloc did poorly, reversals occurred in all generations. In the Danish and Norwegian cases we can speculate about the implications of these patterns of voting among generations *if* they were to persist, since they provide additional insights into the parties' possible difficulties in the future.

For the SD the implications are mixed. The party has acquired only between about one fifth and one third of the votes of the younger generation since the mid-1970s; simultaneously SD support in this generation has fluctuated considerably and has usually been at least 10 percentage points lower than in the oldest generation. Hence the prospects of further electoral decline loom large unless the SD can break these trends and improve its standing among younger voters. In two respects, however, the implications may be favourable for the SD. First, the likelihood of a socialist majority in the electorate seems greater now than in the past. Second, although the vote for the parties to the left of the SD has tended to increase steadily, so has fragmentation of these parties. Despite the electoral successes of the radical socialists, the SD is clearly the largest socialist party – even among voters in the youngest generation. As both the largest party and the largest socialist party, the SD is likely to remain a prime candidate to form the government.

The quandary of the DNA is quite different from that of the SD in as much as young Norwegians have a strong proclivity to vote non-socialist. To the extent that this tendency is a firmly established voting pattern, it casts a serious shadow over the future prospects of the Norwegian Social Democrats. The volatility of young voters, in general, suggests that their electoral choice may not be based on firm attachments to a particular party. On the other hand, the tendency of young electors to vote non-socialist has existed since the 1973 election.

In conclusion, this analysis of enduring sources of partisan attachment and the voting patterns among generations has identified substantial differences in the predicaments of the three Social Democratic parties. The SD appears to be in the most serious trouble, compared to the other parties. Erosion in enduring partisan attachments is most extensive for the SD. The party's record in attracting young voters has not been very good during the past decade. One of the SD's main trump cards is the weakness of other Danish parties. An additional asset may be the strengthening of socialist sentiments in the younger generation.

The position of the DNA is stronger than that of the SD in several respects. Generally the DNA's polling strength is much superior. However, the Norwegian party's predicament becomes more serious when it is viewed against the backdrop of the overall decline in socialist voting since the 1973 election. But the gravest question mark concerns young voters and whether this weakness of the DNA is a generational phenomenon or the product of 'period' forces.

The SAP has experienced the least amount of deterioration in enduring partisan attachments. Generational differences in socialist voting are small. Irrespective of generations, there is basically a 50–50 split in socialist and non-socialist voting. The somewhat paradoxical result is that in the Scandinavian country where the enduring sources of socialist partisanship have been subject to least erosion, the delicate balance of voting strength between the two blocs may heighten the importance of short-term influences on electoral choice since they may tip the scale in favour of one of the blocs.

Finally, it needs to be pointed out that the enduring partisan attachments of many non-socialist parties also weakened during the 1970s, and in some instances the deterioration was far-reaching. In short, the voting support of the Social Democrats may have become more fluid during the past decade, but the electoral backing of the other parties is generally characterised by even greater fluidity.

NOTES

1. See, for example, F.G. Castles, 'Scandinavia: The Politics of Stability', in Roy Macridis (ed.), *Modern Political Systems: Europe* (Englewood Cliffs, NJ: Prentice-Hall, 1977).

2. For analyses of these elections, see Ole Borre, 'Denmark's Protest Election of December 1973', *Scandinavian Political Studes*, Vol. 9 (1974); Henry Valen and Willy Martinussen, 'Electoral Trends and Foreign Politics in Norway: The 1973 Storting Election and the EEC Issue', in Karl Cerny (ed.), *Scandinavia at the Polls* (Washington, DC: American Enterprise Institute, 1977).

3. Giovanni Sartori, *Parties and Party Systems* (Cambridge: Cambridge University Press, 1976), pp. 150–51.

4. For a comparative discussion of the governmental status of Social Democratic parties in Western Europe, see F.G. Castles, *The Social Democratic Image of Society* (London: Routledge & Kegan Paul, 1978), Chapter 1.

5. For an interesting analysis illustrating the effects of this constraint on various policy areas, in comparison to Sweden, see Gösta Esping-Andersen, *Social Class, Social Democracy and State Policy* (Copenhagen: New Social Science Monographs, 1980).

6. For a discussion of the most impressive case of the recent growth of conservative parties in Scandinavia, the Norwegian Party, see Bjarne Kristiansen and Lars Svåsand, 'The Conservative Party in Norway: From Opposition to Alternative Government', in Z. Layton-Henry (ed.), *Conservative Politics in Western Europe* (London: Macmillan, 1982).

7. For a broader discussion of electoral change in Scandinavia, see Ole Borre, 'Critical Electoral Change in Scandinavia', in Russell J. Dalton, Scott C. Flanagan and Paul Allen Beck (eds.), *Electoral Change in Advanced Industrial Democracies: Realignment or Dealignment?* (Princeton, NJ: Princeton University Press, forthcoming).

8. For comparative discussions of the radical socialist parties, see Daniel Tarschys, 'The Changing Basis of Radical Socialism in Scandinavia', in Karl Cerny (ed.), *Scandinavia at the Polls* (Washington, DC: American Enterprise Institute, 1977); John Logue, *Socialism and Abundance. A Study of the Danish Socialist People's Party* (Copenhagen: Akademisk Forlag, 1982), Chapter VIII.

9. Maurice Duverger, *Political Parties* (London: Methuen, 1954), pp. 95, 69. Cf. Stefano Bartolini, 'The Membership of Mass Parties: The Social Democratic Experience, 1889–1978', in H. Daalder and P. Mair (eds.), *Western European Party Systems* (London: Sage, 1983), p. 187.

10. For a comparative discussion of unionisation in Western countries, see Walter Korpi, *The Democratic Class Struggle* (London: Routledge & Kegan Paul, 1983), Chapter 3.

11. For a discussion of membership trends, see Diane Sainsbury, 'Functional Hypotheses of Party Decline: The Case of the Scandinavian Social Democratic Parties', *Scandinavian Political Studies* (New Series), Vol. 6, No. 4 (1983).

12. Ivor Crewe, 'The Labour Party and the Electorate', in Dennis Kavanagh (ed.), *The Politics of the Labour Party* (London: George Allen & Unwin, 1982), p. 15.

13. Seymour M. Lipset and Stein Rokkan, 'Cleavage Structures, Party Systems, and Voter Alignments', in S. Lipset and S. Rokkan (eds.), *Party Systems and Voter Alignments* (New York: The Free Press, 1967), pp. 50–56.

14. This discussion draws on data in Torben Worre, 'Social baggrund og parti', in Ole Borre *et al.*, *Vælgere i 70'erne* (Copenhagen: Akademisk Forlag, 1978); Henry Valen, *Valg og politikk* (Oslo: NKS-Forlaget, 1981), pp. 133–45; Olof Petersson, 'Klassidentifikation', in Kent Asp *et al.*, *Väljare Partier Massmedia* (Stockholm: Liber Fölag, 1982). Unfortunately the Swedish time series covers a short period. Moreover, 1968 does not constitute a good baseline for comparison. In many respects, the 1968 election was exceptional.

15. This discussion relies mainly on Per Arnt Pettersen, 'Identification, Agreement and Government Performance: The Relative Impact on Voting', *Scandinavian Political Studies* (New Series), Vol. 4, No. 3 (1981); Sören Holmberg, *Svenska väljare* (Stockholm: Liber Förlag, 1981), Chapter 10; L.K. Pedersen and J. Weber, 'Stabilitet og politisk involvering', in Ole Borre *et al.*, *Efter vælgerskredet* (Aarhus: Forlaget Politica, 1983). In addition, Oddbjørn Knutsen has kindly made available data from the project, 'Democracy in Norway: Participation and Basic Values'.

16. See, for example, Sören Holmberg, *Riksdagen representerar svenska folket* (Lund: Studentlitteratur, 1974), pp. 378–80; Sten Berglund and Ulf Lindström, *The Scandinavian Party System(s)* (Lund: Studentlitteratur, 1978), pp. 16–24, 189-91.

17. See Henry Valen and Willy Martinussen, op. cit., p. 57; Olof Petersson and Henry Valen, 'Political Cleavages in Sweden and Norway', *Scandinavian Political Studies* (New Series),

Vol. 2, No. 4 (1979), p. 317; Henry Valen and Bernt Aardal, *Et valg i perspektiv. En studie av stortingsvalget 1981* (Oslo: Central Bureau of Statistics of Norway, 1983), p. 162; Henry Valen, *Valg og politikk*, op. cit., pp. 282–4. For an analysis of leftist attitudes in the Norwegian electorate in 1981, see William M. Lafferty and Oddbjørn Knutsen, 'Leftist and Rightist Ideology in the Social-Democratic State', *British Journal of Political Science*, Vol. 14, No. 3 (1984), pp. 287–309.

18. See Sören Holmberg, *Svenska väljare*, op. cit., Chapter 12, esp. pp. 248–59. Preliminary analyses of the 1982 election suggest an erosion in favourable attitudes towards state intervention.

19. Hans L. Zetterberg, 'The Public's View of Social Welfare Policy in Sweden', *Sifo* (1980), pp. 4, 26; 'Föreställningar och önskningar om den offentliga sektorns storlek', *Sifo* (1979), p. 4. Cf. Walter Korpi, op. cit., pp. 200–204.

20. See, for example, Harold Wilensky, *The 'New Corporatism', Centralization and the Welfare State* (Beverley Hills: Sage Professional Papers in Contemporary Political Sociology, 1976); Douglas Hibbs, Jr., and Henrik Jess Madsen, 'Public Reactions to the Growth of Taxation and Government Expenditures', *World Politics*, Vol. 33, No. 3 (1981), pp. 414–21.

21. See Ole Borre, 'Recent Trends in Danish Voting Behavior', in Karl Cerny (ed.), *Scandinavia at the Polls*, op. cit., pp. 21–7; K. Lindrup and J. Pedersen, 'Holdninger og politiske spørgsmål ved 1979-valget', in Ole Borre *et al.*, *Efter vælgerskredet* (Aarhus: Forlaget Politica, 1983), pp. 44–50.

22. Jerrold G. Rusk and Ole Borre, 'The Changing Party Space in Danish Voter Perceptions, 1971–73', in I. Budge, I. Crewe and D. Farlie (eds.), *Party Identification and Beyond* (London: Wiley, 1976), pp. 143–9.

23. See Ole Borre, 'Fragmentation and Realignment: Electoral Volatility in Denmark', in I. Crewe and D. Denver (eds.), *Electoral Volatility and Partisan Change in Western Democracies* (London: Croom Helm, forthcoming).

24. *Aftenposten*, 14 September 1983, p. 5.

25. Henry Valen, *Valg og politikk*, op. cit., p. 28; Henry Valen and Bernt Aardal, op. cit., p. 57.

26. These comments on voting among generations in Denmark and Sweden are based on Ingemar Glans, 'Valvindar välter teoribyggnader: Förändringar i klassers och kohorters partival i Danmark och Sverige', *Statsvetenskaplig tidskrift*, Vol. 86, No. 2 (1983), pp. 126–9.

Institutional Constraints and Party Competition in the French Party System

Stefano Bartolini

The turbulent political history of post-war France runs counter to the image of general stability and continuity associated with the party landscape of most other West European countries. Yet the discontinuity which sets France off from its more stable neighbours in the 1950s and 1960s is not the only atypical feature. For, perhaps paradoxically, while the 1970s have witnessed established parties throughout Western Europe being challenged by new political movements (whether ecological, regional, protest or whatever) and while the capacity of many parties to perform satisfactorily their traditional functions of political integration, consensus building and policy formulation is widely questioned, political parties in France appear to have been passing through a golden age. They have seen a growth in both their popular legitimacy as well as in popular confidence in their capacity to solve existing problems.[1] In general, they have experienced a revitalisation of their organisations in both quantitative and qualitative terms, and at both the national and the local level.[2] They have demonstrated a fresh capacity to penetrate both new and traditional social milieux where their presence had declined during the 1960s.[3] Against prevailing traditions in France, they also have increased their internal cohesion and discipline, at the parliamentary level[4] as well as in terms of the capacity of the central party to enforce a national political and electoral strategy throughout the whole country. They have been the principal agents of a process of politicisation and nationalisation of the French local political life to a level never attained in the past.[5]

Each of these developments in the 1970s – which together could be considered as crucial indicators of the (comparatively) late 'modernisation' of French mass partisan politics – is sufficiently important to merit a paper of its own. At the same time, these developments represent individual elements of an overall process in which the French party system has been restructured and revitalised. This paper will therefore concentrate on the transformation of the party system itself, making only marginal reference to changes at the level of the individual parties. Moreover, in analysing party system changes, particular emphasis will be given to the interplay between the structural constraints deriving from the institutional context of party competition and the spatial distribution of the political opinions of the electorate.

The three following sections will be devoted respectively to a short description of the major changes in the party system, to an analysis of the causes of such changes and, finally, to a discussion of the nature and direction of such changes.

FEATURES OF PARTY SYSTEM CHANGE

Given the importance of the original positions taken towards the new Gaullist regime in 1958, and with a view towards analysing long-term electoral dynamics, the most useful grouping of parties in France is one which distinguishes the long-lasting Gaullist and pro-regime majority from the various forms of opposition to it which were manifested during the period: (1) an extreme right opposition profoundly opposed to de Gaulle as a result of his betrayal of 'Algérie Française'; (2) a centre opposition originally rejecting de Gaulle's new institutions, personalism and foreign policy, but politically moderate and located in an intermediate position between the Gaullist majority and the left opposition; and (3) a left opposition opposing de Gaulle as a leader as well as his new institutions and, finally, his specific economic policies. Figures 1 and 2 represent the electoral fate of these four major poles and can help to summarise the basic structural changes in the party system since 1958. These changes may be summarised as follows:

(a) the disappearance of an extreme right opposition;
(b) the eventual disappearance of a centre-located opposition; and
(c) the electoral re-equilibrium within the left and right blocks, that is between communists and socialists on the one hand and Gaullist and 'other majority' on the other.

(a) The Disappearance of an Extreme Right Opposition

Though this aspect may appear a minor element in the electoral development of the Fifth Republic, it has been of immense significance in terms of party competition. An extreme right opposition had been particularly strong during the Fourth Republic and continued in the first years of the Fifth, merging somewhat diverse elements favouring French Algeria, as well as a reactionary and pseudo-fascist tendency expressing itself under different political labels. It must be emphasised that these forces were significantly underrepresented in electoral terms in 1958 (see Figure 1), as in great part they initially identified with Gaullism. As such, their defeat in 1962, when they openly opposed de Gaulle, appears less significant than was actually the case.

The political pole was actually destroyed by the extraordinary electoral aggregation of the right created by de Gaulle's charismatic appeal in the period 1958–65;[6] while later remnants of this extreme right persisted culturally in France, they remained politically insignificant due to an electoral system which could not offer any hope to such a small electoral force. What is necessary to underline is that, since 1962, the French party system no longer displays one of its long-standing features: the existence of an anti-system right opposed to the existing regime and which is at the same time not accessible in terms of a governmental majority. It was precisely this crucial development which helped the Gaullists to gain a majority of seats and thereby to initiate the entire process of party system realignment.

FIGURE 1
ELECTORAL DEVELOPMENT OF THE FOUR FRENCH MAJOR POLITICAL POLES

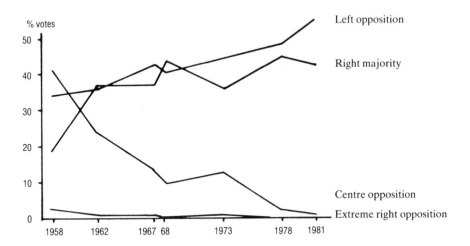

Legend: Left includes all parties left of the SFIO–PS + Left Radicals + various left parties.
   Right includes Gaullists + Independent Republicans and since 1968 all ex-centre
   opposition groups joining them (ex-CDP and ex-Reformists).
   Centre opposition includes MRP and Conservatives (1958–62), CD (1967–68),
   Reformists (1973), Ecologists (1978–81) + various centre candidates.
   Extreme right opposition includes candidates regrouped in this category by the
   Ministry of Interior's data.

(b) The Eventual Disappearance of a Centre-Located Opposition

It is important to understand that in this context the reference is not to the
actual electoral disappearance of centrist parties or of a centrist set of
opinions and orientations in the electorate and/or political elites; rather, it
refers to the virtual disappearance of political forces *centrally located* in
spatial terms, that is, in a position of equidistance between the blocks of the
majority and the opposition. In the first phase of the new Gaullist regime
this central positioning was occupied by a group of parties of Catholic,
Radical, liberal – and sometimes even socialist – orientations which, having
originally supported de Gaulle in 1958, later moved into opposition. At the
basis of their ideology was – as it always had been – an assumption that the
extreme wings represented a political danger, as well as a belief in the
negative value of a block versus block confrontation and of the superiority of
government based on the moderation of the centre.
   With the rise of the Gaullists to a majority position, therefore, and as a

result of the new cross-cutting of the traditional left–right cleavage with the new Gaullism–anti-Gaullism institutional cleavage, the Catholic, Radical and liberal parties of the Fourth Republic found themselves in a centre position *vis-à-vis* the left and the Gaullist majority. Indeed, the predominance of the latter institutional cleavage during the 1960s acted to create a centre location for these moderate forces, in that they would align with the left opposition on matters concerning Gaullist constitutional practices – and sometime foreign policy – and with the Gaullist majority on matters concerning socio-economic policy. Their capacity to maintain an autonomous centre position was therefore *based on the persistence of the combined effect of the two cleavages*. With the death of de Gaulle and the progressive acceptance of the new political institutions at both mass and elite level, the *raison d'être* of these forces was undermined. The break-up of the Fifth Republic centrist opposition began with the second ballot of the 1968 elections – when the Duhamel group of the Centre Démocrate agreed to an electoral alliance with the majority – and ended ten years later when, under the leadership of the then President Giscard d'Estaing, all the remnants of the ex-centrist opposition formed part of the majority and united electorally with the Republican Independents to form the Union pour la Démocratie Française (UDF).

This realignment with the Gaullist majority was facilitated by the constraints imposed on party strategy by the new political institutions – particularly the electoral law and the presidential competition. All of the political strategies which had been developed by the centrist forces in order to maintain and foster their autonomous position and appeal ran counter to the logic of party competition induced by the existence of a homogeneous Gaullist majority on the one hand and the electoral and political *rapprochement* between Communists and Socialists on the other. More precisely, as a result of their long-standing cooperation during the Fourth Republic, the centrist forces were able to establish political alliances among themselves and even with the SFIO, but were unable to make these alliances electorally effective. The crucial problem faced by these parties in 1962 with the anti-Gaullist Cartel des Non, during the Centre Démocrate experience, and also eventually the Réformateur experiment, was how to direct their supporters to vote at the second ballot when no centrist candidate was actually in the running. The double-ballot majority system obliged the centrists to offer clear indications to their supporters according to the kind of contest which was occurring in any given constituency; moreover, it required the supporters to act in a disciplined fashion at the second ballot. Yet, since the dramatic failure of the Cartel des Non in 1962, the centrists have been plagued continually by their incapacity to offer clear-cut, unified and consistent instructions concerning second-ballot contests between, for instance, Gaullists and Communists, Socialists and Independent Republicans, and so on; and even where indications were given, the centrists also have been plagued by the indisciplined way in which their respective electorates have followed these indications. At the time of the Cartel des Non the SFIO required its electors to vote for Communist candidates when the contest was between the latter and the Gaullists; the CNIP gave the opposite advice. In

1968 one section of the CD stipulated a general electoral alliance with the majority, asking its electors to support majority candidates in the second ballot, while another section – led by Lecanuet – asked the same electors to support the candidates of the FGDS against Gaullist candidates, and gave no guidance in the case of the not-infrequent Communist–Gaullist confrontations.[7] Even more paradoxical was the situation in 1973 during the last attempt of the Radicals and Catholics to maintain an intermediate position between the two blocks. The Mouvement Réformateur was politically more homogeneous, in a moderate sense, having already shed a great part of its ex-centrist electors with left leanings. However, such political homogeneity in terms of the left–right cleavage was precisely the factor which left it in an untenable position: its candidates won a promising 13 per cent of the votes in the first ballot, which, if maintained in the second ballot, would have weakened the anti-left and anti-Communist vote and thus increased the chances of the left gaining victory. Inevitably, Lecanuet and Servan Schreiber were thus pushed to seek an electoral agreement with the majority, an agreement which represented the first step towards their full integration into the majority.

It should also be noted that in this period the position of the centrists was further undermined by a specific feature of the French double-ballot electoral law regarding the high threshold of first-round votes necessary to have the right to run a candidate in the second round. This threshold was originally five per cent of the votes cast, but this was raised to 10 per cent of the total electorate in 1967. In 1976 this percentage was further raised to 12.5 per cent. The 1967 modification significantly weakened the capacity of the centrists – and of all minor parties – to maintain any relevant electoral role. The centrist parties had grounded their electoral strategy on the presentation of a large number of candidates in the first round with the possibility of negotiating their withdrawal in certain constitutencies in the second round in exchange for similar withdrawals in others by the Socialists, Left Radicals and Independent Republicans. The increase of the threshold, however, meant the *automatic* exclusion from the second ballot of most non-left or non-majority candidates, and reduced to almost nil the blackmail potential of the minor formations.

A final crucial element contributing to the incapacity of the centrist forces to maintain themselves was the impossibility of a centrist force in the logic of a presidential contest institutionally devised to allow only two candidates to participate in the second and decisive round. Although in completely different political situations, both the Lecanuet and Poher candidacies in 1965 and 1969 demonstrated the impossibility of competing seriously for the presidency from an intermediate position. Given the increasing electoral salience of the presidential contest, the centrists found themselves in the unpleasant position – in terms of the institutional setting of the Fifth Republic – of being unable to provide a *realistic* presidential candidate, and therefore, unlike the Socialists and Independent Republicans with the candidatures of Mitterrand and Giscard d'Estaing, proved unable to take political or electoral advantage of the presidential contests.

In terms of the changing perception of cleavages among their electors, therefore, as well as in terms of electoral and presidential logic, a centre position proved more and more untenable after the departure of de Gaulle. A closer electoral analysis would show how in both the decisive legislative and presidential second ballots the parties located at the centre proved increasingly irrelevant to the electoral realignment occurring around them, while also proving unable to influence and control the second-round choice of their declining numbers of supporters, who increasingly tended to choose according to their own ideological affinities vis-à-vis the two blocks. In 1974, the final incorporation into the majority of the last centrist party – after another section of it had already opted for an alliance with the socialists – had the character of an elite ratification of what was already an electoral *fait accompli*.

Since then, the history of the ex-centrist parties is part of the history of the rightist alliance. A centre positioning in the French political spectrum did reappear in the 1978 and 1981 elections with the ecology lists (see Figure 1). However, their location is the result of an emphasis on a particular issue and is important only to the extent that the concerns of ecologically minded electors influence the tactics of other parties willing to gain their preferential support, namely the PS–RG and the UDF.

(c) The Electoral Re-equilibrium Within the Left and Right Blocks

The third fundamental change in the French party system has been the electoral growth of the centre-left and centre-right, that is, the Socialist–Radical alliance, and, more recently, the UDF. Figure 2 gives a clear picture of the mounting strength of these formations between 1967 and 1981 and, at the same time, the significant decline of the extreme parties – PCF and Gaullists. The result is that we find a new equilibrium in both blocks. Since the processes occurring within each block are different, however, it is necessary to look at them separately.

(i) The left. The problem of the French left in the Fifth Republic is the problem of Communist–Socialist relations, a point which finally became clear to the Socialists following the failure in 1964 of the last attempt to follow a political and electoral strategy based on the centre-left – the aborted Defferre candidacy for the Presidency.[8] However, notwithstanding the fact that during the 1960s and 1970s the advantages of a PC–SFIO (PS) alliance at the electoral level were as evident as were the disadvantages of disunity, Socialist–Communist relations have been characterised by a continuous see-saw of cooperation and conflict: extremely conflictual after 1958 following the support offered by the SFIO to de Gaulle; increasingly friendly between 1962 and 1967 to the extent of forming an electoral alliance; again hostile in 1968–69 as a consequence of the reciprocal recrimination following the events of May 1968 and the 1969 presidential campaign; a new *rapprochement* between 1970 and 1974 leading to both an electoral alliance and a common governmental programme and fostering major successes for the left in the presidential (1974) and local government elections; after 1974 a new phase of growing conflict which, in September 1977, just before the 1978 legislative elections, led to the break-up of the common governmental

FIGURE 2

ELECTORAL RE-EQUILIBRIUM WITHIN LEFT AND RIGHT COALITIONS

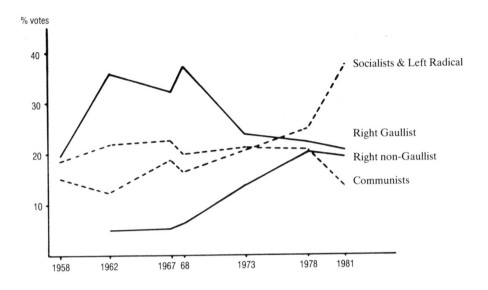

programme and in 1980, just before the 1981 presidential elections, to the break-up of the electoral alliance, that is, the mutual agreement to withdraw at the second ballot in favour of the best-placed candidate;[9] finally, since the 1981 presidential election, there has been a new sudden appeasement which led to the legislative triumph in June and, since then, to relatively friendly, although often critical, relations. What is the rationale of this dialectic of conflict and consensus? It is the contention of this article that party strategies within the French left can be explained largely as a result of the structural constraints inherent in the transformation of the party system and the new French electoral process.

When the SFIO finally oriented itself towards an alliance with the PC in 1965 it did so on the basis of three fundamental lessons received through the failure of the Cartel des Non and the Defferre candidacy: (1) that the discipline of its electors was greater in terms of casting their second ballot vote for PC candidates than for centre-right candidates; (2) that the discipline of Communist electors in voting for Socialist candidates at the second ballot when competing against any right-wing candidate was enormously higher than the discipline of centrist electors in voting for Socialist candidates competing against Gaullists; finally, (3) that to look for centrist electoral support in order to beat a Communist candidate was a suicidal move in the face of a very big Gaullist party. As such, the decision to seek electoral agreement with the forces to its left was imposed on the SFIO by the distribution of the second-party preferences of its own electorate, as well as – if not more so – by those of the Communist and centrist electorates.

Although born as a marriage of convenience, the electoral and later political alliance led to the growing success of the united left, but also increasingly provided evidence of the mechanisms inherent in the new logic of party competition which had been determined by the rise of Gaullism and by the electoral law. The germs of the problem had already appeared in 1968, but were not to come completely to light until the 1970s. In the 1968 elections the left alliance lost 2.4 per cent of the votes and 52.8 per cent of their seats. Results of opinion polls showed that the *débâcle* in terms of seats resulted from the polarisation of the contest and the negative image of the Communist Party.[10] The implications of the results were clear: in addition to the global electoral strength of the two parties, the governmental destiny of any left alliance would depend on two additional factors: first, the level of discipline with which the electorate of each party would vote for the leading left candidate at the time of the second round, and second, the number of centrist or undecided electors who would opt to vote for the candidates of the left.

It would seem that in this initial period the PC leadership believed this to be only a temporary problem. In the long run they thought the alliance would benefit all its component parts, and in the first half of the 1970s the party engaged in a campaign of renewal of its internal structure and external image, still regarding itself as the stronger electorally, the better organised and the more disciplined party of the left. The leadership made every effort to overcome the resistance to the Common Programme still present in large sections of the Socialists and Radicals, reassuring the allies of their non-hegemonic aims, soft-pedalling the extent to which they were in ideological competition, and also making many electoral concessions.[11]

In the middle of the 1970s, following the strong showing of the left in the legislative and presidential contests, the PC leadership began to look differently at the situation. It was increasingly evident that not least because of the aggregative power of the presidential candidature of Mitterrand, the re-establishment of the PS had proven to be a success. But even more important was the Communist realisation that the PS enjoyed a *positional advantage* in the unitary strategy. At both national and local elections, the PC tend to gain less from the alliance than do the Socialists, and its second-ballot results continue to be disappointing: when represented by a Communist candidate in the second round, the alliance fares badly, and in 1973 as well as in 1978 and in 1981 barely managed to get the same vote as that obtained by the two parties separately in the first ballot. This suggests a continued reluctance among Socialist and Left Radical supporters to vote for a Communist candidate, and reflects the incapacity of the latter to attract additional electors from the group of centrist and/or undecided electors.[12]

The Communist Party had hoped that the long practice of cooperation and the signing of the Common Programme would have acted to overcome any diffidence *vis-à-vis* Communist candidates. But while this may well have been the case for many Socialist electors, the growth of the new Socialist Party and of its Radical allies resulted primarily from the absorption of voters of the centre and moderate left.[13] Thus, even if the discipline of traditional Socialist electors was increasing, this was cancelled out by the greater unwillingness of the *new* electors to vote for Communist candidates. In 1978, for instance, only 65 per cent of those voting PS at the first run transferred their vote to the Communist candidate when the alternative was a UDF candidate,[14] while almost all PC voters became disciplined second-ballot Socialist voters when needed.

In addition, the specific effects of the electoral system should also be noted, in that it is a mechanism which *amplifies in terms of seats the decline or growth of one party within an electoral alliance*. Figure 3 provides clear evidence of this trend. From 1967 to 1978, despite losing only 1.8 per cent of its votes, the PC had lost about 18 per cent of the leading positions of the left alliance in the second round. In 1978 it still represented 41.7 per cent of the combined left vote, but accounted for only 32.2 per cent of second-ballot left candidatures. In this context, it is not enough for a party in a block alliance to simply maintain its electoral strength since, if the alliance tends to expand, the 'primary block election' role of the first round produces a disproportion-ately large decline of the party's second-round candidates. The effect becomes dramatic if one party declines and the other grows electorally, as Figure 3 shows clearly. In other words, in such a situation, a decline in its share of votes in the alliance may entail the reduction of the weaker party to the role of a small parliamentary supporting group.

Already in the middle of the 1970s, therefore, and more so later, the PC appears as the non-dynamic, blocked component of the coalition. Because of features intrinsic to party competition in the 1970s, the fate of the left alliance rested on the capacity of the Socialist–Radical component to expand towards the area of centrist or undecided electors. In such a context, it is therefore not surprising that the PC decided to revise its attitude towards the PS and the united left. The direction of this strategic change was, however, 'traditional': after 1975 the party attacked the Socialists with traditional accusations of 'reformism' and 'opportunism',[15] relaunched its image as a militant revolutionary party, and realigned itself towards Moscow on inter-national questions.[16] Interpreting its difficulties as stemming from the lack of an autonomous identity – which it saw as having been diluted in the name of the Union of the Left – it decided to revitalise along traditional militant lines, even at the risk of endangering the chance of an overall electoral victory for the left. In the 1978 legislative elections, this strategy of 'killing' the united left in 'self-defence' proved not to be electorally damaging, and the results convinced the party that it could push its new strategy even further to the extent that, during some of the local elections in 1980, it even refused to recommend support for the better-placed Socialist candidates in the second ballot.

It is obvious that by emphasising its internal centralism and ideological profile, the party became less acceptable to Socialist and centrist voters, and therefore reduced the chances of a left electoral majority being translated into a left parliamentary majority. However, in a situation in which the growth of the united left implied a reduction of the strength and role of the PC, to sacrifice governmental chances in order to revitalise the identity of

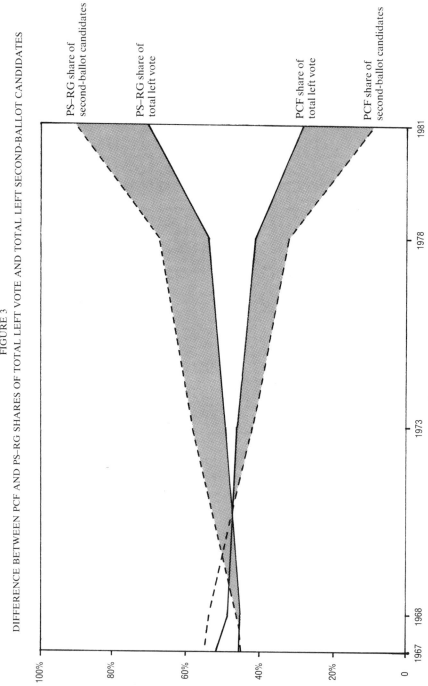

FIGURE 3

DIFFERENCE BETWEEN PCF AND PS–RG SHARES OF TOTAL LEFT VOTE AND TOTAL LEFT SECOND-BALLOT CANDIDATES

the party was not an irrational choice, provided of course that the party's belief in its capacity to maintain the loyalty of its electorate and the unity of its militants and cadres proved correct.[17]

It is in this sense that the 1981 presidential and legislative elections proved to be a crucial electoral turning point. Firstly, in the first ballot for the Presidency – when 25 per cent of the Communist electorate voted directly for Mitterrand rather than for Marchais – and later in the June legislative elections when the PC lost 4.5 per cent of the votes (22 per cent of its own electorate). In contrast to the experience of 1978, the Communist break-up of the Union of the Left and its realignment towards the Soviet Union on the Afghanistan and Polish questions proved to be directly damaging in electoral terms. Indeed, the Marchais débâcle in the first round of the presidential elections (15 per cent) actually obliged the PC suddenly to dismantle its strategy. Having decided initially to offer reasonably soft support to Mitterrand in the second ballot, maybe hoping for his eventual defeat, it found itself obliged to offer strong support and to revert to the discipline of the left union for fear of being abandoned *en masse* by its electorate. In-depth electoral analysis showed that the PC losses could be attributed neither to abstentionism, nor to the logic of *vote utile*, but rather that Communist dissidence proved the key factor.[18] Perhaps ironically, in 1981 the PC paid for the unitary habits induced in its electorate since 1965: the sudden reconstruction of the Union de Gauche between presidential and legislative elections was virtually imposed on the party by the dissidence of its marginal voters. Moreover, since 1981 the PC can no longer be guaranteed of its capacity to pull its electorate behind whatever strategy the party leadership wishes to adopt. On the contrary, the party has become increasingly subject to a centripetal drive through the defection potential of part of its constituency.

In conclusion, it is therefore somewhat paradoxical to note that the victory of Mitterrand, and later that of the PS, were partly fostered by the breaking up of the Union of the Left and by the consequent isolation of the PC, insofar as this facilitated the increased likelihood that centrist voters could support Socialist candidates. In the second ballot of June 1981 legislative elections, 90.5 per cent of the candidates leading the left were Socialists and only 9.5 per cent were PC (see Figure 3).

(ii) The right. Despite many similarities there are two crucial differences between the development of the left block and that of the right block – ex-*majorité* since June 1981 – which need to be emphasised. As can be seen in Figures 1 and 2, despite overall block stability, the 1970s have witnessed a significant new equilibrium emerging within the alliance which has acted to the advantage of the formation placed nearer to the centre of the political space. Whereas from 1962 to 1968 the majority was entirely monopolised by the monolithic Gaullist party, the decade since 1973 has witnessed a new internal balance. The parties of the right alliance which obtained their last parliamentary majority with 45.9 per cent of the votes in 1978 had, in 1962 – when some of them were in opposition – won 54.6 per cent of the votes. The absorption of the centre into the majority has occurred, therefore, at a

considerable electoral cost, particularly to the PS–RG. These electoral changes within the right block must be understood in the light of first, the crisis of the Gaullist party, which lost de Gaulle in 1969, the Presidency of the Republic with the death of Pompidou in 1974, and even the premiership with the resignation of Chirac in August 1976; and second, the capacity of Giscard d'Estaing to use the resources of the Presidency to constitute himself as the centre of an aggregation of centrist forces flowing together into the majority, a process which was completed in 1978 when the three components – the RI of Giscard d'Estaing, the right-wing Radicals and the remnants of the Catholics – formed the UDF.

Even the right block, however, does not lack evidence of internal competition similar to that present in the left. In terms of electoral competition, ex-centrist forces have to a certain extent enjoyed a positional advantage vis-à-vis the Gaullist party as a more acceptable second choice for a large sector of the undecided and switching electorate, as well as even in some sectors of the Left Radical and Socialist electorate. Moreover, the advantage which they gained in the eyes of the electorate as the party of the President was substantial, and contributed to their capacity to achieve an electoral balance vis-à-vis the Gaullists. Even in this case – and in a way very similar to the PC – the Gaullist party reacted by reorganising and relaunching itself ideologically in an effort to compete more directly with the Giscardiens at both legislative and presidential levels.[19] This renewed competition within the right alliance appeared at its most significant in the Gaullist independent candidatures at the 1978 legislative elections and in the Chirac–Giscard d'Estaing contest in the first round of the 1981 presidential election.

In 1967, 1968 and 1973, the majorité had presented a single first-ballot candidate in almost all constituencies. The internal distribution between the different parties occurred case by case, normally through the offices of the Prime Minister acting as coordinator of the campaign and the candidatures of the majorité. In 1978, however, with the aim of reaffirming the independent identity and the principal role of the Gaullist party, Chirac broke with traditional practice and presented independent candidates at the first ballot, choosing to treat this first round as a primary election in which voters would choose which candidate of the right would eventually contest the seat against the left. Thus in 1978, and for the first time, Gaullist candidates competed against other majorité candidates in as many as 316 constituencies. In itself, this new strategy may have helped the early reunification of ex-centrist forces with the RI in the UDF, particularly as the 12.5 per cent threshold necessary in order to be admitted to the second ballot risked the exclusion of many non-Gaullist candidates. While the modification of the threshold probably had been directed against candidatures external to the two dominant blocks – particularly against potential ecology or regionalist movements – nevertheless it also had an impact within the majority, encouraging the Radicals, Christian Democrats and Republicans to overcome mutual differences and party-specific loyalties.[20] Confronting an independent Gaullist candidate, these parties simply could not afford to remain electorally distinct. In the event, the Chirac strategy of open competition within the block proved disappointing to the Gaullists: the UDF managed to win 21.4 per cent of the votes and 137 seats.

Similar disappointment faced Chirac in his attempt to regain the Presidency. Most analysts have argued that his sharply fought struggle with Giscard d'Estaing in the first ballot facilitated the subsequent victory of Mitterrand. It certainly is true that, in 1974, 79.5 per cent of the first-ballot Chaban Dalmas supporters voted for Giscard d'Estaing, while in 1981 only 71.5 per cent of Chirac first-ballot supporters voted for Giscard d'Estaing.[21] In any case, the *majorité* suffered electorally as a result of its internal disunity, and if in 1978 it had managed to win a majority of seats notwithstanding its poor electoral performance, this was due primarily to the disarray of the left. At the legislative elections of 1981 the right attempted to reduce its level of internal competition by resorting once again to a first-ballot agreement on single candidates, settling on 385 such candidates in Metropolitan France as against only 88 cases of double candidatures. In the event, however, the RPR–UDF *rapprochement* was too late, too unconvincing and too full of recriminations to allow it to balance the Socialist *montée* under the Mitterrand presidency.

However similar to those of the left they may appear, the vicissitudes of the rightist alliance in the 1970s occurred in a different context of party competition. In terms of sociological composition, ideological profile and spatial location the RPR and UDF electorates in the 1970s and 1980s are sufficiently similar[22] that the electoral acceptance by one party of the other is normally very good – and certainly far better than in the left block. This in turn means that for one party to compete centripetally in order to distinguish itself from its partner could cost that party dearly. The tendency of rightist voters to display a less intense identification with a specific party than those of the left allows these electors to act more in the interests of the coalition rather than of any political force: in this sense, the supporters of the ex-*majorité* parties can cast a *vote utile* even at the first run.[23] The fact that the levels of acceptance or refusal of the two parties in the mass electorate is broadly similar – although slightly favouring the UDF – permits the alliance to agree on single candidatures at the first ballot, or at least to establish a code of 'good behaviour' in order to attenuate the competitive effects of the first-ballot primaries – as was the case in the 1982–83 local elections – *without risk of electoral losses*. The same practice is impossible on the left, as the nomination of single Communist candidates would almost certainly imply electoral losses for the Union of the Left as a whole.

CAUSES OF PARTY SYSTEM TRANSFORMATION

This short analysis of the main phases of reconstruction of the party system allows us to systematise the main factors which have been influential. In general, major electoral realignments result from three kinds of phenomena: a decline in the importance of traditional cleavages; the emergence of important new lines of division; and changes in the main political institutions. All three have occurred in France: the aggregative capacity induced by the enormous personal appeal of de Gaulle which ran counter to the traditional lines of division of the French electorate (particularly of the centre-right electorate); the influence of the new political–institutional cleavage concerning the acceptability of the Gaullist institutions; and the impact of new political institutions – particularly the highly competitive presidential competition and the electoral law. The difficulty, therefore, is not the simple identification of major factors of change, but that of judging their relative importance and the extent of their mutual interaction.

Clearly one of the first elements to be considered in terms of both importance and chronology is the impressive aggregation of the French centre-right electorate in the Gaullist party.[24] By solving the Algerian problem – and more generally the recriminations of French decolonisation – de Gaulle deprived the extreme right in France of its main *raison d'être*. At the same time he managed to assuage the *fronde* of the Army, encouraging its modernisation from a traditional base to a nuclear one, with the growing influence of highly specialised and technically professionalised officers. The regulation in 1959 of the issue of religious schools deprived the Catholic movement of a claim which had previously constituted the key element of its political distinctiveness. Allowing economic policy to be determined by such classic liberals as Pinay, Rueff and Giscard d'Estaing meant the loss to the liberals of parts of their electorate. In the last analysis, however, only de Gaulle's extraordinary personal appeal made it possible for these policies to result in the formation of a great right-wing party rather than simply in the fragmentation of the moderate forces.

But while this original impetus proved particularly important, a second and often neglected effect of the Gaullism–anti-Gaullism cleavage must also be emphasised: the fact that this cleavage divided the French mass electorate along lines quite different to those in which it divided the French political elites. At the elite level, the Gaullist–anti-Gaullist institutional cleavage divided the Gaullists and the small group of RI from all other political parties; at the mass level, however, the main dividing line concerning the acceptability of Gaullist institutions was situated much more to the left, dividing the entire centre-right from the left. It also should be noted that certain sectors of the Radical and Socialist electorate had an image of de Gaulle and of the new institutions which was much more positive and less polarised than that of the political elites of the parties for which they traditionally voted. In the long run it was this separation of mass electorate and political elites in the 1960s which provided a new dynamic for the party system and which lies at the basis of the restructuring in the 1970s. In the last resort, the original element which is necessary, albeit not sufficient, to interpret the change of the party system was the fact that for a long time the political parties, formerly of the Fourth Republic, based their electoral alliances on a cleavage – the institutional cleavage – which was not perceived with the same intensity by the mass of their electors. In such circumstances, it is understandable that the centrist parties continually faced difficulties in getting their supporters to follow their second-ballot strategy, difficulties similar to those experienced by the SFIO when it adopted a 'reactionary' strategy aimed at the restoration of the political institutions of the Fourth Republic.

However, the separation of mass electorate and political elites concerning their perception of the cleavage was not of itself sufficient to produce a large scale electoral realignment. Dissonance between the perceptions of mass and elite can have a direct repercussion on electoral behaviour only when specific mechanisms exist to foster the individual elector's perception of these incongruities. In France, the new double-ballot electoral law played precisely this role, acting as a mechanism which could demonstrate and even amplify the separation between the mass electorate and the political elites regarding the figure of de Gaulle, the new regime and the presidential reform, and, at the same time, offering the *institutional opportunity* to substantiate this dissonance in behavioural terms.

The second ballot and its high electoral threshold are at the heart of this process. Political parties are frequently obliged to indicate to their supporters which other party they should vote for; and when the dissonance between voters and elites is real and diffused, it is bound to be strongly perceived by those voters when the second-ballot preference of the elite does not correspond to their own. Whereas with systems of proportional representation party leaders can ask the electorate to support them, and at the same time remain free to use such support for different political strategies, in a double-ballot system the party *must* select its political and electoral alliances not only in advance but also in a way which is *congruent with the second-party preference of the bulk of its electorate*. As has been emphasised above, the failure of the ideologically heterogeneous anti-system electoral and political alliances of the parties which had governed the Fourth Republic was decided by the electoral behaviour of the marginal electorate of each party in the second ballot. In the long run, the numerical strength of parties and their ideological affinity in left–right terms progressively selected the only alternative alliances which were possible given the distribution of opinion of the different electoral segments.

At the end of the 1970s and in the 1980s the electoral law operated in a different political reality to that of the realignment period. Following the disappearance of a centre political position, opposition between two large electoral blocks highlighted other influences of the electoral system and, in particular, the tendency of the system to favour the moderate parties of each block given their ability to appeal to the bulk of undecided/switching voters located primarily at the centre of the political space. Moreover, when little separates the electoral strength of the two alliances, the electoral system tends in the second ballot to favour the internal coherence of each block in terms of the ideological affinity of the electors of the parties which compose it. From this point of view, the right has so far enjoyed a clear advantage over the left. Nor has this been contradicted by the victory of the left in 1981. In 1978, despite a majority of votes in the first ballot, the left had been defeated at the second round as a result of its internal ideological and pragmatic divisions. In 1981 the left won – but not because it had overcome this problem; rather, the victory resulted from the extraordinary success of the Socialists under the impetus of Mitterrand's presidential success which, in turn, caused the PC virtually to disappear in the second ballot, leaving the left represented almost wholly by Socialist candidates. In any case, it took

55.8 per cent of the votes to produce a majority of seats for the left, whereas the right had won a majority of seats in 1978 with less than 50 per cent of first-ballot votes.

Paradoxically, therefore, the French double-ballot majority system imposes the need to form block alliances while, at the same time, it creates the conditions for the high level of competitiveness and instability within these alliances. This said, however, it is incorrect to attribute to the electoral system *tout court* the bipolarisation effect said to exist in the party system. First, in analytical terms, there is a distinction to be made between the role played by the high threshold and that played by the electoral formula itself, in that a high threshold can be applied in every electoral formula with fairly similar effects. As far as the electoral formula in itself is concerned, experts tend to agree that: (1) the direct influence of the formula on the *number* of parties cannot be determined precisely; (2) its effect on small parties is not so clear as that of the plurality system and depends very much on their spatial positioning and coalition strategy; (3) it has the clear effect of operating to the disadvantage of those parties perceived by the bulk of the electorate as anti-system or, at least, as ideologically distant from the median position.[25]

If these are the only generalisable effects of the double-ballot majority formula (see Figure 4 for French party disproportionality) it is doubtful if it can be regarded as solely responsible for the change in the French party system, and, in particular, its tendency towards coalition bipolarisation. Rather, it is first necessary to reassess the importance of the high threshold[26] and, second, to consider the specific effects of the electoral system as resulting from the interplay between its generalisable effects on the one hand and the specific changes in the cleavage structure of the 1960s on the other; in other words, the so-called bipolarisation was not 'produced' by the system, but only reinforced by it when and only after its preconditions in terms of the French cleavage structure had already been independently established.[27]

The final important factor accounting for the transformation of the party system is, of course, the impact of the presidential reform. Since this has been already discussed at length, it is not necessary here to enter in a detailed analysis.[28] Suffice it to recall the specific effect it has had on party competition. It is often argued that the explicit constitutional norm which permits only the two leading candidates to participate in the second ballot has contributed directly to the aggregation of the political parties in two competing alliances. However, this generalisation needs further specification. First, in a similar way to the impact of the electoral law, the French presidential system also proved an electoral mechanism contributing to demonstrate the potential dissonance between the orientations and/or preferences of the political elites and the mass electorate. Since there could be only two second-ballot candidates, many political parties were compelled to indicate their second preferences to their electorate, staking their political credibility and legitimacy on the correspondence between their choice and that of their supporters. As such, even the presidential contest tended to oblige those political parties which were unlikely to have successful second-ballot candidates to select political alliances in line with the prevalent second prefer-

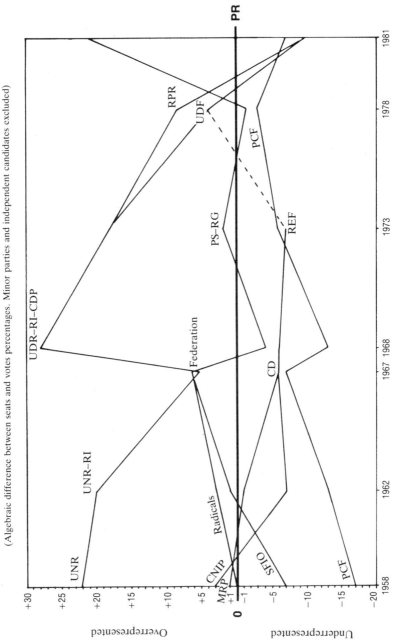

FIGURE 4

DISREPRESENTATION IN PARLIAMENT OF THE FRENCH POLITICAL PARTIES (1958–81)

(Algebraic difference between seats and votes percentages. Minor parties and independent candidates excluded)

ences of their first-ballot electors. Moreover, parties were also obliged to be consistent at all three electoral levels – presidential, parliamentary and local – since, in the interests of coherence, no party could afford to offer the same electorate different suggestions according to the level of competition. Very much in the same way as the double-ballot electoral system, so also binary presidential elections break the intrinsic logic of the extreme multi-party system by imposing on the parties the prior need to define their political alliances; as such, it also contributes to the failure of those alliances which are not based on ideologically homogeneous sectors of the electorate.

Finally, presidentialism acts in the long run as a means of strengthening the leadership within the political parties and political alliances, and favours the emergence of political personalities for whom the publicity obtained through the campaign (or through the presidency) guarantees autonomous political resources and, therefore, the opportunity to act as the focus of any regrouping or reorganisation of political forces. This 'presidential effect' is very evident in the case of the Gaullist party. But it has also been extremely important for the new UDF and PS, both of which have grown and re-organised under the umbrella of the Giscard d'Estaing presidency in the one case, and of Mitterrand's reasonably successful campaigns in 1965 and 1974 in the other. As such, three of the four political parties which dominate contemporary French politics can be said to have benefited at different times from the 'presidential effect'.

The 1970s have witnessed the growing conviction among both electors and elites that a credible presidential candidate is a necessary condition for the electoral success of a political party. In a system pervaded by presidential logic, a party which lacks such a credible candidate ends up by becoming the second-rank partner of an alliance. At the same time, however, this develop-ment also has contributed to exacerbating the internal competition within each block, in that each party has an immense incentive to push its own candidate towards the Elysée. Here again, we can note an important differ-ence between the left and right blocks. Within the right, both the Gaullists and the UDF have an opportunity to run for the presidency, and, as such, competition between the two parties in the first ballot may go so far as to jeopardise the overall chances of the coalition in the second ballot; this indeed was the case in the 1981 presidential elections. Within the left block the situation is different; competition between PC and PS candidates does not really exist at the level of the presidency, since it is obvious that a Communist candidate – even if achieving a plurality in the first ballot – would have no chance of victory in the second. The presentation of a first-ballot Communist candidate is therefore primarily designed to publi-cise party policies and to maintain Communist electoral identity, even though such a strategy may weaken the party electorally as a result of a *vote utile* of Communist electors for the Socialist candidate even in the first ballot. In the 1981 presidential elections, for instance, roughly one fourth of those voters who had supported Communist candidates in the legislative elections voted directly for Mitterrand in the first ballot for the presidency. In sum, it is important to note that the Communist Party is the only party in the system which has no opportunity to benefit from the 'presidential effect';

rather, even presidential contests contribute to its finding itself in a strategic *cul de sac*.

WHAT TYPE OF PARTY SYSTEM IN THE 1980s?

Much of the literature on the French party system assumes that behind the multi-party system of the Third and Fourth Republics were concealed only two fundamental political tendencies or temperaments,[29] the internal fragmentation of which was facilitated if not promoted by 'weak' political institutions, and electoral laws in particular, lacking aggregative potential.[30] Within this basic framework, therefore, developments of the party system in the 1970s and 1980s have been seen mainly in terms of a final and explicit realisation of political competition between these two traditional conservative and progressive tendencies, a realisation facilitated by the new institutional mechanisms (the electoral law and semi-presidentialism). Under this interpretation the change in the party system is therefore not seen to be problematic, but rather as a process of 'normalisation', bringing party politics eventually in line with the fundamental continuity of a conservative and a progressive temperament.

Although this view deserves to be discussed in more detail, it is an interpretation which seems to oversimplify the change which has been taking place. For the purposes of this paper, therefore, we have found it more useful to situate the analysis of change in the French party system in the context of a slightly modified version of Sartori's typology of party systems. The relevant dimensions on which Sartori bases his general typology are:

(a) *the number of relevant parties*, counted according to a precise rule of systemic relevance;
(b) *the degree of ideological polarisation of the system*, that is, the ideological distance which separates its extreme components;
(c) *the number of ideological poles* around which party competition is articulated;
(d) *the direction (centripetal or centrifugal)* of party competition, that is, the direction of the most electorally rewarding competition tactics for parties.[31]

It is necessary to state immediately that the fundamental variables in Sartori's typology are the first two, the number of parties and the degree of polarisation, while the others are presented as 'properties' of party systems which are largely determined by the two primary criteria.[32] In short, Sartori establishes a relationship between the number of parties and the ideological distance on the one hand, and the number of poles and the direction of competition on the other. A large number of parties in a context of ideological polarisation is causally related to a multipolar configuration and centrifugal party competition; a limited number of parties, on the other hand, and a limited ideological distance, tends to produce a bipolar party system and centripetal competition.

This said, it is necessary to add that, in the present analysis, dimensions (c) and (d) will be considered as *autonomous dimensions of change*, in that the development of the French party system over the past 15 years calls into question the causal nature of the link between number of parties and the ideological distance on the one hand, and the number of poles and the direction of party competition on the other. This point will become more clear when looking at the four dimensions one by one in reference to French political developments.

As far as the format of the party is concerned – the number of relevant party organisations – there has been a substantive reduction since the 1960s. Only four major parties now dominate French politics. In 1978, they were of remarkably similar electoral strengths: 20.7 per cent for the PCF; 25 per cent for the PS–MRG; 21.4 per cent for the UDF, and 22.5 per cent for the RPR. Together, these parties obtained 89.6 per cent of first-ballot votes. Other parties or independent candidates together collected only 10.4 per cent of the votes, while actually none of these latter could afford to elect any candidate without prior agreement with one of the major parties, that is, none of them enjoyed any real coalition or blackmail potential. In 1981 there was an important change in the balance within the left, but together the four parties won 93.9 per cent of votes, leaving only 6.1 per cent to others (extreme left – PSU; Ecologists; extreme right; and Independents). There is, therefore, no doubt whatsoever that in terms of the number of parties with systemic relevance, the French party system is a four-party system, and that from the beginning of the Fifth Republic it has moved from the category of *extreme multi-partism* to that of *limited multi-partism*.

At the level of ideological distance and polarisation among the parties, however, there is no evidence of a change of similar magnitude. Since the end of the 1960s, certain deep ideological conflicts in French politics – such as those stemming from decolonisation, Gaullist constitutional reform and practice, and church–state relations – have weakened, fostering a growing basic consensus and ideological depolarisation. However, as has been emphasised above, French Communism in the 1980s is still perceived as a rather extraneous force, largely unacceptable to vast electoral sectors which deny it any democratic credentials. Rather than weakening over time, this perception was actually reinforced by the behaviour of the Communist Party, particularly since its efforts at democratisation and ideological revision at the beginning of the 1970s proved to be inherently tactical, and were reversed since 1976–77. For most commentators, the PC position in the 1980s is seen as a step back, even with respect to its relatively late and limited 'westernisation'.[33] Opinion polls consistently show that large elements of the electorate continue to perceive the party as democratically unacceptable and illegitimate and as being isolated in a far-left position. Hence those elements of discontinuity in the space of party competition, the effects of which have been discussed above.[34] Indeed, in comparative terms, and particularly on the left, the distribution of political opinion on the left–right scale in France remains one of the most polarised in Europe.[35] It is thus important to realise how, despite almost 20 years of electoral and political alliance with the Socialists and Left Radicals, Communist electors still constitute a significantly distinct ideological pole (see Figure 5).

In the French case, therefore, patterns of party fragmentation and ideo-

FIGURE 5

LEFT–RIGHT LOCATION OF DIFFERENT SECTORS OF THE FRENCH ELECTORATE IN 1978

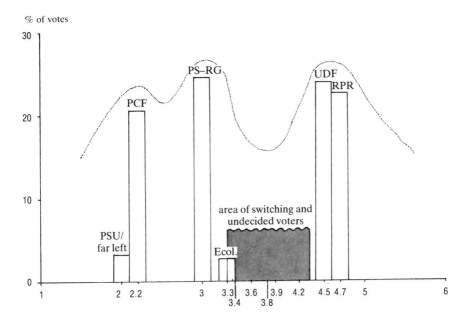

Legend: 3.4 = mean location of electors voting right in the presidential election of 1974 and left in the legislative elections of 1973 and 1978.

3.6 = mean location of electors voting left in 1973 and right in 1978.

3.8 = mean location of electors voting right in 1973 and left in 1978.

3.9 = mean location of electors abstaining.

4.2 = mean location of electors voting right in 1974 and abstaining in the legislative election.

Source: Elaborated from 1978 post-electoral SOFRES survey.

logical distance are not associated with a system of moderate pluralism. A substantial reduction of the party system format up to now has not been associated with a correspondingly large ideological depolarisation. As such, it is difficult to derive a *causal* relationship between these two variables and other properties of party system competition – the number of ideological poles around which the competition is articulated and the direction of this competition itself. With the disappearance of parties located in the centre of the political space, and with the growing shift of electors directly from one block to the other, the bulk of floating and undecided voters is now mainly located in the centre of the political space (see Figure 5). This in itself would suggest a trend towards centripetal competition with its moderating effects on parties. However, as has been argued above, despite ample evidence that competition is indeed centripetal in tendency, nevertheless this does occur in the context of a continuing ideological polarisation. This means that the frequently quoted tendency towards a 'bipolarisation' of the French party system, and its description as a *'quadrille bipolaire'*,[36] is both imprecise and misleading. If by bipolarisation is meant a tendency towards a 'bipolar' coalition configuration, then this is obviously the case; but the crucial question is whether this bipolarity – bipolar in the sense that it is character-ised by *only two* competing alliances – also signifies, or tends to produce, an effective reduction to two ideological poles, a change which would entail the effective structural change towards moderate multi-partism. This is clearly not the case. The Communist position remains such that, in terms of its ideological distance from the other components of the system, the party system is even now characterised by the articulation of competition on *three* distinct poles, *notwithstanding the fact that there are only two coalition blocks*. This is demonstrated not only by the analysis of the distribution of political opinion and the acceptability of the parties, but also by the strategic behaviour of the PC itself, which cannot be explained through the assump-tion of a bipolar distribution of opinion. Indeed, rather than coming to terms with centripetal drives, the PC actually tries to counter them.

In conclusion, to describe the French party system in the 1980s as a *système bipolaire* on the *prima facie* fact that there are only two competing electoral coalitions is to ignore those specific features which distinguish it from moderate bipolar competitive systems, and hence fail to explain the *rational* polarisation strategy of the PC.

In terms of Sartori's typological criteria, therefore, the French party system presents inconsistent and mixed characteristics. As a result of the incongruity between format and polarisation, the continuing multi-polarity of electoral opinion is associated with a type of competition which – as a result of institutional constraints – is centripetal in tendency. This mixed configuration provides one of the keys to understanding the strategic and tactical choices of parties in the past ten years. Centripetal competition rewards the moderate parties' tendency to move towards the centre to gain the support of the centre-located electorate. However, this logic is not entirely acceptable to the extreme parties, with the result that there is increased competition within each block, and particularly in the left. It is even more important to recognise that the multi-polar distribution of opin-ion allowed the Communist Party to maintain its strength in the 1970s without being obliged to accept the logic of moderation and centripetal competition. In other words, in order to gain electorally in such a configura-tion, it is necessary to accept the centripetal logic; at the same time, however, and unlike in the case of pure moderate pluralism, to refuse to compete centripetally is not to run the risk of severe electoral defeat.

Before the 1981 elections, the key theoretical question concerning the future development of the French party system was whether a fundamental ideological polarisation would persist in opposition to the centripetal drives fostered by the institutional mechanisms or, on the contrary, whether such drives would dominate and so trigger off a definite process of depolarisation, involving also the PC and its electorate. The results of the 1981 legislative elections and the 1982–83 local elections seem to suggest the second alternative. For the first time the PC's strategy of polarisation has been heavily and explicitly penalised by a sector of its electorate. However, it remains to be seen whether this is the first sign of a process of depolarisation of the Communist electorate which may push the Communist leadership to an unambiguous revision of their ideology and strategy.

NOTES

1. Compare the survey data concerning French attitudes towards political parties in the 1960s and 1970s respectively in J. Charlot (ed.), *Les Français et de Gaulle* (Paris: Plon, 1971), and *L'Opinion française en 1977 – SOFRES* (Paris: Presses de la Fondation Nationale des Sciences Politiques, 1978).
2. For a general synthesis of the large literature on this point see F.L. Wilson, 'The Revitalisation of French Parties', *Comparative Political Studies*, Vol. 12 (1969), pp. 82–103.
3. Cf., for instance, K. Evin and R. Cayrol, 'Les partis politiques dans les entreprises', *Projet*, No. 106 (June 1976), pp. 633–48, and D. Wess, *Politique, partis et syndicats dans l'entreprise* (Paris: Les Éditions d'Organisation, 1979), pp. 56–79.
4. Cf. F.L. Wilson and R. Wiste, 'Party cohesion in the French National Assembly', *Legislative Studies Quarterly*, Vol. 1 (1976), pp. 467–90.
5. Cf. A. Mabileau (ed.), *Les Facteurs locaux de la vie politique nationale* (Paris: Pedone, 1973).
6. See M. Dogan, 'Le personnel politique et la personnalité charismatique', *Revue française de sociologie*, Vol. 6 (1965), pp. 305–24.
7. For the internal problems of the centrists in this crucial period see F. Goguel, 'Bipolarisation ou rénovation du centrisme?', *Revue française de science politique*, Vol. 17 (1967), pp. 918–28; R. Cayrol and J.-L. Parodi, 'Le centrisme deux ans après', *Revue française de science politique*, Vol. 18 (1968), pp. 93–106; C. Ysmal, 'Unité ou pluralité du centrisme?', *Revue française de science politique*, Vol. 19 (1969), pp. 171–82.
8. See J. Gras, 'La Fédération de Gaston Defferre', *Esprit* (September 1965), pp. 326–41.
9. Cf. *Humanité*, 27 September 1980, and G. Le Gall, 'Sénatoriales: la fin de la discipline républicaine?', *Revue politique et parlementaire*, Vol. 82, No. 888 (1980), pp. 9–14.
10. See the data in B.A. Campbell, 'On the Prospect of Polarisation in the French Electorate', *Comparative Politics*, Vol. 8 (1976), p. 285.
11. For a good example see *Le Monde*, 13 October 1972.
12. Empirical evidence of this incapacity can be drawn from every electoral opinion poll. A well documented case is the ecology vote. The ecology electorate, located in a centre position on the left–right scale (see Figure 5), voted predominantly for the left in the second ballot of 1978 legislative election, but not where the left was represented by a Communist candidate. Cf. J.R. Frears and J.-L. Parodi, *War Will Not Take Place. The French Parliamentary Elections March 1978* (London: C. Hurst, 1979), p. 95.
13. Cf. J.-L. Parodi, 'L'union et la différence: les perceptions de la Gauche après la crise de Septembre 1977', in *L'Opinion française en 1977*, op. cit.
14. Cf. the post-electoral survey SOFRES, April 1978. In 1973 the corresponding figure was 68 per cent.
15. On the revival of old propaganda themes and their use against the Socialists see the excellent work by D. Labbé, 'Les discours communistes', *Revue française de science politique*, Vol. 30 (1980), pp. 46–77.
16. For a synthetic analysis of these changes see J. Bourdouin, 'Le PCF. Retour à l'archaisme?', *Revue politique et parlementaire*, Vol. 82, No. 889 (1980), pp. 30–40.
17. In this period dissent within the party was growing and was often expressed publicly: See J. Bourdouin, 'Les phénomènes de contestation au sein du Parti communiste français', *Revue française de science politique*, Vol. 30 (1980), pp. 78–111.
18. See, F. Platone and J. Ranger, 'L'échec du Parti communiste aux élections du printemps 1981', *Revue française de science politique*, Vol. 31 (1981), pp. 1015–37; and G. Le Gall, 'Le nouvel ordre électoral', *Revue politique et parlementaire*, Vol. 83, No. 893 (1981), pp. 1–32.

19. On the Chirac reorganisation and relaunching of the Gaullist party see C. Crisol, *La machine RPR* (Paris: Fayolle, 1977); and P. Lecompte, 'Horizon 1981: Les forces en présence dans la majorité', *Revue politique et parlementaire*, Vol. 82, No. 887 (1980), pp. 20–48.

20. On the formation of UDF see D. Seguin, *Les nouveaux Giscardiens* (Paris: Colmann-Lévy, 1979).

21. Cf. J. Charlot, 'Le double enchaînement de la défaite et de la victoire', *Revue politique et parlementaire*, Vol. 83 (1981), pp. 15–28.

22. See evidence in J. Capdeville *et al.*, *France de Gauche vote à droite* (Paris: Presses de la Fondation Nationale de Science Politique, 1981), pp. 240–49.

23. Ibid., p. 27.

24. On this process see P.G. Cerny, 'Cleavage, Aggregation, and Change in French Politics', *British Journal of Political Science*, Vol. 2 (1972), pp. 443–55.

25. Cf. D.W. Rae, *The Political Consequences of Electoral Laws* (New Haven: Yale University Press, 1971), pp. 109–10; and D. Fisichella, *Sviluppo democratico e sistemi elettorali* (Florence: Sansoni, 1970), pp. 213–21.

26. Goguel is among the very few who have adequately underlined the enormous role of this exceptionally high threshold, which as an electoral device does not have any specific connection with the double-ballot majority system. See F. Goguel, 'Mode de scrutin et alternance', *Revue politique et parlementaire*, Vol. 84, No. 899 (1982), pp. 20–21.

27. This interpretation therefore differs from those believing that the electoral bipolarisation around a Gaullist and an anti-Gaullist left block emerged because it had been imposed by the plurality character of the second round. This thesis was originally advanced by A.J. Milnor, *Elections and Political Stability* (Boston: Little, Brown & Co., 1969), pp. 63–4, and later accepted by many others.

28. See V. Wright, *The Government and Politics of France* (London: Hutchinson, 2nd ed. 1983), Chapter 6.

29. 'Concerned above all with reality, I concentrated less on parties, superficial and constantly changing categories, than on fundamental tendencies,' A. Siegfried, *Tableau politique de la France de l'ouest sous la IIIe République* (Paris: Colin, 1913), p. XXIV. This interesting introductory statement by Siegfried may be considered as characterising an interpretative paradigm shared also by Goguel and Duverger. Although they have devoted greater attention to a moderate and centrist third tendency, they have tended to regard it not as an autonomous tendency in public opinion, but rather as a governmental geographical location, a meeting point of opinions belonging to the two basic tendencies. See F. Goguel, *Géographie des élections françaises de 1870 à 1951* (Paris: Colin, 1951); and M. Duverger, 'L'éternel marais. Essai sur le centrisme français', *Revue française de science politique*, Vol. 14 (1964), pp. 118–20. A voice dissenting from this interpretative framework is that of R. Aron, 'Réflexions sur la politique et la science de la politique française', *Revue française de science politique*, Vol. 5 (1955), pp. 5–20.

30. Cf. F. Goguel and A. Grosser, *La Politique en France* (Paris: Colin, 1954), pp. 78–80; and J. Chapsal, *La Vie politique et les partis en France depuis 1940* (Paris: Les Cours de Droit, 1960), pp. 13–14.

31. See G. Sartori, *Parties and Party Systems: A Framework for Analysis* (New York: Cambridge University Press, 1976), especially Chapters 5, 6.1 and 6.3.

32. To be precise, Sartori attributes the status of independent variable primarily to the numerical criterion, while he regards ideological distance as an intervening variable linked and interacting with the first. Cf. ibid., p. 286.

33. See the conclusion of two recent analyses of G. Lavau, *A quoi sert le PCF?* (Paris: Fayard, 1981); and J.-J. Becker, *Le Parti communiste veut-il prendre le pouvoir?* (Paris: Seuil, 1981).

34. For the relevance of this continuum as an effective dimension of competition and of the perception of the political space by French electors and parties, see the evidence provided by the studies of S.H. Barnes and R. Pierce, 'Le preferenze politiche degli italiani e dei francesi', *Rivista italiana di scienza politica*, Vol. 2 (1972), pp. 335–52; G.A. Mauser and J. Freyssinet-Dominjon, 'Exploring Political Space: A Study of French Voters' Preferences', in I. Budge, I. Crewe and D. Fairlie (eds.) *Party Identification and Beyond: Representation of Voting and Party Identification* (London: John Wiley & Sons, 1976), pp. 203–24; H.

Rosenthal and S.K. Sen, 'Spatial Voting Models for the French Fifth Republic', *American Political Science Review*, Vol. 81 (1977), pp. 1447–66.

35. Comparative data are available in R. Inglehart and H. Klingemann, 'Party Identification, Ideological Preference and the Left–Right Dimension Among Western Mass Publics', in I. Budge, I. Crewe and D. Fairlie (eds.), *Party Identification and Beyond*, op. cit., pp. 253–5; and in G. Sartori and G. Sani, 'Polarisation, Fragmentation and Competition in Western Democracies', in H. Daalder and P. Mair (eds.), *Western European Party Systems – Continuity and Change* (London: Sage Publications, 1983), pp. 307–40.

36. Cf. M. Duverger, *Le Monde*, 27 January 1976.

The Emerging Spanish Party System: Is There a Model?

Antonio Bar

Most traditional views of European party systems, particularly those which began to proliferate in the 1960s, tended to consider these systems as stable structures in which no radical change had taken place over years of electoral history, and which were largely independent of any changes which might have occurred in the heart of the societies in which they functioned. Thus Lipset and Rokkan stated at the end of that decade that 'the party systems of the 1960s reflect with few but significant exceptions the cleavage structures of the 1920s',[1] while in the same vein, and based on their analysis of long-term electoral data, Rose and Urwin concluded that 'the electoral strength of most parties in Western nations since the war has changed very little from election to election, from decade to decade, or within the lifespan of a generation'.[2]

However, more recent studies have shown that, since the 1960s, European party systems have undergone certain transformations which, though not very radical, counter the suggestion that they are absolutely stable structures. Pedersen's analysis of changing patterns of electoral volatility[3] is the most obvious example, particularly as far as the changes between 1969 and 1977 are concerned, but other authors also have provided similar evidence,[4] to the extent that the conception of party systems as having been frozen by the cleavage structures established in an earlier era is now generally questioned by virtually all the scholars concerned with this question.[5] Finally, as Maria Maguire has put it, while it can be argued that the traditional alignments are still visible, albeit in a weaker state, nevertheless

> there can be little doubt that the electoral stability that characterised European party systems for much of the post-war period has recently given way to a situation of greater change and instability. Not only has this affected a larger number of countries, but it has also been very generalised in terms of the number and variety of parties affected.[6]

If we were to attempt to specify the real evidence of change which is hidden beneath analytical indices or categories, it could be concluded, following Pedersen,[7] that the most important changes are (a) an increase in the number of competing parties, (b) changes in the distribution of electoral strength, and (c) a changing relationship between voters and parties, which is detectable in some cases as a tendency towards decreasing party identification, in others in the increased frequency of unconventional political behaviour, and in yet others as a defection of large portions of the electorate from older parties to new parties which are classifiable neither as traditional mass parties nor as 'catch-all' parties.

But if all this is true for those Western European party systems which form part of pluralist and democratic political systems that are at least almost half a century old, it becomes paradigmatic in the case of Spain, where the most recent democratic experience, coming after over 40 years of dictatorship, is still very new. The Spanish party system, after three general elections and several other by-elections (regional and local) held in this democratic period, has been characterised by extreme instability which is manifested in (a) a change in the number of parties, (b) a change in their electoral strength, and (c) a substantial weakening of the party–electorate bond. While this instability might be considered as normal in a young party system in the throes of formation, the actual amount of change is surprising – particularly if compared to such similar transitional situations as those experienced by various other European countries at the end of periods of dictatorship.

A DESCRIPTIVE CHARACTERISATION

The contemporary Spanish party system is a young system, which came into being only a few months prior to the June 1977 general election, when the first political parties began to be legalised after many years of prohibition under the Francoist dictatorship.[8] The period of dictatorship had meant the disappearance of virtually all the old parties of the republican period and, of the more than 200 political parties which became legal shortly before those first elections, only some four or five could lay claim to being the continuation of parties that already had been in existence prior to the dictatorship; all the rest had begun as clandestine groups in the final years of the dictatorship or immediately after Franco's death. Of the national parties on the left, only the Socialist Party (PSOE)* and the Communist Party (PCE) were more than 40 years old. Even then, however, both had experienced substantial changes in both their ideological content and political strategy. On the right, all the parties were of recent creation: both the Union de Centro Democratico (UCD) of Adolfo Suarez and the Alianza Popular (AP) of Manuel Fraga came into existence only very shortly before and because of the 1977 elections.[9] On the other hand, however, the ruling elites and even bases of both of these parties evince a substantial continuity with the political class of the Francoist regime.

Together with its newness, and partially as a consequence of it, the Spanish party system is also characterised by a lack of consolidation. This was shown conclusively when the most recent general election, in 1982, resulted not only in the majoritarian triumph of the PSOE on its own, for the first time in Spanish history, and in the virtual disappearance of the political centre – the UCD – which had been in office up to that time, but also in the reduction of political competition to a virtual bilateral left–right confrontation between the PSOE and the AP.

*A 'Key to Parties and Coalitions' can be found on pp.152–3.

TABLE 1

PARLIAMENTARY ELECTIONS IN SPAIN: CONGRESO DE LOS DIPUTADOS

Parties[1]	15 June 1977				1 March 1979				28 October 1982			
	votes	%	seats	%	votes	%	seats	%	votes	%	seats	%
UCD	6,337,288	34.61	166	47.4	6,268,890	34.95	168	48.0	1,494,667	7.14	12	3.4
PSOE	5,358,781	29.27	118	33.7	5,469,813	30.50	121	34.6	10,127,392	48.40	202	57.7
PCE	1,718,026	9.38	20	5.7	1,911,217	10.65	23	6.5	865,267	4.13	4	1.1
AP[2]	1,525,028	8.83	16	4.6	1,067,732	5.95	9	2.6	5,478,533	26.18	106	30.3
PSP	816,510	4.46	6	1.7	–	–	–	–	–	–	–	–
UN	–	–	–	–	370,740	2.10	1	0.3	–	–	–	–
CDS	–	–	–	–	–	–	–	–	604,309	2.89	2	0.6
CDC[3]	514,647	2.81	11	3.1	–	–	–	–	772,726	3.69	12	3.4
UDC	173,375	0.95	2	0.6	483,353	2.70	8	2.3	–	–	–	–
PNV	314,409	1.72	8	2.3	275,292	1.53	7	2.0	395,656	1.89	8	2.3
CAIC	37,183	0.20	1	0.3	–	–	–	–	–	–	–	–
PAR[4]	–	–	–	–	38,042	0.21	1	0.3	–	–	–	–
EE	60,312	0.33	1	0.3	85,677	0.48	1	0.3	100,326	0.48	1	0.3
ERC	143,842	0.78	1	0.3	123,452	0.69	1	0.3	138,116	0.66	1	0.3
HB	–	–	–	–	172,110	0.96	3	0.8	210,601	1.01	2	0.6
PSA	–	–	–	–	325,842	1.82	5	1.4	–	–	–	–
UPC	–	–	–	–	58,953	0.33	1	0.3	–	–	–	–
UPN	–	–	–	–	28,248	0.16	1	0.3	–	–	–	–

Notes: 1. Only those which won seats in the Congreso de los Diputados (Lower Chamber).
2. AP took part in the elections always as a coalition with smaller parties: as AP in 1977, as CD in 1979, and as CP in 1982.
3. CDC and UDC took part in coalition as CiU in 1979 and 1982.
4. In 1982 it took part in coalition with AP.

Following the second general election of March 1979, when the Spanish party system had already given the impression of heading towards a certain consolidation, scholars both in Spain and abroad[10] began to define it in terms of general typologies. It was then my contention that the very structural characteristics of the political system in general, and those of the party system, prevented the latter from being included in any of the existing typologies as though it were already a consolidated structure, and that the best that could be hoped for would be a description of the party system and the conditions of its functioning. For that very reason, I then characterised the Spanish party system as one still in the process of formation, weak, and unconsolidated,[11] a characterisation which I believe to be still valid today, and particularly since the third general election of October 1982. The reasons for this are as follows.

(1) *The brief history of some of the most important parties of the system*, to which I have referred above. This means that the process of political alignment of the different social sectors, in accordance with their needs and interests, has had to occur in a very short time span. Consequently, the overall structure of the party system should not be considered as having totally adapted to the changes produced in the social coalitions at the end of the dictatorship, while the social structure itself and the changing alignments of the different groups and sectors should not be considered as having been stabilised, particularly given the impact of the economic crisis which occurred precisely at the moment of the consolidation of the new political system. Finally, the present period is one of political dealignment and realignment,[12] of transition and of change, in which the parties have had insufficient time to establish bonds that are solid, stable and consistent with the social structure and the different interests. All of this is evidenced by the virtual non-existence of more or less stable bonds of party identification and, as will be seen later, by low levels of party membership, by high electoral volatility and by the accentuated polarisation of the system.

(2) *The lack of organisational consolidation and of well-defined and differentiated ideological party programmes.* While this is a defect which is relevant to a greater or lesser extent to almost all the major parties of the system,[13] the case of the UCD is particularly telling: having been formed from the top down as an electoral coalition in 1977, it shortly afterwards became a single party which grouped together a wide range of diverse ideological components – Christian democrat, moderate liberal, social democrat, centrist with no ideological definition, and a reformist component of the old Francoist techno-bureaucracy; in fact, so diverse was this range of political components that it could be said to coincide with the entire parliamentary political spectrum of some European countries. This complicated cocktail, brought together under the auspices of forming a centre, exploded between late 1981 and 1982. While the social democratic component finally joined the PSOE, the more conservative sectors went over to the AP, the Christian democrats formed their own party (Partido Democrata Popular – PDP), which would later also form a coalition with the AP, and other sectors formed small groups of a centrist and liberal nature (one of them, the Centro Democratico Social – (CDS) – being presided over by

ex-Prime Minister Suarez), which are at this moment in the process of reconstitution. This kind of pre-electoral harakiri, together with certain governmental mistakes, could not but culminate in the UCD's crushing defeat in the October 1982 general election (the party's seats fell from 168 to 12) and in its subsequent self-dissolution in February 1983.[14]

A similar picture is to be found in the PCE which, after redefining itself as 'eurocommunist' at its Fourth Congress of 1978, and after managing to win 23 seats in the 1979 general election, suffered numerous internal difficulties and tensions between the different components which, to simplify matters, can be termed as the Eurocommunists, the moderate Eurocommunists and the pro-Soviets. These problems were to lead to numerous defections and secessions which seriously weakened the party and caused it to suffer a clear electoral defeat in 1982 when it managed to win only four seats.

The AP, on the other hand, has demonstrated its lack of ideological consolidation in the way that it has tended to dispose of the Francoist character with which it began in 1976 and in its efforts to form a conservative party – liberal–conservative, as it defined itself at its congress of January 1983 – based on the British model, which would provide the right-wing axis in Spain. The goal of the party, since the UCD's disappearance, is to take over the entire old centrist vote and to form what Fraga – its undisputed leader – calls the 'natural majority'. As such, a major effort is now being made to change the party's ideological profile and public image. For the moment, the success of this policy is only relative: while a coalition with the Christian democrats of the PDP and other smaller minority groups has been formed, only a small proportion of the UCD vote has been captured; nevertheless, its parliamentary representation has increased spectacularly, from nine seats in 1979 to 106 in 1982.

The PSOE is perhaps the most consolidated and stable party of the political spectrum. Reorganised after 1974, it has continually grown both organisationally and electorally. One of the most important phases in this process was, undoubtedly, its extraordinary congress of September 1979, when it dropped its exclusively Marxist definition in favour of an ideological syncretism of the social-democratic left. Its policy represents a clever mix of a certain terminological radicalism with a pragmatism that always seeks out efficacy over doctrine, and it is this which had led to its progress and to its overwhelming victory in the 1982 election (increasing its share from 121 seats in 1979 to 202 in 1982), in which it obtained an absolute parliamentary majority. Internal tensions are not absent, however, and together with a formally recognised and critical left wing – Izquierda Socialista – the greatest problems of the PSOE may come from its trade union organisation, the UGT, due to the difficult economic circumstances in which Spain currently finds itself.

(3) *Archaic operational methods within the parties.* This signifies the presence of a certain clientelistic and subjective method of operating, in which internal power derives from specific personal relations rather than from objective criteria and personal merit. There is also, of course, a strong tendency towards bureaucratisation which, although it could be considered as normal, is perhaps too accentuated for such a young party system. All of

this acts to prevent full intra-party democracy and corrupts the party machinery.

(4) *The popular fear or mistrust of the parties.* This is a phenomenon which is caused as much by historical circumstances as by factors of a more structural nature. In the first place, the memory of the harsh repression suffered by political militants during the last two military dictatorships in Spain has combined with the strong political socialisation towards demobilisation and specific anti-partism during that period. Second, there is the traditional lack of interest in joining associations, which is demonstrated by the low levels of membership in voluntary associations (only seven per cent) or trade unions (only 14 per cent).[15] All this has resulted in extremely low levels of party membership, which barely came to six per cent of the population[16] – a very much lower percentage than the 15 per cent which is calculated as the average figure for party membership in Europe[17] – the weak support for other channels and participative forms such as neighbourhood, ecologist and pacifist associations, and, of course, the virtual absence of stable bonds of party identification beyond a certain persistence, even intergenerational, of ideological sympathies for either the left or right.[18]

(5) *The great difficulty in establishing stable relations or coalitions between parties.* Here, however, an exception is the parliamentary right, where the AP has managed to set up more or less lasting coalitions with small but similar parties and independents. In general, the problem of coalitions is caused principally by (a) the relatively large ideological distance separating the major parties of the system which are capable of forming majoritarian governments (see Table 9.2); (b) the parties' lack of consolidation and the absence of an identification with a sufficiently broad and stable electorate, which requires them to differentiate themselves from one another and also to find a space on the political spectrum capable of adequately representing their respective support groups or social coalitions; and (c) the constitutional regulation of government–parliament relations, which permits the existence of minority government and so removes the necessity for majoritarian coalitions. It is for this reason that, after the first two general elections of 1977 and 1979, despite the relatively small success of UCD, winning 47 per cent of seats in 1977 and 48 per cent in 1979 (see Table 1), minority governments were formed which, in turn, led to significant governmental weakness and a popular reaction against what was felt to be a lack of political leadership. Only the consensus politics adopted during the 1977–79 period, which allowed the Constitution of 1978 to be drafted and adopted concealed this problem. The problem re-emerged in 1979–82, however, when confrontational politics came into play, despite the fact that after the frustrated coup of February 1981 the UCD and the PSOE came to a tacit agreement that the latter would support the government. This agreement enabled the construction of the autonomous regional structure of the state to be accomplished and allowed the government to continue, although not without difficulties, until the election of October 1982. Following this election, the absolute victory of the PSOE made it once again possible to form a homogeneous government which could maintain its independence without having to engage in any form of political collaboration.

However, these relations at governmental level have not prevented stable coalitions being established between the different parties at the local and regional level. Thus the united left of the PSOE and the PCE and some others have governed the more populated cities of the country since 1979. Since the local and regional elections of May 1983, however, the PSOE has also increased its majority at these levels and has tended to govern, likewise, alone.

In short, until the PSOE entered office in October 1982, the minoritarian governments of the UCD had based themselves exclusively on a search for changing support with regard to specific issues, while always rejecting the idea of a stable governmental coalition.

(6) *The limitation of the role of the party system as an active subject in the political system and the consequent presence within the latter of other determining forces of great importance.* This is partly due to the historic conditions under which the political transition to democracy took place in Spain, a transition in which a whole set of different forces converged as active elements, and in which the political parties *per se* played only a minor role. These conditions have partly transferred themselves to the new democratic situation. The King, the armed forces, the police, the bureaucracy and the Church, together with other social groups, have maintained autonomous roles, and their strength has been decisive when it came to determining the functioning of a political system characterised by weak parties, lacking both internal consolidation and stable and solid bonds with their electorates.

(7) *The presence in Spain of an important regional subsystem of parties.* While this cannot be examined at length, it is nevertheless necessary to emphasise the importance of this factor in the functioning of the Spanish party system as a whole. Its importance is evident not only in quantitative terms, but also qualitatively. First, a considerable part of the total vote goes to the regional or *nationalist* parties, thereby giving them a reasonable number of seats in the Congreso de los Diputados: in the 1977 elections they obtained seven per cent of the vote and 24 seats (seven per cent); in 1979 ten per cent of the vote and 28 seats (eight per cent); and in 1982, nine per cent and 24 seats (seven per cent). These percentages are even higher if considered within the exclusive sphere of each Autonomous Community, or if the results of the elections for the regional parliaments are taken into account. As far as the areas of the country where the regional parties have gained their best results are concerned, it should be noted that these parties have managed to obtain an absolute majority in all the general and regional elections carried out in the Basque country, and only slightly lower results in Catalonia, Galicia and other regions (see Table 2).

Yet, in qualitative terms, the importance of this element is, if anything, even greater, in that the regional parties have introduced into political competition the nationalism–centralism cleavage as a factor which operates quite independently of the classic left–right opposition. This is clearly evident in the way these parties act both at regional and national levels, to the extent that some of them become actual anti-system parties[19] in a way completely independent of whether they are on the ideological left or right. However, in some cases, there is a strong coincidence between the extreme

TABLE 2

ELECTORAL STRENGTH OF THE NATIONWIDE PARTIES AND
THE REGIONAL PARTIES (PERCENTAGES)

		1977^1	1979^1	1980^2	1982^1
Basque Country	Nationwide[3] parties	51.25	44.03	31.53	44.30
	Regional[4] parties	35.23	50.69	64.46	54.38
Catalonia	Nationwide[5] parties	66.90	68.80	51.60	68.20
	Regional[6] parties	26.90	20.60	39.20	26.20
Galicia	Nationwide[7] parties	65.29	82.20	79.80	92.87
	Regional[8] parties	4.32	11.22	12.73	4.69

Notes:
1. National parliamentary elections.
2. Regional parliamentary elections. Those for Galicia were held in 1981.
3. UCD, PSOE, PCE, AP.
4. PNV, EE, HB.
5. PSC–PSOE, PSUC–PCE, CC–UCD, SC–AP.
6. CiU, ERC.
7. UCD, PSG–PSOE, AP, PCG–PCE.
8. BNPG–PSG, UG, EG, PG.

positions of both the left–right and the nationalism–non-nationalism con-
tinua. If we take as an example the Basque party subsystem (see Figure 1) it
can be seen how at the two extremes of the line of maximum polarisation
there appear the two parties which possess the highest degrees of nationalism (regionalism) and leftism (HB – Herri Batasuna) on the one hand, and of
non-nationalism (centralism) and rightism (AP) on the other. In the Basque
case, therefore, the most extreme left positions also coincide with the most
radical nationalist postures while the most right-wing positions coincide with
the strongest centralist, *'españolista'* attitudes. Yet, as we approach the
centre of this line, the positions begin to vary much more and the level of
correlation between nationalism and leftism, as well as between centralism
and rightism, is far smaller. Furthermore, although a detailed study cannot
be included here, the same phenomenon tends to occur in the other regions
where the *national* problem is deeply entrenched, that is in Catalonia and
Galicia (I refer only to those parties which either hold or have come close to
holding seats in Parliament, and not to marginal groups, where the variations are greater).

On the other hand, the intensity of the regional question in most cases has
led to the national parties themselves appearing in the more problematic
regions as actual regionalist parties, either by transforming their internal

FIGURE 1
TWO-DIMENSIONAL DISTRIBUTION OF PARTIES BY THE ELECTORATE
IN THE BASQUE PARTY SYSTEM

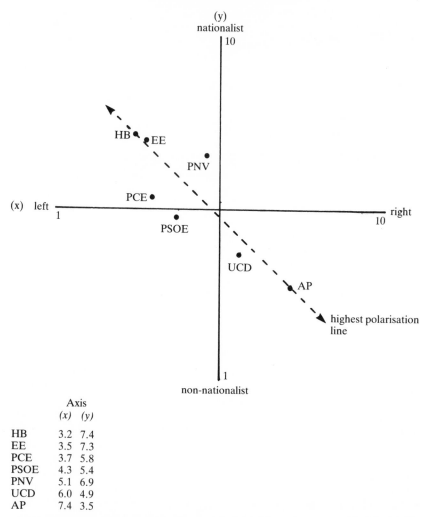

| | Axis | |
	(x)	*(y)*
HB	3.2	7.4
EE	3.5	7.3
PCE	3.7	5.8
PSOE	4.3	5.4
PNV	5.1	6.9
UCD	6.0	4.9
AP	7.4	3.5

Source: Data from F.J. Llera Ramo, 'La estructura electoral y el sistema de partidos en las Comunidades Autónomas del País Vasco y Foral de Navarra después de las elecciones generales de 1982', *Revista de estudios políticos*, No. 34 (1983), pp. 147–202.

structure into a federal one – which makes it seem that the regional sections are operating with entire autonomy, like virtually independent parties – or by forming stable alliances or coalitions with authentic regional parties of a similar ideology in those regions where their introduction was either too weak or previously non-existent.[20] In addition, the results of political competition at a regional level also have immediate repercussions at the national level, thereby conditioning the functioning of the national party system. In this sense it should be emphasised that the electoral disaster of the UCD in October 1982, which brought about its very disappearance, had been preceded by a series of successive regional defeats.[21]

Finally, the Spanish political system, based upon strong political decentralisation, has the effect of turning the *Comunidades Autonomas* into peripheral centres of power with their own regional party subsystems which develop and consolidate themselves in patterns which often differ from the national party system in terms of both configuration and dynamics.

AN ANALYTICAL CHARACTERISATION

This description of the Spanish party system, albeit an essential starting point in the explanation of its phenomena and changes, is nevertheless insufficient if we wish to understand its distinctive features in comparative terms. Accordingly, and following from ideas presented in the most recent writing on the comparative study of party systems,[22] I would suggest that there are three aspects of the Spanish system which should be analysed: (i) the number of major parties – with parliamentary representation – present in the system and the degree of concentration or dispersion of the overall vote among them; (ii) the amount of change in the vote and therefore in the system as a whole after each of the three general elections; and (iii) the kind of relations and political competition that exist between the parties in the system. In order to study these variables adequately, three analytical indices will be used which allow us to characterise comparatively the Spanish party system: (a) Rae's 'fractionalisation index', which is a good indicator not only of the number of parties present within the system, but also of the level of vote concentration; (b) Pedersen's index of volatility, which serves both to quantify the electoral change taking place in the party system, and also to indicate the rise or decline in the level of stability and of consolidation of the system; and (c) the degree of polarisation[23] which allows us to discuss the nature and direction of the prevalent pattern of inter-party competition.

1. A Fragmented System?

The establishment of democratic liberties in Spain led to a proliferation of parties, amounting to 200 or more parties at the time of the second general election.[24] In that election, 34 national parties or coalitions actually presented candidates, as did 36 regional or provincial groups. In practice, however, the number of parties is far smaller, and after the three general elections which have so far been held there are only 18 political formations which, in one or other of the legislatures, have actually formed part of the Congress. And, indeed, of these 18, only 10 have been present since the general election of October 1982 (see Table 1).

While legal, economic and political circumstances have all contributed to the drastic reduction of this party atomisation, what is of particular relevance is the electoral law. The prevailing electoral system in Spain, pending the elaboration of a definitive electoral law, is that set out by the

Real Decreto-Ley of 18 March 1977, when it was originally envisaged only for the first general election, but which was then extended also to the subsequent elections. As far as the Lower House or the Congress is concerned, it is a proportional system based on the D'Hondt formula, which lays down a minimum requirement of three per cent of the total vote in each electoral district in order for a party or group to be included in the vote count. There is, however, the further difficulty created by the existence of electoral districts of unequal size – the provinces – which are guaranteed a minimum number of representatives (two formally, three in practice – out of a total number of 350 seats) and which leads to the overrepresentation of underpopulated areas. Finally, as is well known,[25] the proportionality of the D'Hondt formula is rather limited, and tends to favour larger parties; smaller parties, on the other hand, unless their strength is concentrated in only a few electoral districts, as is the case of the regionalist or nationalist parties in Spain, fail to gain parliamentary representation or, at least, win relatively few seats in terms of their voting support.

This 'reductive' effect was already evident after the first general election of June 1977, and yet again in the subsequent elections of March 1979 and October 1982. The number of parties or coalitions with parliamentary representation has declined and, what is even more important, as a result of a natural process of political selection by the electorate the vote also has tended to centre on the more representative political groups.

In this sense, the level of fragmentation, both electoral and parliamentary, has gradually decreased, with fewer parties and greater vote concentration on the two major groups. These latter groups have extended their lead over the other groups, both in terms of votes and seats, while the leading party – especially in the 1982 election – has also increased its lead over the second party (see Tables 3 and 4).

TABLE 3

ELECTORAL AND PARLIAMENTARY FRAGMENTATION IN SPAIN AND EUROPE

	Spain			Mean	
	1977	1979	1982	Spain	Europe
Electoral fr.	.775	.768	.688	.743	.714
Parliamentary fr.	.655	.644	.572	.623	.616

Sources: Keesing's Contemporary Archives, D.W. Rae, *The Political Consequences of Electoral Laws* (New Haven: Yale University Press, 1971), and Junta Electoral Central.

According to the Rae index[26] the Spanish party system therefore displays relatively low fragmentation, particularly since the most recent election, when the fractionalisation index fell below the European average at electoral and parliamentary levels. Overall, as one can see in Table 3, mean fractionalisation in Spain is only slightly higher than the European mean, and is similar to that in such countries as Italy (0.74 and 0.65) or West Germany (0.73 and 0.69).

Despite the turnaround in the leading political groups since the first parliamentary elections, the vote has tended increasingly to concentrate on the two parties holding the dominant positions since the first parliamentary elections (see Table 4). Two points should be noted about this vote concentration, however. First, it affects only those parties of a national orientation, which are also those which have undergone the greatest changes, whereas the regional parties (with one or two exceptions)[27] tend to stay within a more or less stable percentage of votes and seats which never reached four per cent (see Table 1). Second, the level of vote concentration between the two principal political groups does not reach a sufficiently high percentage to designate Spain as a two-party system. According to Rae, a two-party system can be indentified in simple terms when the sum of the votes of the two major parties exceeds 90 per cent of the total, while the leading party wins less than 70 per cent of the total. As can be seen in Table 4, the Spanish party system is still far from this format, even though it has to be recognised that the total percentage of seats won by the two major political groups is quite close to the minimum required by Rae. In fact, in the elections for the regional parliaments held in 1983 – excluding Galicia, Andalucia, the Basque country and Catalonia – this vote concentration was even more evident, with the two leading parties winning 81.8 per cent of the votes.

TABLE 4

PERCENTAGE OF TOTAL VOTE AND SEATS IN
THE CONGRESO DE LOS DIPUTADOS OBTAINED BY THE FOUR LEADING PARTIES

Rank	1977		1979		1982	
	% v.	% s.	% v.	% s.	% v.	% s.
1st	34.61	47.4	34.95	48.0	48.40	57.7
2nd	29.27	33.7	30.50	34.6	26.18	30.3
3rd	9.38	5.7	10.65	6.5	7.14	3.4
4th	8.83	4.6	5.95	2.6	4.13	1.1
1st + 2nd	63.88	81.1	65.45	82.6	74.58	88.0
1st + 2nd + 3rd + 4th	82.09	91.4	82.05	91.7	85.85	92.5

1st: UCD in 1977 and 1979, and PSOE in 1982.
2nd: PSOE in 1977 and 1979, and AP in 1982.
3rd: PCE in 1977 and 1979, and UCD in 1982.
4th: AP in 1977 and 1979, and PCE in 1982.

The Spanish system can therefore be characterised as (a) a moderate multi-party system, with four important political groups of a national orientation,[28] and with another four parties which are much smaller and exclusively regional; (b) a system with an average level of fragmentation (according to the Rae index), the increase of which has been caused partially by the presence of smaller regional parties; and (c) a system which is still far from being a purely two-party system.

2. A Stable System?

The lack of consolidation of the Spanish party system is evident in the extremely high levels of electoral volatility,[29] particularly in the 1982 election. In that election, not only did the PSOE win a landslide victory, being the first party to gain an absolute majority, but there was also an important change on the right as the UCD was pushed aside by the AP. Thus the party which had come first in 1977 and 1979, the UCD, not only lost this position to the left, but also saw itself supplanted by the right-wing coalition led by the AP.

The level of volatility over the first two general elections had remained relatively low, at a level comparable to that of other older and more consolidated European party systems (see Tables 5.1 and 5.2). While this led more than one analyst to think that Spain already had a consolidated, crystallised and stable party system, the radical change in 1982 has underlined the fact that it is a system still in the process of formation, lacking consolidation and highly unstable. These are characteristics which may now have begun to wane, but this, in any case, cannot be confirmed until there has been a greater succession of elections under circumstances of relative political normality. It must be emphasised that the situation in which the new Spanish political system has moved ever since its creation is one of tension and democratic instability which, of course, has also made itself felt in the instability of the party system.

In this sense, the Spanish situation may be considered similar to those pertaining in countries such as France, Germany or Italy after the Second World War. Even more to the point, it is also similar to the case of Portugal, which also had to establish a new party system after a long period of dictatorship, a process which began only a few months earlier than that in Spain. Moreover, the highest levels of volatility in Europe have been registered precisely in these countries and at the times nearest to their emergence from dictatorship (see Tables 5.1 and 5.2). In Italy, for example, the level of electoral volatility between 1946 and 1948 was 23 per cent, and 14.1 per cent between 1948 and 1953.[30] What is exceptional in the Spanish case, however, is that its level of volatility is far greater than that recorded by those countries at these times, while the tendency in Spain is also now in the ascendant, as against a declining pattern in those other cases. The high level of aggregate vote change means that at least some 9,000,000 voters transferred to another party between the second and third elections, whereas only just under 2,000,000 had done so between the first and second elections. While this change has occurred on the right and the left, it has been greater in the former block (Vt 26 per cent) than in the latter (Vt 12 per cent). On the right, the disintegration and electoral defeat of the UCD opened the way for the great triumph of the AP. On the left, the PSOE confirmed its hegemonic position, increasing its number of votes at the expense of not only the PCE but the UCD as well.

According to available data for 1982,[31] almost half of the PSOE's votes (45 per cent) came from other political groups – principally the UCD (16 per cent) – or from abstentions; in the case of the AP, on the other hand, only 35

TABLE 5.1

THE VOLATILITY OF SPANISH AND PORTUGUESE PARTY SYSTEMS 1976–83

	A	B	Average	
			National	European
Spain	4.60	36.80	20.70	9.2
Portugal	8.23	7.90	8.07	

A: 1977–79 for Spain, and 1976–79 for Portugal.
B: 1979–82 for Spain, and 1979–83 for Portugal.

TABLE 5.2

THE VOLATILITY OF FIVE EUROPEAN PARTY SYSTEMS 1948–77

	Period			National
	1948–59	1960–69	1970–77	average
France	21.8	11.9	10.6	16.8
Denmark	5.5	8.9	18.7	11.0
Germany	15.2	9.5	4.9	9.8
Netherlands	6.3	7.9	12.7	9.1
Italy	10.3	8.0	6.8	8.4

Source: M. Pedersen, 'The Dynamics of European Party Systems', European Journal of Political Research, Vol. 7 (1979).

per cent of its 1982 vote is accounted for by its 1979 support, while the other 65 per cent came from other political groups – principally the UCD (43 per cent) – or from previous abstentions (see Table 6). In short, the major losers of the October 1982 election were the UCD and the PCE. In the first case, the UCD's defeat and dissolution weakened the political centre, which is now represented by the minoritarian CDS (two seats), by the Basque regionalists of the PNV (Partido Nacionalista Vasco) (eight seats) and by the Catalonians of the CiU (Convergencia i Unió) (12 seats), thereby favouring a bipolarisation of the system. Indeed, more than half of the UCD's 1979 vote was divided up almost equally between the AP (33 per cent) and the PSOE (30 per cent) in 1982 (see Table 7). In the second case, the PCE lost almost half its 1979 votes (48 per cent) to the PSOE, thereby leaving the latter with a virtual monopoly of the parliamentary left (see Table 7).

3. A Polarised System?

If it is true that 'the best single explanatory variable for stable versus unstable, functioning versus non-functioning, successful versus immobile, and easy versus difficult democracy is polarisation',[32] then clearly an examination of this characteristic or variant of the Spanish party system provides an essential key to the explanation of the system's dynamics and its functioning.

TABLE 6

ORIGIN OF THE 1982 VOTE WITH RESPECT TO 1979 VOTE (PERCENTAGES)

	Vote in 1982							
	PSOE	AP	UCD	PCE	CDS	Regionalists	Others	(1)*
Vote in 1979								
PSOE	55	3	4	2	3	3	5	4
AP	-	35	3	-	3	-	-	-
UCD	16	43	87	-	76	7	12	10
PCE	5	-	1	83	-	-	6	1
Regionalists	1	1	1	-	-	80	18	2
Others	1	2	-	2	3	-	44	1
(1)*	22	16	4	13	15	10	15	82
Total	100	100	100	100	100	100	100	100

*(1) = did not vote + blank vote + no answer.

Source: CIS study no. 1327.

TABLE 7

VOTE SWING BETWEEN 1979 AND 1982 (PERCENTAGES)

	Vote in 1979						
	PSOE	AP	UCD	PCE	Regionalists	Others	(1)*
Vote in 1982							
PSOE	90	-	30	48	9	22	22
AP	2	92	33	-	2	17	5
UCD	1	3	20	-	1	-	-
PCE	-	-	-	44	-	2	1
CDS	-	1	5	-	-	2	-
Regionalists	1	1	2	-	73	-	1
Others	-	-	1	2	5	37	-
(1)*	6	3	9	6	10	20	71
Total	100	100	100	100	100	100	100

*(1) = did not vote + blank vote + no answer.

Source: CIS study no. 1327.

Polarisation as a measure of the ideological distance existing between the parties forming a system is not merely a descriptive element, but is also analytic, allowing us to judge the viability of the party system itself and of the political system in general. It is not necessary here to refer to the now familiar debate concerning the validity of the spatial models of competition based on the right–left ideological continuum. I consider the points in favour of such approaches already sufficiently well argued. It does seem appropriate, however, to point out that the left–right continuum is meaningful as far as the Spanish electorate is concerned; respondents are not only capable of locating themselves at different points along this continuum, both generally and with reference to specific questions, but are also capable of locating consistently the different parties of the system in terms of left and right according to both their own ideology·and that of the parties. The proportion of the respondents unable to locate themselves or the parties along this continuum rarely exceeds 20 per cent, and normally averages around 15 per cent.

Looking at the electorate in general it can be said that the Spanish population has overcome the highly conflictual and radically polarised situation of the Second Republic. Nowadays, Spanish society is far more consensual, and the establishment of the democratic system has proved to be generally accepted.[33] Political confrontation today is focused on more contingent problems, there being broad agreement on the fundamental questions – at least among the more ample and decisive sectors of society. Moreover, the degree of polarisation on contemporary political matters is also relatively low, particularly if one takes into account the circumstances from which the new democratic system has emerged and under which it has developed.

In general terms, and in keeping with the findings of virtually all of the numerous sociological studies that have been carried out on the political transition and the new democratic regime, it can be said that the vast majority of the Spanish population locates itself in a central position; while there are slight deviations to the right and, principally, to the left, nevertheless the point of equilibrium lies in the central area of the left–right ideological spectrum. On a ten-point scale, the average of the mean positions recorded in the numerous studies carried out between 1976 and 1983 lies at 4.7, in a centre-left position, very similar to that recorded in countries such as Italy (4.3) or France (5.0) during the same period, and evident also in the results of October 1982 elections (see Table 8 and Figure 2.1).

TABLE 8

DISTRIBUTION OF VOTES AND SEATS IN THE LOWER CHAMBER
BY IDEOLOGICAL AREAS

Area	1977		1979		1982	
	% v.	% s.	% v.	% s.	% v.	% s.
Left	44.22	41.7	45.43	44.2	54.68	60.0
Centre	40.29	53.7	39.18	52.3	15.61	9.7
Right	8.83	4.6	8.42	3.5	26.18	30.3
Centre + Right	48.92	58.0	47.60	55.8	41.79	40.0
Centre + Left	84.51	95.4	84.61	96.5	70.29	69.7

Left: PSOE, PCE, PSP, UPC, EE, ERC, HB, PSA, UPC.
Centre: UCD, CDC, UDC, CiU, PNV, CAIC.
Right: all the coalitions led by AP; UN, PAR, UPN.

Moving from a general characterisation of the electorate to the closer analysis of ideological polarisation[34] between political parties, however, the picture becomes more complex. Taking as a reference point the four most important national parties of the parliamentary spectrum – the PCE, PSOE, UCD and AP[35] – and considering where on the left–right continuum they are located by the electorate in general, we can see how this polarisation index has oscillated with minimal variations between 0.64 following the 1977 election and 0.63 after 1979, rising to 0.67 after 1982. It is, then, one of the highest indices in Europe, similar to the Italian (0.63) and the Finnish (0.64). However, the degree of polarisation drops slightly if one considers solely the location of the individual parties on the same left–right scale by their own respective voters, or if one takes into account the location the voters of each party give to themselves. In both instances, the results are more moderate and centre-locating than those in which the political parties are placed by the electorate in general. In this case, the degree of polarisation oscillates between 0.50 and 0.57. In this sense, one can argue that the electorate in itself is less polarised than it considers the political parties to be. This difference should have a centripetal effect on political competition,[36] in as much as the party system tends to adapt itself to the general conditions of the political system; this has not happened, however, and, after having dropped in the second general election, the degree of polarisation rose slightly in 1982, suggesting a potential centrifugal dynamic. Finally, the distances between the mean positions of the parties considered to be at the extremes of the parliamentary spectrum (in terms of the four most important parties taken as a reference point, these are the PCE and the AP) are not only greater than the distances existing between the mean position of the electorate self-located to the left and to the right, but also have increased at a greater rate than have these latter in the last elections (see Tables 9.1 and 9.2).

If we analyse the evolution of the electorate's self-location at the time of the three elections, we can see how the distribution of opinion presented a unimodal curve which was virtually unchanged after the first two elections and which shifted slightly to the left after the 1982 elections, when there was a considerable increase in the percentage of respondents with a self-location in the area of the centre-left and left (see Figure 2.1). Comparing these curves with those produced by the location of the parties on the same left–right continuum and by the percentage of the votes they obtained in each of the three elections (Figure 2.2), we can see how they run practically parallel in 1977 and 1979 (Figures 2.3 and 2.4); in 1982, however, there is a drastic break (Figure 2.5), due to the collapse of the centre, now formed only by the remnants of the UCD (UCD + CDS in Figure 2.5) and by the regional parties PNV and CiU (which are not represented in Figure 2.5) and because of the sudden increase in support for the electoral coalition headed by the AP. This result produces an enormous distortion in the correlation between the ideological positions of the electorate and those of the political parties: whereas the former continue to present a unimodal curve, the vertex of which has now shifted further to the left, the latter presents a bimodal distribution.

TABLE 9.1

DISTANCE BETWEEN THE MEAN POSITIONS OF THE
ELECTORATE'S LEFT AND RIGHT[1]

	left	distance	right	polarization
1977	2.55	2.90	5.45	0.48
1979	2.63	2.77	5.40	0.46
1982	2.53	2.90	5.43	0.48

TABLE 9.2

DISTANCE BETWEEN THE MEAN POSITIONS OF PARTIES
ON THE LEFT–RIGHT CONTINUUM[1]

parties		1977 distance	parties		polarization
PCE	2.05	3.85	AP	5.90	0.64
PCE	2.05	2.30	UCD	4.35	
PCE	2.05	0.75	PSOE	2.80	
PSOE	2.80	3.10	AP	5.90	
PSOE	2.80	1.55	UCD	4.35	
UCD	4.35	1.55	AP	5.90	

		1979			
PCE	1.85	3.75	AP	5.60	0.63
PCE	1.85	2.45	UCD	4.30	
PCE	1.85	0.75	PSOE	2.60	
PSOE	2.60	3.00	AP	5.60	
PSOE	2.60	1.70	UCD	4.30	
UCD	4.30	1.30	AP	5.60	

		1982			
PCE	1.85	4.02	AP	5.87	0.67
PCE	1.85	2.51	UCD[2]	4.36	
PCE	1.85	0.94	PSOE	2.79	
PSOE	2.79	3.08	AP	5.87	
PSOE	2.79	1.57	UCD	4.36	
UCD	4.36	1.51	AP	5.87	

Notes:
1. Scale 1–7.
2. UCD + CDS.

There is a variety of factors which can account for these differences, and
also for both the increase in the party system polarisation relative to the
population in general and the increase in polarisation which occurred
between the last two elections. As far as the last point is concerned and in
purely analytic terms, it can be argued that the increase in polarisation
between 1979 and 1982 is due to the PCE's shift to the left after 1979 (on a
scale of 1 to 7, it shifts from 2.05 to 1.85), a change which was not compen-

FIGURE 2.1
DISTRIBUTION OF THE SPANISH
ELECTORATE ON THE LEFT–RIGHT
CONTINUUM (SCALE 1–7)

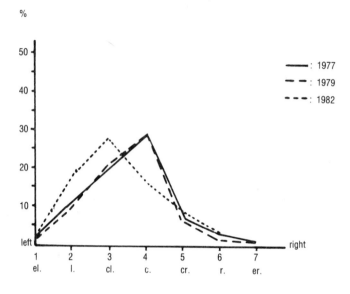

FIGURE 2.2
SPATIAL LOCATION OF PARTIES
AND PERCENTAGE OF VOTE

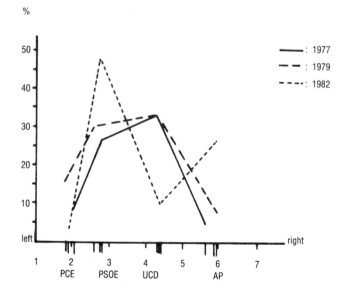

FIGURE 2.3
SPATIAL LOCATION OF PARTIES
AND THE ELECTORATE IN 1977

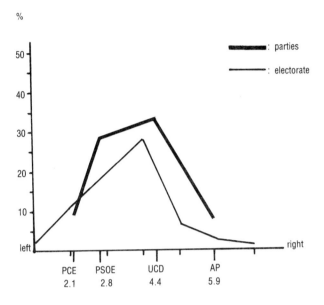

FIGURE 2.4
SPATIAL LOCATION OF PARTIES
AND THE ELECTORATE IN 1979

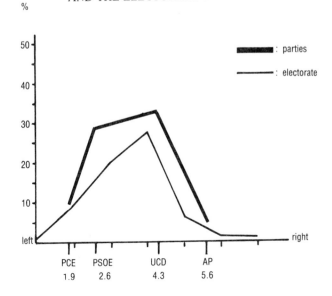

FIGURE 2.5
SPATIAL LOCATION OF PARTIES AND THE ELECTORATE IN 1982

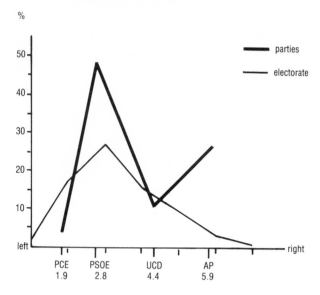

sated for by a substantial movement of the AP towards the centre. On the contrary, and despite its electoral success, the AP has remained in virtually the same position. The PSOE, on the other hand, has shifted significantly towards the centre (from 2.60 in 1979 to 2.79 in 1982). This partially explains its huge success in the 1982 election, but does not affect the index of polarisation of the system as a whole (see Figure 2).

After the 1979 general election, the PCE gradually adopted a more radical posture than that which it had maintained during the transitional period and immediately after the 1977 general election. This transformation was accompanied by a series of internal upheavals that culminated in several splits and a significant drop in party membership, all of which led to its electoral defeat in 1982 and the loss of many of its votes to the PSOE (see Table 7). Since then, the PCE's efforts to reconstruct itself have led to an even greater emphasis on radical tactics, as for instance can be seen in the fact that its opposition to the PSOE government is considerably more severe than had been its opposition towards the UCD. As far as the AP is concerned, its conservative politics have undergone no major changes since abandoning its earlier Francoist character. Indeed, the electoral success of the AP in 1982 owes more to the UCD's inability to consolidate itself as a coherent centre party and its serious governmental mistakes than to any significant shift towards a more moderate and central position on the part of the AP itself. Finally, as far as the PSOE is concerned, there is no doubt that the changes in ideology and attitude that have been taking place since 1977 as well as its deliberate intention to become a modern centre-left party in the

European social-democratic mould have led to its increasing acceptance by the electorate. With the collapse of the UCD, this increased acceptance finally led to its landslide victory in 1982, with 16 per cent of its present vote coming from the UCD, and only five per cent from the PCE (see Table 6).

All these data emphasise the need to make a clear distinction between the ideological and political positioning of the electorate and that of the political parties. Whereas the former define the position of the electorate as regards basic questions concerning the society and the political system, the latter are based on issues of more immediate, short-term politics, which necessarily create an increase in the range of distance between them. It is, therefore, not surprising that the range of political parties appears greater and more polarised than that of the electorate.

While in general terms this factor can explain the difference in the degrees of polarisation that exist between the location of the electorate and that of the political parties on the left–right continuum, the enormous difference that exists in the particular case of the AP (see Figure 2.5) clearly indicates the necessarily critical and transitional nature of the 1982 elections. Whereas the PSOE is situated in a position which more or less coincides with that of the majority of the population – a factor which thereby explains much of its electoral success – the percentage of those who locate themselves in the same position as the AP is much lower than the percentage of votes obtained by the AP – 23 points of difference. Moreover, while the self-location of most of those who voted for the PSOE (3.02 on a 1–7 scale) is fairly similar to the position held by the party (2.79) in the eyes of the electorate at large, this difference is much greater in the case of the AP, the mean location of its voters being 4.98, with the party being at 5.87. This would suggest that if the AP wishes to consolidate its electoral position and further increase its electoral support, it will have no choice but to make substantial changes in its ideology and occupy a position which is as close as possible to the mean position occupied by its electors. Otherwise, what is at present a virtually empty gap in the centre will be taken over by other political groups which are currently in the process of reconstruction.[37]

The Spanish party system, thus, is a bipolarised system whose oscillating dynamics, after being slightly centripetal in the 1979 general election, have once again become slightly centrifugal since the 1982 election.

CONCLUSION: IS THERE A MODEL?

As can be seen from the previous sections, the conclusion to be drawn is that the Spanish party system remains a non-crystallised, non-stabilised system, much as it had been from the very beginning and following the 1977 election. The political parties remain in indefinite positions vis-à-vis their own ideology and that of the electorate, a dissonance which suggests that the election outcomes are themselves not definitive and that major new changes may well take place in future elections, despite the present hegemony of the PSOE. Moreover, the sheer number of parties is itself unstable; the break-up of the UCD and the internal crises of the PCE have both given rise to a great deal of transferring of party membership and to the creation of new parties, including parties which undoubtedly are striving to gain the centre of the political spectrum and which have the greatest chances of growing and consolidating themselves in the future. Indeed, everything depends on the capacity of these parties to offer a solid and cohesive alternative.

In practice, however, the wide range of parties in existence today can be reduced to five different options: the PCE, which occupies the left; the PSOE on the centre-left; the remains of the UCD and the CDS – the latter a split from the former – in the centre; the coalition formed by the AP–PDP–UL (Union Liberal) and other smaller regional parties on the right; and the Basque moderate regionalists of the PNV and the Catalonians of CiU, which would be in the centre, even though in terms of ideology it is their position as nationalist parties which tends to carry more weight. Alongside these, there are also the radically nationalist EE (Euskadiko Ezkerra) and HB, even though the former is totally minoritarian both at a national level (one seat) and in its own region, while the latter is a genuine anti-system party which refuses to take up its parliamentary seats and which therefore fails to carry out any active politics in this ambit.

In terms of the election results, however, this apparent fragmentation is reduced drastically in that the vote centres on only two principal parties, which managed to accumulate 74.6 per cent of the vote in the most recent general election (see Table 4). Paradoxically, far from increasing electoral or parliamentary fragmentation – as one might have expected to happen as a result the presence of many small parties seeking to fill the void left by the UCD – the virtual disappearance of the centre has helped in its reduction (see Table 3). Political fragmentation in Spain has gradually diminished and today is relatively low. In this sense it is perfectly possible to characterise the Spanish party system as a moderate pluralist party system which is still, however, rather far from being a pure two-party system.

The lack of party system consolidation leads to an extremely high level of electoral volatility, among the highest in Europe since the Second World War. Judging from the dynamics of the system, it is likely that this volatility will continue to be high in future elections, in that it is still necessary to create more stable electoral bases in line with the political orientations of both the parties and the electorate.

The degree of polarisation of the party system is relatively high and, in general, is increasing: the tendency therefore seems to be centrifugal. Nevertheless, it is here that the system's dynamics could lead to more important changes: unless the Spanish electorate undergoes a radical trans-formation of its primarily centrist, or more recently centre-left, ideological orientation (see Figure 2.1), which is highly unlikely, then the most normal thing would be for the party system to adapt to this and thereby effect not only a reduction in the level of volatility but also in the degree of polarisa-tion.

On the other hand, and this is yet another example of the incongruities typical of a party system still in the process of formation and consolidation, the present polarisation is at odds with the low level of fragmentation. The low level of fragmentation of the Spanish system, which has led to its being occasionally classified as two-party since the 1982 election, is more typical of systems of very low or minimal polarisation – such as West Germany (0.28), Austria (0.29) or the United Kingdom (0.31) – than of highly polarised systems – such as France (0.57) or Italy (0.63). As has been argued, a greater distance between the extreme parties on the parliamentary spectrum could be expected to allow for the occupation of the intermediate positions by a larger number of parties with a substantial total vote and, thereby, for a high level of fragmentation.[38]

Having said this, which party system model, if any, is appropriate for the Spanish case? The Spanish party system does not fit the two-party model – not only because the result of the 1982 election was quite evidently transitory, but also because the percentage of votes obtained by the major parties was not sufficiently great to allow this. Nor do I believe it is a two-and-a-half party system, in that there is no strategically located 'half' party which can condition government formation. In purely numerical terms, the present Spanish party system would fit the predominant party system model[39] because of the number of relevant parties involved and the difference at present between the percentages of votes of the first and second parties. At the same time, however, this model is inappropriate to the situation after the first two elections and, as such, it is therefore impossible to include the Spanish system in this model on a fixed basis, as though it were a frozen system.

It also seems difficult to fit the Spanish case to the more complex model of moderate pluralism.[40] First, although the number of relevant parties is compatible with such a classification, the level of ideological polarisation is much higher in Spain as a result of the greater ideological distance between the parties. Second, there is neither a governmental system with alternative bipolar coalitions nor consistently centripetal competition, as the characteristics of this model demand.

Finally, it is also clear that the Spanish party system will not fit properly in the polarised pluralism model, at least not without distorting or impairing either reality or the model itself. If we look only at those characteristics which Sartori suggests as the defining features of the model, it is easy to see how some of them cannot be applied to the changing reality of the Spanish party system. First, as already has been mentioned, with respect to the number of relevant parties the Spanish system does have the necessary minimum to allow for its inclusion in this model, especially during the first two legislatures (although it is necessary to note that, at the parliamentary level, the gap between the two leading political groups and the other parties renders the latter of little significance to political competition).

Second, even if the presence of anti-system parties is detectable in Spain, none of these is considered relevant or is even present on a national scale. The HB, of course, is an obvious anti-system party, but not only is it merely regional, it has also never won more than three seats in the national parliament nor a vote which accounts for more than 0.8 per cent at national level. Nor do the PCE or even the AP, despite its original Francoist character, easily fit this category, in that both parties have played a crucial role in the very creation of the present political system and in its maintenance.

Third, one could argue that there did exist in Spain a system of bilateral, yet incompatible, oppositions, such as during the UCD mandate, as a result of the latter's central role in the system. Nevertheless, on the right, the AP opposition was then insignificant because of its small number of seats in the Congress, and opposition politics centred around the PSOE, which played a hegemonic role on the left. Moreover, since the 1982 election the situation has changed drastically into a system of unilateral opposition – PSOE–AP – in which other groups play only a virtually symbolic role. The present Spanish system is therefore not now characterised by plurilateral oppositions, even though this was the case during the first two legislatures.

Fourth, although the political centre was occupied by the government party during the first two legislatures, it is now occupied only by the remnants of the UCD and the moderate regional groups, all of which together barely account for 16 per cent of the votes and 10 per cent of the seats. This characteristic is therefore now also absent from the Spanish system, in that the PSOE, the party in office, has a majoritarian position and is located between centre and centre-left.

Fifth, though the system is polarised and though it is this bipolar tension which has led to the practical disappearance of the centre in 1982, I do not believe this to be a stable situation and would argue that the circumstances are such that an inversion of this centrifugal dynamic will take place.

Finally, with regard to the other characteristics of polarised pluralism, it cannot be argued that at present there exists in Spain serious and fundamental disagreement over the political system itself, nor that opposition is totally irresponsible. Although there is always some kind of electoral outbidding, for the most part it is relatively insignificant as far as the general functioning of the party system is concerned.

In conclusion, the Spanish party system is still in the process of formation and crystallisation, and it is extremely difficult to attempt its typological characterisation. There are some consistent dynamics which provide the only aspects from which one could formulate some kind of characterisation, such as its progressively decreasing fragmentation, its extreme volatility and its increased polarisation; but, apart from offering an interpretation of these phenomena, one can do little more than present a largely factual description of the contemporary Spanish party system.

KEY TO PARTIES AND COALITIONS

AP: Alianza Popular
CAIC: Candidatura Aragonesa Independiente de Centro
CD: Coalicion Democratica
CDC: Convergencia Democratica de Catalunya
CDS: Centro Democratico Social
CiU: Convergencia i Unio
CP: Coalicion Popular

EE: Euskadiko Ezkerra
ERC: Esquerra Republicana de Catalunya
HB: Herri Batasuna
PAR: Partido Aragones Regionalista
PCE: Partido Comunista de España
PDP: Partido Democrata Popular
PNV: Partido Nacionalista Vasco
PSA: Partido Socialista de Andalucia
PSOE: Partido Socialista Obrero Español
PSP: Partido Socialista Popular
UCD: Union de Centro Democratico
UDC: Unio Democratica de Catalunya
UL: Union Liberal
UN: Union Nacional
UPC: Union del Pueblo Canario
UPN: Union del Pueblo Navarro

NOTES

The empirical data mentioned in this paper, if not otherwise indicated, are taken from the studies 1137, 1138, 1141, 1157, 1165, 1183, 1327, 1340, 1346 and 1351 of the Centro de Investigaciones Sociolgicas (CIS) of the Office of the Presidency. I should like to express my thanks to the CIS, and especially to Pilar Alcobendas, for all the help given to this research.

1. S.M. Lipset and S. Rokkan, 'Cleavage Structures, Party Systems and Voter Alignments: An Introduction', in S.M. Lipset and S. Rokkan (eds.), *Party Systems and Voter Alignments: Cross-National Perspectives* (New York: Free Press, 1967), p.50.
2. R. Rose and D. Urwin, 'Persistence and Change in Western Party Systems Since 1945', *Political Studies*, Vol.18 (1970), p.295.
3. M. Pedersen, 'The Dynamics of European Party Systems: Changing Patterns of Electoral Volatility', *European Journal of Political Research*, Vol.7 (1979), pp.1–26.
4. A. Zuckerman and M.I. Lichbach, 'Stability and Change in European Electorates', *World Politics*, Vol.29 (1977), pp.523–51; and S.B. Wolinetz, 'The Transformation of Western European Party Systems Revisited', *West European Politics*, Vol.2 (1979), pp.4–28.
5. See O. Borre, 'Electoral Instability in Four Nordic Countries', *Comparative Political Studies*, Vol.13 (1980), pp.141–71; H. Daalder, 'The Comparative Study of Parties and Party Systems: An Overview', in H. Daalder and P. Mair (eds.), *Western European Party Systems: Continuity and Change* (London: Sage, 1983), pp.1–28; P. Mair, 'Adaptation and Control: Toward an Understanding of Party and Party System Change', ibid., pp.405–29; G. Sjoblom, 'Political Change and Political Accountability: A Propositional Inventory of Causes and Effects', ibid., pp.369–404.
6. M. Maguire, 'Is There Still Persistence? Electoral Change in Western Europe, 1948–1979', ibid., p.29.
7. M. Pedersen, 'Changing Patterns of Electoral Volatility in European Party Systems: 1948–1977', op. cit., p.35.
8. The most significant parties to be legalised were the Socialists (PSOE) in February 1977, and the Communists (PCE) in April of the same year.
9. The PSOE was founded in 1879, as a result of a split in the Spanish section of the First International. The PCE came into being as a result of two splits from the PSOE, in 1920 and 1921. The AP began in 1976 as a federation of parties integrated by well-known members of the political class of the Francoist regime, and became a single party in March 1977. The UCD owes its origins to a coalition of small parties – the Democratic Centre – formed in

January 1977, which was to consolidate itself in March of that same year under the presidency of Adolfo Suarez – the then President of the Government. In August 1977, after its success in the June elections it became a single party, and in February 1983, after its electoral defeat of October 1982, it broke up.

10. See M. Ramirez, 'Aproximacion al sistema de partidos en Espana, 1931–1981', in S. Castillo *et al.*, *Estudios sobre historia de Espana* (Madrid: UIMP, 1981), p. 223; J.J. Linz, 'The New Spanish Party System', in R. Rose (ed.), *Electoral Participation: A Comparative Analysis* (Beverley Hills, CA: Sage Publications, 1980), pp. 100–89; and G. Sartori, *Partidos y sistemas de partidos*, I (Spanish version) (Madrid: Allianza, 1980), p. 210.

11. See A. Bar, 'El sistema de partidos en Espana: Ensayo de caracterizacion', *Sistema*, No. 47 (1982), pp. 3–46.

12. See P. McDonough, A. Lopez Pina and S.H. Barnes, 'The Spanish Public in Political Transition', *British Journal of Political Science*, Vol. 11 (1981), pp. 49–79.

13. See J. de Esteban and L. López Guerra, *Las partidos politicos en la España actual* (Barcelona: Planeta, 1982).

14. See C. Huneeus, 'La Union de Centro Democratico, un partido consociacional', *Revista de politica comparada*, Vol. 3 (1980), pp. 163–92; L. Garcia San Miguel, 'The Ideology of the Union de Centro Democratico', *European Journal of Political Research*, Vol. 9 (1981), pp. 411–47; R. Chamorro, *Viaje al centro de UCD* (Barcelona: Planeta, 1981); E. Attard, *Vida y muerte de UCD* (Barcelona: Planeta, 1983).

15. See A. Bar, 'La participacion politica en Espana: Analisis de dos factores determinantes', *Revista de estudios politicos*, No. 23 (1981), pp. 211–31; A. Bar 'Los factores sociodemograficos de la participacion politica en Espana', *Revista de estudios politicos*, No. 27 (1982), pp. 171–90.

16. The data are from July 1978 (CIS), when party membership in general was at a peak, with the political transition to democracy being fully under way.

17. See J.R. Montero, 'Partidos y participacion politica: Algunas notas sobre la afiliacion politica en la etapa inicial de la trasicion espanola', *Revista de estudios politicos*, No. 23 (1981), pp. 33–72; S. Bartolini, 'The Membership of Mass Parties: The Social Democratic Experience, 1889–1978', in H. Daalder and P. Mair, op. cit., pp. 177–220.

18. See J.M. Maravall, *La politica de la transicion, 1975–1980* (Madrid: Taurus, 1981), p. 42.

19. I am adopting the terminology of G. Sartori, *Parties and Party Systems: A Framework for Analysis* (Cambridge: Cambridge University Press, 1976), p. 132.

20. The most evident case is that of Catalonia where virtually all the national parties took part in the elections either in coalition with exclusively Catalonian parties, or with sectors of their own that were federated and functioning autonomously.

21. After its success in the second parliamentary elections of 1979, the UCD gradually lost every subsequent election that was held: in the local elections of April 1979 it was defeated in the larger cities; in the referendum on Andalucian autonomy in February 1980 its proposal was defeated; it was also defeated in the elections to the Basque and Catalonian parliaments in March 1980; in the partial elections to the Senate in Seville and Almeria; and in those to the Galician and Andalucian parliaments in October 1981 and May 1982 respectively.

22. For all, see H. Daalder and P. Mair, op. cit.

23. See G. Sani and G. Sartori, 'Polarisation, Fragmentation and Competition in Western Democracies', in H. Daalder and P. Mair, op. cit., pp. 307–40.

24. See the list in J. de Esteban and L. Lopez Guerra, *Las elecciones legislativas del 1 de Marzo de 1979* (Madrid: CIS, 1979), pp. 89–93, and in M. Martinez Cuadrado, *El sistema politico espanol y el comportamiento electoral regional en el Sur de Europa* (Madrid: ICI, 1980), pp. 234–40.

25. See D.W. Rae, *The Political Consequences of Electoral Laws* (New Haven: Yale University Press, 1971); and D. Nohlen, *Wahlsysteme der Welt: Daten und Analysen* (Munchen: Piper, 1978).

26. The calculation for Rae's fragmentation index is based on the following formula:

$$F = 1 - \left[\sum_{i=1}^{n} Ti^2\right]$$

Ti being the percentage of votes or seats for each party.

27. The PSA (Partido Socialista de Andalucia) burst onto the parliamentary scene with five seats in the Congress (1.4 per cent of the total vote) in 1979, only to leave just as suddenly in 1982.

28. Given the temporary situation in which they are to be found, I consider that the remnants of the UCD and its splinter, the CDS, together with the reformist movements currently undergoing reorganisation, effectively constitute a single political group, since they all occupy the same central ideological space.

29. The degree of volatility has been calculated according to Pedersen's formula:

$$Vt = \frac{1}{2} \times \left[\sum_{i=1}^{n} \Delta Pi,t \right]$$

where $\Delta Pi,t$ is the change in the percentage of the votes of each party from one election to the next.

30. See the data in the Appendix of S. Bartolini and P. Mair, 'The Class Cleavage in Historical Perspective: An Analytical Reconstruction and Empirical Test', paper presented at the meeting of the German Political Science Association, Mannheim, October 1983.

31. The data used here come from study no. 1327 of the CIS of November 1982, which is chronologically closest to the October elections.

32. G. Sani and G. Sartori, op. cit., p. 337.

33. In 1978, 83.4 per cent of the Spanish population considered democracy as the best form of government, whereas, for example, in West Germany between 1967 and 1978, the percentage of people holding that opinion varied between 68 per cent and 74 per cent; see J.J. Linz *et al., Informe sociologico sobre et cambio politico en Espana, 1975–1981* (Madrid: Euramerica, 1981), pp. 613–14. According to Maravall (op. cit., p. 108), only one per cent of the population was against the democratic system in 1980, while those indifferent to it reached 12 per cent.

34. I calculate the polarisation index according to the formula proposed by Sani and Sartori (op. cit., p. 231), that is, 'the absolute difference between their mean self-location divided by the theoretical maximum'.

35. These parties won 82 per cent of the vote in 1977 and 1979, and 86 per cent in 1982 (see Table 4). One should bear in mind that the references to the AP consider not only the party itself but also those smaller groups that formed a coalition with the AP for all the elections held so far and which, therefore, have obtained seats in parliament. With regard to the later study of the 1982 elections, and, on account of its break-up, the UCD has been assimilated with Adolfo Suarez's CDS as representative of the weakened centre.

36. See J.M. Maravall, op. cit., p. 49.

37. At present there is a move in Spain aimed at uniting, in a single national centrist party, liberal sectors and other residual groups from the UCD with the Catalonian regionalists of CiU, whose intention it is to regain the currently scattered centrist vote. Nor should the possibility be ignored that the PDP Christian democrats might back out of their present coalition with the AP and go it alone in an attempt to occupy the centre, with which they themselves feel more closely identified.

38. See G. Sartori, *Parties and Party Systems,* op. cit., p. 135.

39. See J. Blondel, *An Introduction to Comparative Government* (London: Weidenfeld & Nicolson, 1969).

40. See G. Sartori, *Parties and Party Systems,* op. cit., pp. 173–185.

The Greek Party System: A Case of 'Limited but Polarised Pluralism'?

George Th. Mavrogordatos

A THREE-PARTY SYSTEM

This article is not concerned with change in established party systems follow-ing protracted periods of normal operation. It deals, rather, with the forma-tion and consolidation of a party system following a period of suppression of party politics.[1] Indeed, it would make little sense to speak already of 'change' in the party system that has emerged in Greece since the demise of the Colonels' regime only a decade ago. Besides this difference in perspec-tive, it is also doubtful whether an analysis of the formation and consolida-tion of party systems can benefit from the accumulated, if not cumulative, research on system change. After only three elections measures such as electoral volatility and fractionalisation may be difficult to interpret.

The return to constitutional rule in July 1974 set in motion a restructuring of the Greek party system that seven years of military rule had frozen but had also manifestly failed to eradicate. Seven more years and three elections later, this restructuring had run its course, resulting in a three-party system, with three major (and 'relevant') parties sharing between them 95 per cent of the vote and all the parliamentary seats (see Table 1).[2] In this respect at least, structural continuity with the (pre-1967) past was fully restored.

To speak of structural continuity rather than mere similarity with the past, one must go beyond obvious changes in party labels and programmes to the very roots of the party system, which are to be found in two successive historical conflicts of this century. The first was the 'national schism' between Venizelists and Antivenizelists over Greek participation in the First World War, which was transformed and perpetuated in the inter-war period as an irreconcilable conflict between Republicans and Royalists.[3] The second was the new schism between the bourgeois parties and a Communist-dominated left which erupted during the Second World War and culminated in the Civil War of 1946–49.[4] The succession and super-imposition of these two historical cleavages has produced a deeply rooted and lasting division into three political camps or 'families', the centre, the right and the left, as they were called in the post-war period.

On the eve of the dictatorship, in 1967, each of these three historical political families had been assembled under the roof of a *single* party: the Centre Union (EK), the National Radical Union (ERE), and the United Democratic Left (EDA) respectively (the latter effectively controlled by the then illegal Communist Party from abroad).[5] After the demise of the dicta-torship in 1974, however, this was no longer the case: each political family was deeply divided by a bitter internal struggle over its authentic representa-

TABLE 1
RESULTS OF GREEK PARLIAMENTARY ELECTIONS, 1974-81

Parties	1974		1977		1981	
	Votes %	Seats	Votes %	Seats	Votes %	Seats
Extreme Right[1]	1.1	-	6.8	5	1.7	-
New Democracy[2]	54.4	220	42.9	173	35.9	115
Center[3]	20.6	60	12.0	16	1.5	-
PASOK[4]	13.6	12	25.3	93	48.1	172
KKE Esoterikou[5]	9.5	3	2.7	2	1.4	-
KKE		5	9.4	11	10.9	13
Extreme Left	0.0	-	0.5	-	0.2	-
Other	0.9	-	0.4	-	0.4	-
Total	100.0	300	100.0	300	100.0	300

Notes:
1. In 1974, the National Democratic Union (EDE); in 1977, the National Front (EP); in 1981, the Party of Progressives (KP).
2. The 1977 figures also include the short-lived New Liberals, who subsequently joined New Democracy.
3. In 1974, the Centre Union–New Forces (EKND) and a local list in the Dodecanese; in 1977, the Union of Democratic Centre (EDIK); in 1981, EDIK, the Liberal Party and the allied Party of Democratic Socialism (KODISO) and Party of Peasants and Working People (KAE).
4. Those elected on PASOK lists in 1981 include G. Mavros, former leader of EDIK (until 1977), and M. Glezos, representing the United Democratic Left (EDA).
5. The 1974 and 1977 figures also include EDA.

tion in the new historical era which was about to begin. It may even be argued that both the first two elections (that of 1974 and especially that of 1977) involved a struggle for power *within* each political family rather than *between* them (the victory of New Democracy being certain on both occasions).[6] This transitional struggle was over by 1981. The election of that year was the first since 1974 actually to involve and effect a change in government. It also demonstrated that each political family was again effectively represented by *one* major party, as before the dictatorship.

KKE: THE TRADITIONAL LEFT

It is ironic that it is within the left that the forces of tradition have won their most easy, clear-cut and irreversible victory, that is, the triumph of the orthodox KKE (Communist Party of Greece) over its Eurocommunist rivals of the so-called KKE Esoterikou ('of the interior'). Unconditional loyalty to the Soviet Union and the other myths of the past, together with incomparably greater financial resources, gave the orthodox KKE an enormous advantage not only among the perennially persecuted and thereby profoundly traditionalist masses of the old left – the vanquished of the Civil War – but also among a younger generation radicalised *in vitro* under (and against) the dictatorship. With the traditionalist old guard in complete control since the split of 1968 (which led to the formation of KKE Esoterikou), the orthodox KKE remains one of the most old-fashioned Communist Parties in Western Europe. It is also probably the most secretive: party membership, finances, and even the actual composition of the Central Committee remain shrouded in a cloud of mystery, reflecting the party's clandestine past. Since 1974, dissent within the KKE has produced a series of expulsions and walkouts, particularly among younger cadres. Otherwise, very little transpires about intra-party debates, while the image projected is one of unquestioned unanimity and discipline. Sectarian rigidity may account for the party's remarkable organisational strength, especially in the labour movement, but has also placed insuperable limits on the growth of its popular and specifically electoral appeal, as shown in 1981.

ND: A NEW RIGHT?

For its part, the right underwent in 1974 a traumatic break with its royalist and authoritarian past, which had been irreparably discredited by its ultimate consequence: the military dictatorship of 1967–74. With the return to parliamentary politics, the future prospects of the right urgently required a swift liquidation of this legacy and a novel political project. Both might have been unthinkable without the charismatic authority and consummate statesmanship of Konstantinos Karamanlis, who returned to Greece in July 1974 as the providential 'man of destiny' amidst the national crisis provoked by the disintegrating dictatorship over Cyprus. Saving the nation, he then also saved the right. On the one hand, he proceeded with the swift liquidation of the past by (a) legalising the Communist Party (outlawed since 1947), (b) presiding over a selective but substantial purge and punishment of those associated with the dictatorship and its worst excesses, and above all (c) abandoning the monarchy to its final defeat in the referendum of December 1974. On the other hand, he imposed a novel political project of liberal-bourgeois modernisation, crowned by Greek accession to the European Community, by founding New Democracy (ND) as a new party of the right or even of the centre-right.

Nevertheless, the party proved inferior to the task. Despite the infusion of some new blood, it was immediately dominated by unreformed notables of the old ERE and eventually failed to develop an effective mass organisation independent of personal clienteles. The initial organisational drive culminated in 1979 with the election of 334 local party committees by some 130,000 'members' and with the holding of the first regular party congress, but had no comparable sequel and obviously failed to transform ND into a democratic mass party. Moreover, ND's endeavour to absorb the old centre by simply recruiting individual politicians of centrist background failed to produce substantial nationwide results, whereas its electoral support was ominously eroded in 1977 by a breakaway extreme right, the so-called National Front (EP) which was composed of assorted diehard royalists, those nostalgic for the dictatorship, religious fanatics and fascists.

Eventually, ND was also deprived of the charismatic appeal and strong leadership of its founder when Karamanlis became President of the Republic in May 1980 and thereby ostensibly removed himself from party politics. Under his weak successor Georgios Rallis (barely elected by the parliamentary party over his conservative rival Evangelos Averof), the divided party gradually drifted towards the past in an effort to recapture and reintegrate the extreme right. Although this was achieved in 1981, it did not avert electoral disaster.

Following the election, Averof's accession to the leadership was the logical consequence of defeat and of the concomitant contraction of ND to the limits of the traditional right. But it has also accelerated the party's retrogression in both ideological and organisational terms. Averof speaks for those party regulars and supporters who remain viscerally attached to the overall legacy of the Civil War, while his old-fashioned autocratic style has reduced ND's operation to that of a traditional parliamentary party of notables, relegating unlimited authority to the leader alone. Ideological differences, personal rivalries and factionalism have been exacerbated thereby. Nevertheless, vociferous opposition to the PASOK government has provided a measure of party unity and has produced a spectacular mobilisation of party cadres and supporters. It remains to be seen whether and how mass mobilisation will change the party itself.

PASOK: THE NEW CENTRE

In 1974, one should have expected that the old centre would be absorbed by ND or else would disappear. What had been historically the centre's reformist programme was largely appropriated by Karamanlis, whereas republicanism as a distinctive partisan banner was definitively buried together with the monarchy in the referendum of December 1974. Despite the 20 per cent won in the 1974 election, the centre was indeed bound to disappear insofar as it was represented by unreformed survivors of the past such as Georgios Mavros and Ioannis Zigdis. It was, however, reborn under 'the green sun', symbol of PASOK.

The genius of Andreas Papandreou had been to recognise already during the dictatorship that in terms of both structure and programme the model of the old Centre Union was no longer viable. By creating his own Panhellenic Liberation Movement (PAK), he effectively refused to assume the leadership of the Centre Union upon the death of his father Georgios Papandreou in 1968. The parallel with Karamanlis is obvious in this as in other respects. As charismatic leaders, both had the vision to break with tradition *and* the authority to impose this break. Unlike Karamanlis, however, Papandreou could afford to take his time and to unfold a strategy in three stages, which underlies the growth of the Panhellenic Socialist Movement (PASOK) that he founded in September 1974, upon his return to Greece.[7]

In 1974, the immediate priority was to establish PASOK as an entirely new party, with an unambiguously unique identity and no ties with the past. This goal was successfully achieved, but at the price of a poor electoral result. Its socialist label, ideology, grassroots organisation, and even the odd party symbol of the green sun firmly established the total novelty and originality of PASOK. On this basis, expansion could begin and continue unabated.

The next goal was to become the country's second largest party and achieve unchallenged supremacy within the divided opposition, as the sole credible alternative to ND. This goal was also successfully reached, in 1977, thanks to the remarkably easy discredit of EDIK (the old centre) which disintegrated after its disastrous defeat in that election. It was also achieved thanks to a populist catch-all strategy, which had been readily provided with an elaborate theoretical foundation from the outset. The fundamental cleavage in Greek society was simply defined as one between an all-embracing 'non-privileged' majority and a minute privileged 'oligarchy' representing foreign and domestic 'monopolies'. Moreover, what had been initially a dogmatic conception of 'third-world' socialism was gradually diluted and supplanted by a generic promise of 'change'. Fierce nationalism drew upon dormant anti-Western sentiment and was crucial in legitimising PASOK even among the most unlikely traditionalists.

Finally, after 1977, a parliamentary majority appeared within reach at last. PASOK systematically cultivated an image of increasing pragmatism, moderation and responsibility – the accepted image of a governing party. Its populist catch-all strategy was further developed in February 1978 under the slogan 'National Popular Unity', aimed at turning the overwhelming social majority of 'non-privileged' Greeks into a parliamentary majority as well. Essentially, this involved an appeal to all the 'non-privileged' over their traditional party loyalties. As Papandreou would often stress in his campaign speeches, there were no 'leftist, centrist or rightist' salaries, pensions or prices. This strategy of appealing to voters on both the left and the right of PASOK reached its tangible culmination just one month before the 1981 election with the inclusion on the PASOK ticket of both Georgios Mavros, former leader of EDIK, and Manolis Glezos, wartime resistance hero and EDA spokesman. Whereas the EDA addition was by then marginal, it was towards its right that PASOK needed the reassuring, if uninspiring, trade mark 'Mavros'.

Frequent and often abrupt readjustments of the party line have continued since PASOK came to power in 1981. They have been possible only because PASOK remains essentially a movement around an undisputed charismatic leader. As such, Papandreou is largely exempt from normal requirements of consistency and is not bound by previous statements, including his own. He also remains the only effective source of legitimate authority within the party. He has thus had no great difficulty in repeatedly crushing intra-party dissent, whether by expelling his opponents or else by playing off one tendency against the other, as the supreme and sole arbiter.

Party membership has reportedly grown dramatically from around 27,000 in 1977 to twice that number in 1980 and eventually to over 200,000 in 1984, after two years of PASOK government. Nevertheless, this spectacular growth has not transformed PASOK into a democratic mass party. The groups and individuals who might have spearheaded such a transformation have been systematically expelled or silenced. The parliamentary group has been relegated to a subordinate position within the party, which was weakened even further by a reform of the electoral system in October 1982, abolishing personal preference votes and instituting straight party lists. Both the composition and the order on PASOK tickets are to be determined by the party's President (Papandreou) in the next election. The Central Committee itself has functioned essentially as a rubber stamp for decisions and documents emanating from the President and his chosen associates in the Executive Bureau. It is highly doubtful whether this situation will change after the party's first congress ever, scheduled for May 1984. Limited expressions of dissatisfaction and criticism may well be allowed as an innocuous ritual, as has been the case in some recent sessions of the parliamentary group and the Central Committee. But the documents prepared for the congress make it plain, in quasi-Stalinist language, that any dissenting views will continue to be treated with suspicion and intolerance.

Impressed by the undeniable novelty of its ideology and structure, many have tended to ignore or deny any link between PASOK and what used to be the centre. Nevertheless, PASOK claimed from its inception the legacy not only of wartime resistance (1941–44) and resistance against the dictatorship (1967–74), but also of the Centre Union and its two 'relentless struggles' (1961–63 and 1965–67). As all other claimants to the centre legacy were gradually discredited after 1974 (until they were finally crushed in 1981), PASOK has abandoned its earlier reticence and has smoothly appropriated this legacy all the way back to Eleftherios Venizelos himself. Moreover, PASOK supporters and members, including Papandreou, have not emerged *de novo*. To the extent that they have had any previous party identification and involvement, this was overwhelmingly with the Centre Union of 1961–67 and especially its youth organisation. In the end, however, what is most decisive is that PASOK has clearly inherited the *structural* position of the old centre within the Greek party system.

A TRIPOLAR STRUCTURE

For all the spectacular changes, the underlying pre-1967 structure of the Greek party system has remained essentially intact: it is still divided into three irreducible political camps or families, each represented by one major party. The persistence of this structure has been unambiguously confirmed by the first survey data on the distribution of the Greek public along the standard (ten-point) left–right scale (see Figure 1).[8] As elsewhere, an individual's self-placement on the scale has two main components: ideological preference and party identification.[9] Whereas the ideological component is reflected in the attitudes associated with self-placement, one should expect the party-related component to be particularly significant and salient in Greece, where the actual terms 'left', 'right' and 'centre' have designated three historical political families rather than abstract belief systems. Post-war political loyalties have consequently been defined in those precise terms to a degree probably unknown in other countries. In effect, there is a close link between self-placement and party choice. Six parties may be placed on the left–right scale according to the mean

FIGURE 1

DISTRIBUTION OF THE GREEK PUBLIC ALONG LEFT–RIGHT SCALE

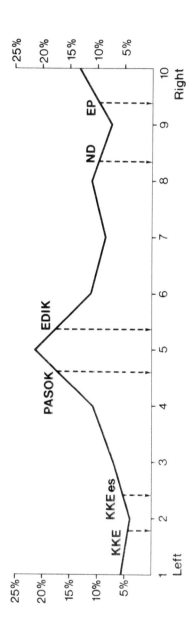

self-placement of their supporters (see Figure 1), while the more reliable data on the three largest parties can also be charted separately (see Figure 2).

The first and foremost conclusion to be drawn from these data is the spectacular confirmation of the historic tripolar structure which has been the single most stable element of the Greek political landscape since the beginning of this century. The six parties are neatly grouped in twos according to the three political families, at three corresponding segments of the spectrum: KKE and KKE Esoterikou on the left, PASOK and EDIK at the centre, ND and EP on the right (see Figure 1). The tripolar structure emerges even more sharply from the distribution of the supporters of the three largest parties (see Figure 2).

Both the centrality and the universal appeal of PASOK across the entire spectrum are also striking. The distribution of its supporters clearly confirms the structural position of PASOK as the new centre (despite its understandable reluctance to acknowledge the term, now reserved for the remnants of the old centre parties). The distinctly stronger attraction it exerts towards the left should be linked not only to its centre-left image, but also to the dynamics of bipolar competition.

BIPOLAR COMPETITION

Despite the continuing threefold division, actual competition for government power is still effectively restricted to *two* contenders (now PASOK and ND), to the exclusion of the left. It is in this crucial respect that structural continuity appears most striking and the succession of the Centre Union by PASOK most unambiguous. Bipolar competition has been a permanent feature of the Greek party system for over half a century. The left was never within reach of a majority by itself (except, perhaps, briefly in 1944). In contrast, the role of the centre has always been to offer a credible alternative to the right without succumbing to the dangerous temptation of an actual popular front (that is, an open alliance between centre and left against the right), as it once did (in 1956).

The electoral system of so-called 'reinforced' (weighted) proportional representation (in force since 1958) was invented in response to the tripolar structure and bipolar dynamics of the party system and has in turn served to perpetuate them.[10] The purpose of this electoral system is twofold: to manufacture a one-party parliamentary majority each time and to allow alternation over time between two major parties. While allowing the centre to compete with the right, the system has consistently victimised the left since 1961, both by reducing its share of seats to a fraction of its share of the vote and by thereby inducing its actual or potential supporters to vote for the centre rather than 'waste' their ballot. Supporters of small parties in general are similarly induced to vote for one of the two largest parties.

THE ELECTION OF 18 OCTOBER 1981

In 1981, PASOK was the main beneficiary of bipolar competition and of the electoral system in particular, at the expense of all other opposition parties.

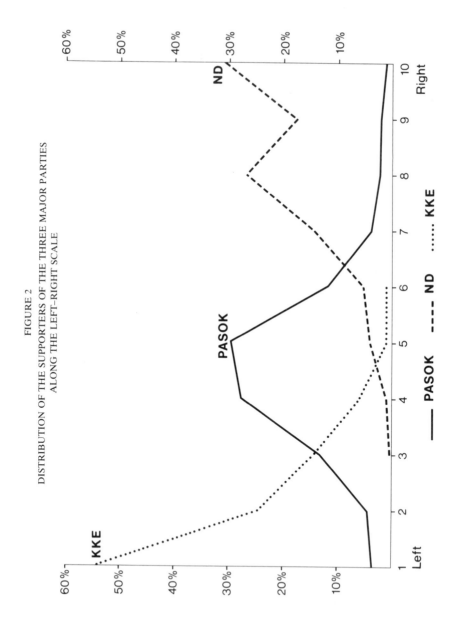

FIGURE 2

DISTRIBUTION OF THE SUPPORTERS OF THE THREE MAJOR PARTIES
ALONG THE LEFT–RIGHT SCALE

Polarisation between ND and PASOK as the only actual alternatives not only drastically limited any potential KKE gains, but also wiped out all the minor parties (see Table 1).

Within the traditional left, the orthodox KKE completed its dominance, but failed miserably in its unrealistic pursuit of '17 per cent' (a critical threshold under the electoral system, whereby the party would have won a proportional share of seats and would have held the balance in the new parliament). Its obsessive campaign around this slogan yielded a gain of only 1.5 percentage points and two seats compared with 1977, indicating the insuperable limits of the party's influence. The election was a Pyrrhic victory for the KKE only insofar as both its most hated adversaries – KKE Esoterikou and the extreme left – lost half their previous electoral strength, while the former was also deprived of parliamentary representation.

For its part, the traditional right rallied massively behind ND to face the PASOK threat. Following the leadership, mass support of the 1977 National Front (EP) was mostly reintegrated by ND, relegating what was left of a breakaway extreme right (the so-called Party of Progressives) back to the status of a negligible protest group, as in 1974. Compared to the five per cent contributed by the extreme right, ND gains from the old centre were meagre indeed and represented the personal clienteles of individual politicians in some districts. In any event, both sets of gains could not offset (as ND had hoped) the staggering loss of almost 14 per cent to PASOK which decided the election.

Apart from this 14 per cent, PASOK also absorbed what remained of the old centre, leaving just 1.5 per cent to be divided among four minor groups, which included the distinctly modern Party of Democratic Socialism (KODISO). This was the *second* time that PASOK almost *doubled* its electoral strength from one election to the next (see Table 1). Such an increase in party support within such a short period may well be unique in comparative terms and may even seem miraculous. It can be understood only if PASOK is recognised as the new centre in Greek politics, following the discrediting and disintegration of EDIK. This has already been shown with reference to the structure and dynamics of the party system as such. But it may also be approached from several other angles. In all these respects, PASOK is the new centre insofar as it approximates to a mirror image of Greek society as a whole.

A MIRROR IMAGE

In the notional left–right space, the distribution of PASOK supporters clearly tends to approximate to the overall distribution of the Greek public, especially around the middle (see Figures 1 and 2). This has its counterpart in physical space – the remarkable homogeneity of PASOK electoral support across the country.

As both maps and appropriate quantitative indicators demonstrate, the geographical distribution of PASOK support in 1981 was far more uniform than that of either ND or KKE. PASOK strength fell below 39 per cent in only three (out of the 56) electoral districts and exceeded 60 per cent in only two. The geographical homogeneity of PASOK support is only the most striking manifestation of the 'nationalisation' of Greek electoral politics – an overall secular trend which affects the other parties as well.[11]

Urban and rural differences constitute a second, far more consequential and significant aspect of the spatial *and* social distribution of electoral support. PASOK homogeneity is here impressive and probably unprecedented (see Table 2). These data should finally lay to rest the widespread myth that PASOK somehow represents an agrarian protest movement, as some hastily concluded – presumably because PASOK support in the countryside did not fit the image of peasant conservatism. This thesis was untenable already in 1974, when the gap between urban and rural PASOK strength was minimal compared to that of all other parties (except, significantly, the centre). In 1981, this gap vanished altogether.

In contrast, it is ND support that became more disproportionately rural in 1981 than ever before since 1974. Party losses in the urban areas were almost double those in rural Greece on a percentage basis (9.6 compared to 5.2). This undoubtedly reflected the enduring hold of conservatism, government patronage and clientelism, exemplified by the centre notables joining ND. But it should also be linked to the reintegration of the extreme right and the overall contraction of ND to the limits of the traditional right.

For its part, the KKE continues to be overwhelmingly urban. Nevertheless, it slightly narrowed in 1981 the previous gap between its rural and urban strength – a significant development if it reflects a trend. Whereas the left should be expected to be disproportionately urban and the right disproportionately rural, it is the hallmark of PASOK as new centre that it should equally represent urban and rural Greece.

In class terms, PASOK is neither a peasants' party nor a workers' party, despite its socialist label, but rather a fairly representative cross-section of Greek society as a whole. Although adequate data are still lacking, it may be said in a nutshell that a measure of class consciousness and class voting is to be found mostly at the extremes of the social structure, among the bourgeoisie and a fraction of the working class, who massively support ND and the KKE respectively. In between, the overwhelming majority of Greek society continues to bask in a distinctly petit-bourgeois mentality, if not ideology, supported and constantly reproduced by the enduring preponderance of small property and small business – a key peculiarity of modern Greek development. The salaried proportion of the economically active population in Greece (42 per cent in 1971) appears to be by far the lowest in Europe, whereas the share of the public sector is large and constantly increasing – another key element of modern Greek development. Otherwise, this society is fragmented into a myriad of narrowly defined and well entrenched sectoral interests. The historic wager of PASOK has been precisely to forge an alliance of all 'non-privileged' Greeks out of this society, behind a vision of radical and generic 'change' – if not exactly socialism.

Charisma has been essential in this respect, as the single most effective cement capable of welding such an alliance together. Charismatic leaders and their movements typically emerge in times of crisis and insecurity.

TABLE 2

URBAN AND RURAL ELECTORAL RESULTS, 1974–81

Parties	1974			1977			1981		
	Urban	Rural	Difference	Urban	Rural	Difference	Urban	Rural	Difference
	%	%	%	%	%	%	%	%	%
Extreme Right	1.0	1.1	+ 0.1	5.5	7.8	+ 2.3	1.5	1.8	+ 0.3
New Democracy	50.1	57.5	+ 7.4	40.5	44.7	+ 4.2	30.9	39.5·	+ 8.6
Center	21.6	20.8	– 0.8	10.3	13.1	+ 2.8	1.8	1.3	– 0.5
PASOK	12.9	14.1	+ 1.2	24.7	25.8	+ 1.1	48.2	48.0	– 0.2
KKE Esoterikou				4.7	1.3	– 3.4	2.2	0.7	– 1.5
KKE	14.7	5.9	– 8.8	13.2	6.6	– 6.6	14.6	8.3	– 6.3

Note: For the parties included in each category, see note under Table 1. The 'urban' category includes all towns with a population of 10,000 or more.

Source: Elias Nicolacopoulos.

Whereas Karamanlis appeared as the providential answer to the immediate political insecurity created by the dictatorship and its disastrous end, Papandreou has similarly embodied an answer to the long-term structural insecurity typical of small property and small business – a generalised insecurity pervading Greek society as a whole.

In a long-term historical (and admittedly schematic) perspective, the emergence of PASOK may be said to represent the final resolution of a contradiction inherent in Venizelism as a historic alliance between the liberal entrepreneurial bourgeoisie and popular, petit-bourgeois and peasant strata.[12] The exhaustion of the alliance, apparent already in the 1930s, and the eventual drift of the erstwhile liberal bourgeoisie to the right are now reflected in the ideological aphasia and political marginality of the last epigones of the Liberal Party. Whereas PASOK, in this perspective, represents the emancipation of the petit-bourgeois and rural masses, freed at last from the fetters of liberal bourgeois politics.

A CASE OF 'LIMITED BUT POLARISED PLURALISM'?

To attempt a classification of the Greek party system in terms of Sartori's typology may provide a fitting conclusion to this summary overview.[13] Counting the 'relevant' parties, there can be little doubt that Greece has a three-party system, falling under the heading of 'limited pluralism' in terms of format. Nevertheless, the numerical criterion alone is neither sufficient nor decisive, if the system is polarised. According to the measure used by Sani and Sartori, the Greek party system undoubtedly is polarised: the distance between the mean self-placement of KKE and ND supporters exceeds *six* points on the left–right scale (it is 6.57 in Figure 1) and actually appears to be greater than the distance found in any other European party system.[14] Consequently, Greece would seem to constitute a deviant case of 'limited but polarised pluralism' – an 'alternative possibility' recognised but not elaborated in the theory.[15]

Among the other features of polarised pluralism, Greece displays most unambiguously the presence of a relevant 'anti-system' party: the KKE. Insofar as the centre has been firmly occupied by PASOK, ND and the KKE may now be regarded as 'bilateral oppositions'. In all these respects, the Greek party system has moved closer to Sartori's celebrated type. Nevertheless, bipolar competition between ND and PASOK seems incompatible with the type's most critical dynamic feature: centrifugal drives. To the extent that bipolar competition has been fostered and preserved by the electoral system, a change to unadulterated proportional representation might indeed activate such centrifugal dynamics. If it also led, sooner or later, to greater fragmentation, the Greek party system would approximate to a normal case of (extreme and) polarised pluralism. But such prospects (and growing popular dissatisfaction) will no doubt affect the eventual choice of a new electoral system by the PASOK government.

NOTES

1. This article is largely drawn from my *Rise of the Green Sun: The Greek Election of 1981* (London: Centre of Contemporary Greek Studies, King's College, 1983), Occasional Paper 1.
2. 'Relevant' in the sense of Giovanni Sartori, *Parties and Party Systems: A Framework for Analysis* (Cambridge: Cambridge University Press, 1976), pp. 121–5.
3. See George Th. Mavrogordatos, *Stillborn Republic: Social Coalitions and Party Strategies in Greece, 1922–1936* (Berkeley: University of California Press, 1983).
4. See, for example, John O. Iatrides (ed.), *Greece in the 1940s: A Nation in Crisis* (Hanover, NH: University Press of New England, 1981).
5. On pre-1967 party politics, see, for example, Keith R. Legg, *Politics in Modern Greece* (Stanford, CA: Stanford University Press, 1969).
6. On the 1974 and 1977 elections, see Howard R. Penniman (ed.), *Greece at the Polls: The National Elections of 1974 and 1977* (Washington, DC: American Enterprise Institute, 1981).
7. The most thorough study of PASOK is Christos Lyrintzis, 'Between Socialism and Populism: The Rise of the Panhellenic Socialist Movement' (Ph.D. thesis, London School of Economics, 1983).
8. These data were collected in the autumn of 1980 and the spring of 1981 for the *Eurobarometer* (Nos. 14 and 15), from a national sample of 1,000 each time. The results of the two surveys are here cumulated.
9. Ronald Inglehart and Hans D. Klingemann, 'Party Identification, Ideological Preference and the Left–Right Dimension among Western Mass Publics', in Ian Budge, Ivor Crewe and Dennis Farlie (eds.), *Party Identification and Beyond: Representations of Voting and Party Competition* (London: John Wiley, 1976), pp. 243–73.
10. On the electoral system, see Phaedo Vegleris, 'Greek Electoral Law', in Penniman, op. cit., pp. 21–48.
11. Elias Nicolacopoulos, 'Les deux guerres civiles et le système des partis politiques en Grèce', (paper presented at the Joint Sessions of the European Consortium for Political Research, Aarhus, 29 March–3 April 1982).
12. Mavrogordatos, op. cit., pp. 111–81 and 328–49.
13. Sartori, op. cit., Chs. 6 and 9.
14. See Giacomo Sani and Giovanni Sartori, 'Polarization, Fragmentation and Competition in Western Democracies', in Hans Daalder and Peter Mair (eds.), *Western European Party Systems: Continuity and Change* (London: Sage Publications, 1983), pp. 307–40.
15. Sartori, op. cit., pp. 286–9.

Party Politics in Contemporary Europe: A Challenge to Party?

Peter Mair

The contemporary literature on parties and party systems in Western Europe is redolent with images of change. The picture of stability which had prevailed in the 1950s and 1960s, and which was presented in its most elaborate form in the work of Lipset and Rokkan and that of Rose and Urwin,[1] gave way in the late 1970s to an emphasis on patterns of change and volatility.[2] And now, as we move towards the mid-1980s, there seems little evidence of a levelling off of the pace of political transformation. Elections in the 1980s have so far witnessed the continuing decline of Labour in the United Kingdom; a record electoral loss for the Christian Democrats in Italy; the entry of the Greens into the German Bundestag for the first time; two defeats out of three elections for the traditionally predominant Fianna Fail in Ireland; the loss of an overall parliamentary majority for the Austrian Social Democrats for the first time since 1971, and a sustained growth of Conservatism in Norway and Denmark. Electoral volatility continues to grow. Table 1 reports the average volatility[3] for elections in Western Europe for each five-year period between 1960 and 1979, as well as for the period 1980 to 1983. With the exception of a slight decline in the late 1970s *vis-à-vis* the early 1970s, it is evident that there has been a steady secular increase in average volatility, such that the figure for 1980–83 is almost half as large again as that for 1960–64.

A Cautionary Note

While most of the literature on party politics in contemporary Europe is emphatic about the fact that things are changing, there is little agreement or consensus on the nature and import of this process, and explanations for

TABLE 1

AGGREGATE ELECTORAL VOLATILITY IN WESTERN EUROPE,[1]
BY FIVE-YEAR PERIODS

	1960–64	1965–69	1970–74	1975–79	(1980–83)
Average Volatility	6.5	7.4	8.8	8.3	(9.3)

Note: 1. All West European countries are included, with the exceptions of Luxembourg, Spain, Greece and Portugal.

Source: Calculated from data in Stefano Bartolini and Peter Mair, 'The Class Cleavage in Historical Perspective: An Analytical Reconstruction and Empirical Test', paper presented to the Annual Meeting of the German Political Science Association, Mannheim, 1983.

what is seen as the transformation of Western European parties and party systems are almost as rife as hypotheses concerning implications for the future. From the mass of relevant literature, it is possible, however, to extract three related themes. The first of these contrasts the electoral volatility of the 1970s with the relative stability of the 1950s and 1960s, and is primarily concerned to counter the hypotheses of Lipset and Rokkan and to suggest that there is a general 'de-freezing' of traditional cleavages. According to this view, various processes of social change – at the level of the class structure, the value system, or even through the growth of the welfare state and the public sector – have rendered increasingly irrelevant traditional lines of partisan division in society and are on the way towards creating a large-scale realignment.

A second approach is more concerned with systemic implications, referring to the recent changes in European politics in terms of changes at the level of the party system itself. Whether for ideological, strategic or even simply tactical reasons, parties now interact and compete with one another in ways different than before, a transformation which is both cause and consequence of the recent growth in electoral volatility. Citizens are seen to have modified their relationship to the parties, while the parties themselves are seen to be more willing to aggregate diverse demands and accommodate to the needs of more heterogeneous clienteles.

The third, and related approach, speaks less of cleavage and/or party system transformation as such, and more of a challenge to party *per se*. Parties in this view are seen in their role as organisations for the expression of interests, as 'active intermediaries' between the citizen and government. As individuals became more educated and politically resourceful, however, and as interests are seen to be increasingly disaggregated and specific, parties are seen to be inadequate instruments of representation and lose their relevance in the face of the mounting competition – and competence – of non-party interest organisations.

All three of these general suggestions carry very far-reaching implications. Whether we are talking about a waning of traditional cleavages, a transformation of party systems or a challenge to party itself, the process of change suggests a very radical rupture with prevailing political practice. And precisely because of this, because the implications of contemporary political change are seen to be so far-reaching on the one hand, and yet are so imprecisely defined on the other, it seems worthwhile to introduce two notes of caution.

In the first place, and most obviously, virtually all the indicators of political change from which the different approaches have been elaborated are simply indices of *electoral* change. Despite the already enormous and continually growing body of work on parties and party systems in Western Europe, there are remarkably few attempts to effect systematic comparisons of change in parties at levels other than the electoral. The recent ECPR-sponsored project on party programmes and manifestos, for instance, represents virtually the first systematic attempt to compare party *ideology* across space and time.[4] At another level, there is remarkably little material available concerning comparative developments at the level of party *organisation* in Western Europe,[5] the understanding of which is surely essential if we are to discuss the growing 'strength' or 'weakness' of parties. The problem here, of course, is to define measures of organisational growth or decline. A falling membership may indicate organisational decay, but at a time when more and more political communication appears to take place via the mass media, and when parties are less reliant on membership subscriptions as a source of finance, a decline in the number of members may be more than compensated for by a growth in, and the more efficacious use of, other resources available to the parties' central offices. If by organisational strength is meant the capacity to mobilise or influence voters, then membership levels may prove a poor indicator of such strength in societies increasingly accessible to new channels of communication.

The second note of caution stems from the fact that virtually all indices of electoral change are based on change at the level of the individual party. Whether one is concerned to examine changes in Rae's fractionalisation index, trends in support for specific parties or overall volatility in the party system as a whole, the measure of change is based on change in each party's percentage vote. Such measures certainly tell us a great deal about the degree of change in any election or over a series of elections. In and of themselves, however, they tell us little about such wider questions of cleavage persistence or party system transformation. In other words, while measuring the *amount* of change, they cannot measure its *relevance*. To invoke a truism, change at the level of the individual party will affect the party system if and only if this change has systemic properties. A shift from the Christian Democrats in Italy to the Republicans and/or the Liberals may register significantly on a scale of electoral volatility, but only under certain specific circumstances will it affect the nature of the Italian party system itself. Even a degree of vote change sufficient to effect the elimination of one or more parties – as happened in Ireland between 1948 and 1957 – need not in itself make a substantial difference to the overall working of the party system.

In a similar sense, change at the level of the individual party will signify a change in the traditional cleavages only if one can establish a one-to-one correspondence between the party and the cleavage, allowing the former to act as the surrogate indicator of the latter. Thus, while a shift from one anti-religious party to another may result in a highly volatile election, it is unlikely to have much bearing on a religious–secular cleavage. To the extent that two or more parties mobilise along the same side of the same cleavage, therefore, measures of cleavage persistence must go beyond simply measures of individual party persistence.[6]

In short, if electoral change is to be seen as a relevant indicator of the broader questions of party system change or cleavage decay, it is not enough simply to know how much change is taking place; rather, one must know where the change is occurring, and which parties are being affected.[7]

The Challenge to Party

Having noted these two caveats concerning systemic change on the one hand, and the problem of the persistence of cleavages on the other, it is now appropriate to return to the third theme identified above, that is, the challenge to party *per se*, which is the main concern of this paper. Here perhaps we are on safer ground, in that if parties are being challenged in their role as active intermediaries between citizens and government, then it seems likely that this will be visible in terms of their electoral performance. The problem here, however, is to know what to look for. The literature which speaks of a 'challenge' to party rarely, if ever, specifies how exactly this is evident electorally, and while frequent reference is made to the idea that parties are now losing their 'hold', precisely what is involved in such a process is difficult to assess. At one level there is little problem, in that the 'hold' of parties refers to their role in the policy-making process, and there is already a growing literature which tries systematically and comparatively to assess changes in that role as well as in that of non-party interest organisations.[8] At the electoral level, however, it is not so easy to establish clear conclusions, since it is difficult to ascertain what is actually implied by the notion of 'electoral hold'. Referring back to the earlier discussion, it may be seen to result from the parties' organisational strength and their capacity to mobilise and influence voters. To the extent that a party maintains or expands this capacity to pull voters along, therefore, it perhaps should be expected at least to retain or possibly even to increase its aggregate electoral support. As such, the increased electoral volatility of the 1970s and 1980s might be seen as symptomatic of a loosening of the hold of party.

There are obvious difficulties attached to such an interpretation, however, the first being the actual amount of volatility itself. To be sure, with a value of 9.3, average volatility in 1980–83 is almost half as much again as that 20 years earlier (Table 1). Nevertheless, this could also be read as showing that there is 90.7 per cent aggregate stability in the early 1980s which, while less impressive than the 93.5 per cent level in the early 1960s, is still substantial. To speak of parties losing their hold or of there being a challenge to party when there is evidence of fewer than one in ten votes changing at the *aggregate* level may therefore be somewhat of an exaggeration. Certainly, individual level data may, and indeed often do, show a greater degree of fluctuation than is evident at the aggregate level, but even then the clearly more exciting task of measuring electoral change often leads one to ignore the sheer volume of electoral stability. Thus, while the SPÖ may have lost its overall parliamentary majority for the first time since 1971, it nevertheless remains the largest party in Austria; while Fianna Fail has suffered two defeats over the last three elections, it too remains the largest party in Ireland, as does the DC in Italy. The Greens may now be in the Bundestag – but if their vote declines by even less than one per cent in the next German election, then they will fall below the five per cent threshold once more. In short, there is evidence of change, but it would be a mistake to underestimate the even greater evidence of stability. Following the premature publication of his obituary, Mark Twain is reported to have telegraphed a newspaper saying that rumours of his death had been exaggerated; European political parties may well live long enough to say the same.

Yet there is rarely smoke without fire, and perhaps Mark Twain may even have been ill. For although the evidence of political stability outweighs that of political change, nevertheless it is undeniable that, in general, there is now a greater degree of aggregate electoral change than at any time since the Second World War. But even to accept this argument means confronting the second, and very obvious, difficulty of using these data to infer that parties are losing their hold. The problem here is simply that, obviously, all parties cannot lose support at the same time. When the different proportions of votes always sum to 100 per cent, then the losses of party X on the swings will inevitably mean gains for party Y on the roundabouts. If the loss of 'hold' is signalled by a loss of votes, then a gain in votes should signal an increased 'hold' which, in turn, suggests that it is difficult to speak of a challenge to party *per se* as opposed to specifying particular challenges to some of the parties for some of the time.

One possible way out of this difficulty is to suggest that a growth in aggregate volatility implies not that all parties are losing at the same time – which clearly cannot be true – but rather that all parties are *vulnerable* at the same time. In other words, because parties are losing their relevance as active intermediaries, and because their hold has weakened, their supporters are now more willing to consider alternative voting choices. Thus the 'core' vote of the party, that degree of support which it can take more or less for granted, could be said to be dwindling, while the 'contingent' component of its vote commensurately grows. As such, the party becomes more vulnerable to loss, even if, at any given election, its vote may remain constant or even increase slightly. More and more of its voters become simply voters, with fewer classifiable as zealots or even converts.

But all of this suggests a process which really cannot be verified on the basis of aggregate patterns of electoral change. To be sure, it could be shown that not only has overall volatility increased, but that most parties are now experiencing greater fluctuations in their overall vote than was the case in the 1950s and 1960s. Even if this is the case, however, there is no reason to believe that such a change is not the consequence of a fairly stable block of floating voters who shift from one party to another, giving each party a highly volatile vote, but also leaving the core support of each reasonably unscathed. If a block of voters shifts to party X at one election, and abandons it at the subsequent contest, then party X would appear to have a highly volatile vote and therefore to be vulnerable. At the same time, however, party X may have retained its core vote over both elections, and therefore be as strongly rooted – to have as strong a 'hold' – as ever.

Either way, one is faced with the persistent problem of extrapolating theories of party strength or weakness from the inevitably crude data provided by aggregate voting patterns. Indices of change are necessarily too all-embracing and too unrefined to permit easy assumptions about what actually is happening to the relationship between parties and voters. In and of itself, aggregate electoral change tells us little about the changing role, if any, of parties as active intermediaries between the citizenry and government.

Remaining at the aggregate level for a moment, however, there remains one avenue yet to be explored. While a closed system in which all valid votes sum to 100 per cent obviously means that not all parties can lose support at the same time, the hypothesised diminished role for parties might be evident in declining rates of turnout and/or in the growth of spoiled or blank ballot papers. In other words, if parties are less relevant as active intermediaries in the process of interest representation, then we might witness a general decline in the number of valid votes expressed in terms of the eligible electorate as we move from the 1950s through the 1960s to the 1970s.

TABLE 2

AVERAGE PERCENTAGE OF VALID VOTES CAST,
BY DECADE AND BY COUNTRY

	1950s	1960s	1970s
Austria	93.8	92.7	91.4
Belgium	88.2	85.4	85.7
Denmark	81.5	87.1	87.0
Finland	76.0	84.7	76.5
France	77.4	74.8	80.6
Germany	83.8	84.7	90.2
Iceland	89.2	89.6	88.8
Ireland	73.6	73.5	75.7
Italy	90.3	89.7	89.2
Luxemburg	87.6	84.2	84.0
Netherlands	93.0	92.5	83.0
Norway	78.4	82.5	81.5
Sweden	78.3	85.9	90.8
Switzerland	67.7	63.0	51.9
United Kingdom	80.3	76.5	74.9
Mean	82.6	83.1	82.1

Source: Calculated from data in T.T. Mackie and Richard Rose, *The International Almanac of Electoral History*, 2nd edition (London: Macmillan, 1982).

Data on the average proportion of valid votes cast in the three decades are reported in Table 2. Far from evidencing decline, however, the picture presented by these data is one of surprising stability. Taking all the fifteen countries together, the average proportion of valid votes cast in the 1950s was 82.6 per cent, as against 83.1 per cent in the 1960s and 82.1 per cent in the 1970s. Nevertheless, five countries do evidence quite dramatic discontinuities, three with decreasing proportions of valid votes – the Netherlands, Switzerland and the UK – and two with increasing proportions – Germany and Sweden. Since the change in the Dutch case can be discounted because compulsory attendance at the ballot box was abolished in 1970, this means that there are two cases of sharp decline balanced by two cases of substantial increase. The remaining ten cases are reasonably stable. Austria has declined steadily, but only slightly; Denmark increased from the 1950s to the 1960s, then fell back to the earlier level again in the 1970s; France declined slightly and then increased quite substantially, and Norway increased in the 1960s, falling back only marginally in the 1970s. In general, then, there has not been a substantial and generalised trend in one direction or the other, a conclusion which concurs with that of Dittrich and Johansen's more sophisticated trend analysis of turnout.[9] If disaffection from parties can be evidenced by declining rates of electoral participation, then these data at any rate fail to offer any support for the argument.

To conclude this discussion, therefore, it was noted at the beginning that the recent evidence of change in party politics in Europe has led to various hypotheses concerning the waning of traditional cleavages, and/or the transformation of party systems, and/or the challenge to party *per se*. However, since the various indices of change are *aggregate* measures of *electoral* change at the level of the *individual* party, and since, moreover, there is also evidence of a substantial degree of stability, then it is suggested that we should be extremely cautious in our extrapolations. If we wish to establish that traditional cleavages are indeed waning, or that party systems are in a process of large-scale transformation, or that party itself is being challenged in its role as a major active intermediary between the citizenry and government, which is the primary concern of this paper, then future research needs to go beyond simply the counting of aggregate votes.

Patterns of Party Identification

One useful area of research which has yet to be fully and systematically explored on a comparative basis concerns individual-level data on affective attitudes to the parties. If parties are ceasing to be relevant as active intermediaries, and if they are indeed losing their 'hold' on voters, then this should be apparent in a declining popular sense of attachment to parties as measured by responses to survey questions which probe the strength of *party identification*. Putting aside the problem of the utility of the concept of party identification in a European context, and also ignoring the obvious differences in what is tapped by the notion of party identification in the different countries, it can be hypothesised that a declining role for party will be directly visible in declining rates of identification or, at least, in a declining intensity in the degree to which partisan loyalists continue to identify. Parties cannot all lose votes at the same time, but they can all lose identifiers.

The measurement of party identification across different political systems and over time is clearly fraught with difficulties. Variations in the meaning of similarly worded questions from one country to the next, as well as changes in question wording from one survey to the next, clearly hinder any systematic comparisons. For the purposes of an initial test of this hypothesis, however, data from the Eurobarometer surveys do offer a useful cache of relevant information. Since at least the early 1970s, the Eurobarometer surveys have included questions about the degree of attachment to parties. And while the wording of these questions has varied over time, leading in some cases to dramatic increases or decreases in reported rates of party identification, there is nevertheless sufficient similarity in certain countries and over certain periods to allow for an initial test.

In the cases of Belgium, France, Germany and the Netherlands, for instance, the question concerning party attachment has remained virtually unchanged between at least October 1975 (Eurobarometer 4) and April 1981 (Eurobarometer 15). Moreover, for all nine EC countries, there is also a run of surveys between October 1978 (Eurobarometer 10) and April 1981 in which the question also remained essentially unchanged.[10] Although these represent quite brief time periods, and although there is therefore no way in which the volatile 1970s and early 1980s can be compared with the stable 1950s and 1960s, nevertheless the data should be sufficient to indicate the presence of any trend which might exist. It should also be emphasised that since the primary concern is with change over time, then variations in the meaning of the relevant survey question between the different systems do not present an obstacle to analysis.

Trends in party identification are shown in Figure 1 and Table 3. Figure 1 reports only the cases of Belgium, France, Germany and The Netherlands – those countries where the party identification question has remained unchanged between 1975 and 1981 – and plots the average proportion of respondents across all four countries who report themselves as 'very' or 'fairly' close to a particular party (continuous line) as well as those reporting 'no ties' to any party (dotted line). The trend in these data is quite evident. Following an initial surge in the sense of attachment between 1975 and 1976, there has been a relative decline, particularly after 1978, with a commensurate growth in the proportion of respondents reporting 'no ties' to any party. The high point in terms of attachment was reached in 1976 with an average of 34.2 per cent (34.1 per cent in 1978),[11] the low point being reached with an average of just 23.2 per cent in 1981. The highest average percentage reporting 'no ties' to parties, 38.0 per cent, on the other hand, was recorded in 1975, which then fell to 29.3 per cent in 1976, fluctuated around that figure until 1979, and then rose to 35.8 per cent in 1980 and to 36.7 per cent in 1981.

A more comprehensive picture is evident in the data in Table 3, which reports the values of an index of party identification for the four countries for the period 1975 to 1981, and for the remaining five countries between 1978 and 1981. The index has been calculated by multiplying the percentage reporting themselves 'very close' to a party by 3, those 'fairly close' by 2, those who are 'merely sympathisers' by 1, and those reporting 'no ties' by 0, and then summing the resultant figures. This gives the index a theoretical minimum value of 0 (100 per cent report no ties to party), and a theoretical maximum of 300 (100 per cent report themselves very close to a party). Dividing this value by 3 then gives a more intuitively meaningful range of 0–100, which is the range which applies to the data shown in Table 3. The index is thus a measure of both the frequency and the intensity of party identification, with larger values of the index indicating a greater sense of partisan attachment.

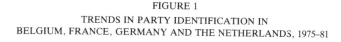

FIGURE 1

TRENDS IN PARTY IDENTIFICATION IN
BELGIUM, FRANCE, GERMANY AND THE NETHERLANDS, 1975–81

Source: Eurobarometers 4,6,8,10,12,13 and 15. The percentages are derived by averaging
results across the four countries having re-computed the data to exclude the non-
respondents. The data were taken from the codebooks published by the ICPSR.

The pattern shown for the four countries in Section A of Table 3 is
obviously similar to that shown in Figure 1 above. The average index rises in
1976, remains reasonably steady until 1978, and then declines dramatically
to just 31.2 in 1981. The pattern is also similar, if more erratic, in each of the
four individual countries, the post-1978 decline being particularly marked in
Belgium, the Netherlands and France. As can be seen from Section B of the
table, the remaining five countries also evidence sharply declining trends for
those years for which comparable data are available. The mean value of the
index falls from 40.3 in 1978 to 33.1 in 1981, the decline being particularly
marked in Britain, Ireland and Luxembourg where the difference between
1978 and 1981 is of the order of 10 points. Overall, rating the nine countries
together, the average index falls from 39.8 in 1978 to just 32.2 in 1981, and
thereby suggests a substantial decline in both the level and intensity of party
identification virtually throughout the Community countries.

TABLE 3
INDEX OF PARTY IDENTIFICATION, 1975–81[1]

	1975 (Oct)	1976 (Oct)	1977 (Oct)	1978 (Oct)	1979 (Oct)	1980 (Apr)	1981 (Apr)
A							
Belgium	23.8	37.0	34.1	36.0	30.9	25.4	26.0
France	31.8	33.4	34.8	36.2	33.8	27.5	27.5
Germany	37.5	42.1	38.9	36.0	34.8	38.1	33.1
Netherlands	41.1	42.8	44.6	48.6	41.2	39.7	38.2
Mean (n=4)	33.6	38.8	38.1	39.2	35.2	32.7	31.2
B							
Britain	na	na	na	39.9	36.7	37.1	30.1
Denmark	na	na	na	41.0	43.9	41.1	36.5
Ireland	na	na	na	38.2	34.6	33.6	28.2
Italy	na	na	na	47.9	49.2	41.6	46.0
Luxemburg	na	na	na	34.6	37.2	32.5	24.5
Mean (n=5)	na	na	na	40.3	40.3	37.2	33.1
Overall Mean (n=9)	na	na	na	39.8	38.0	35.2	32.2

Note: 1. The index has been calculated by multiplying the percentage of those 'very close' to a party by 3, those 'fairly close' by 2, those 'merely sympathising' by 1, those with 'no ties' by 0, summing the results and dividing by 3. The theoretical range is therefore 0 (no ties to party) to 100 (all close identifiers). The percentages used have been recalculated to excluded non-respondents. The 'B' data for 1975 to 1977 have not been included due to the lack of question comparability.

Source: Eurobarometers 4, 6, 8, 10, 12, 13 and 15 (ICPSR codebooks).

It goes without saying that one must be extremely cautious in interpreting these data. The patterns are sometimes erratic; on occasion, there are major and fairly inexplicable changes in certain countries from one survey to the next; the time period concerned is extremely brief, particularly in the case of Britain, Denmark, Ireland, Italy and Luxembourg; finally, data from more recent surveys could show a reversal in the trend. This said, these data, however inadequate they may be, do show a declining sense of party identification in almost all the EC countries. The evidence points unmistakably to a growing disaffection with party.

Organisational Resources and Organisational Relevance

If the trends towards decreasing levels and intensity of party identification evident in the Eurobarometer data are neither spurious nor transitory, then, together with the evidence of increased electoral volatility, they do suggest that the 'hold' of parties in Western Europe is indeed weakening. The evidence should not be exaggerated, however, and certainly there is no way that observers can legitimately consign parties to the dustbin of political ephemera. As has already been noted, fewer than one in ten votes shifts at the aggregate level (Table 1); at the same time, average electoral turnout in the 1970s has remained at more or less the same level as that in the allegedly more gilded age of parties in the 1950s (Table 2); and even allowing for declining rates of identification (Table 3), nevertheless in the European Community in 1981 an average of more than one in four respondents still stated that they were 'very' or 'fairly' close to a particular party. Rather than speak in an exaggerated fashion of the decline of parties, therefore, it may be more useful simply to suggest that they are more vulnerable, and to look for possible explanations for this development.

The most obvious explanations are those which point to change in the social structure and the impact of this on party support. Rudy Andeweg's study of the changing Dutch voter[12] is probably the most exhaustive recent example of such an investigation, but similar if less comprehensive analyses have been carried out in other countries. A second approach emphasises the policy-making function of parties, pointing to the challenge to, and potential failure of, parties in government as a possible source of disaffection.[13] For the purposes of this paper, however, and by way of a conclusion, I would like to touch briefly on the related, if neglected, question of a decline in party organisational resources.[14]

The capacity of parties to influence and mobilise mass publics depends as much on their organisational resources as it does on the particular policies on ideologies which they advance.[15] However attractive a party's programme might be, an organisational infrastructure is necessary if its message is to reach the eyes and ears of its potential constituency. Traditionally, the most obvious organisational resource was the party membership – the organisers, public speakers, canvassers and notables who could carry the party banner to what might otherwise have been an unsuspecting public. In the politics of contemporary Europe, of course, membership is seen to be less relevant, and more weight is being placed on the capacity to use the mass media as the primary channel for communication. But organisational resources have always involved a lot more than simply the card-carrying membership, and include elements which do not properly belong to parties *per se*, but rather to the broader political and social *movement* of which the party is part. And it is the potential loss of these other resources – not substitutable by the mass media – which may have contributed to the contemporary vulnerability of parties.

Eamon de Valera, the founder and long-term leader of the traditionally predominant party in Ireland, Fianna Fail, was always at pains to point out that his was more a movement than a party. Certainly Fianna Fail lacks many of the characteristics associated with modern mass parties: it has no distinct social clientele, but draws support evenly from virtually all groups in the society; despite being, or perhaps because it was so successful, it issued no formal election programme in the post-war period prior to 1977; and more importantly, perhaps, it laid no stress on individual membership, maintaining no central register and not even encouraging a decentralised formal membership. Even now, nobody – not even the party leadership – is really aware of how many people are actually members of Fianna Fail.

While this may constitute somewhat of an extreme example, nevertheless there is a sense in which many mass parties in contemporary Europe are not only parties but movements as well. As Gordon Smith has pointed out,[16] it is often difficult to establish the dividing line between a political party and the movement to which it relates. The constituencies of each overlap, as do their respective leaderships. The goals and strategies of each may differ only to the extent that there exists a division of responsibility. The goals of the British labour movement, for instance, may find their specifically parliamentary expression through the Labour Party, but the party and the unions are each aware of their belonging to a broader cultural, political and even organisational alliance. While this again may seem an extreme example – indeed it was precisely the extended influence of the unions on the party which precipitated the formation of the breakaway SDP – nevertheless there is a sense in which much the same can be said for many of the major European parties, be they Socialist, Communist, Christian Democratic, Agrarian or whatever.

In cases where a party is part of a broader movement, however loosely defined, then that movement provides a substantial, if often informal, infrastructure of organisational support. In this sense, the loyalty which accrues to such a party derives not only from purely partisan socialisation and/or repeated expressions of partisan support – the classic channels for the establishment of a strong party identification – but also from an entire cultural milieu formed by the mutually supportive agencies of party and union, or party and church, or even party and housing estate. In other words, there exists an organisational infrastructure which stretches beyond what one might consider to be purely party-defined bounds. Born themselves from the organisation of social cleavages into politics, parties feed off other non-party organisational structures which also sustain, and are sustained by, those cleavages. If a sense of working-class identification leads one to identify with a socialist party, for example, then the non-party factors which facilitate that class identity – union membership, place of residence and so on – can be seen to be part of the party's extended organisational resources. To the extent that these factors become less important for the individual citizen, therefore, or less associated with a particular party, the party will clearly become more vulnerable to electoral disaffection.

It would be impossible within the scope of this article, and probably also in any other context, to chart the extent to which specific parties rely – either formally or informally – on non-party organisational resources. What is possible to suggest, however, is that their access to such resources may have waned over the past decade or so, and that there has been a growing gap between parties and their supportive networks. In other words, I am suggesting that the party–movement symbiosis – if such it can be described – is increasingly uncharacteristic of contemporary political practice. Parties are being thrown more and more on their own specifically party resources, and find themselves with an ever-diminishing 'movement' infrastructure on which to rely.

While this suggestion is of course extremely speculative, nevertheless there are two reasons why it might be considered plausible. The first is simply because of the waning of some of the traditional movements themselves, through de-confessionalisation in such countries as Italy and the Netherlands, for example, or, on the other side of the coin, through increasing divisions in the labour movement between private and public sector workers. The second reason, which is potentially more interesting, is because of the burgeoning of interest associations in the late 1960s and 1970s, and their increasing independence from party.[17] To the extent that parties have benefited from the solidaristic (as well as financial) support of affiliated and even simply sympathetic interest associations, then the growing independence of the latter removes a potentially invaluable resource.

Parties compete with interest associations to the extent that both mediate the relations between citizens and government. In practice, and as is suggested in Figure 2, such relations are mediated in three ways. First, directly through the parties (a–b–d in Figure 2); second, directly through interest associations (a–c–d), and third through interest associations *and* parties (a–c–b–d).

FIGURE 2
MEDIATED RELATIONS BETWEEN CITIZENS AND GOVERNMENT

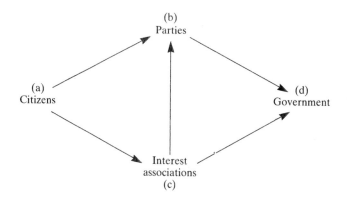

The proliferation and increased popular use of interest associations clearly strengthens the a–c–d link at the cost of the parties. More importantly, however, to the extent that interest associations act independently of party, then the crucial a–c–b–d link is also weakened. And to the extent that the efficacy of parties as intermediaries between citizens and government depends on the maintenance of this link, and thereby on the de-escalation of their potential conflict with interest associations through the incorporation of these associations, then to that extent the parties become vulnerable.

This is perhaps the real challenge to party. It is a challenge which does not so much stem from the emergence of new political demands or even new interests as such, since there is no reason why such new demands or interests could not be organised by party – whether by an old party which adapts or by a wholly new party. Rather, the challenge comes from the growth and increased independence of interest associations which threaten the parties' dominance as intermediaries between citizens and government. Not only do the parties face the loss of organisational resources which accrued to them as part of larger 'movements', but they also face a decline in their own organisational relevance. In such circumstances, voters begin to distance themselves; they feel less attached and have a diminished sense of 'belonging' to a party. Votes continue to be cast, but who actually wins government becomes less important, and so partisan preferences are registered with less consistency. Levels and intensity of party identification decline; electoral volatility increases.

This is probably an exaggerated scenario. As almost a century of mass politics tells us, parties can adapt and do persist. Nevertheless, as we move into the mid-1980s, the signs are that many of the traditional parties in Western Europe are facing the most serious democratic challenge in their history.

NOTES

1. S.M. Lipset and Stein Rokkan, 'Cleavage Structures, Party Systems and Voter Alignments: an Introduction', in S.M. Lipset and Stein Rokkan (eds.), *Party Systems and Voter Alignments* (New York: The Free Press, 1967), pp. 1–64; Richard Rose and Derek Urwin, 'Persistence and Change in Western Party Systems Since 1945', *Political Studies*, Vol. 18, No. 3 (1970), pp. 287–319.
2. Mogens N. Pedersen, 'Changing Patterns of Electoral Volatility in European Party Systems, 1948–1977: Explorations in Explanation', and Maria Maguire, 'Is There Still Persistence? Electoral Change in Western Europe, 1948–1979', both in Hans Daalder and Peter Mair (eds.), *Western European Party Systems: Continuity and Change* (London: Sage, 1983), pp. 29–66 and 67–94 respectively.
3. Measures of volatility are based on the index adopted by Pedersen, op. cit.
4. For a first report, see Ian Budge, David Robertson and Derek Hearl (eds.), *Party Strategy* (forthcoming).
5. Though see Angelo Panebianco, *Modelli di partito* (Bologna: Il Mulino, 1982), and Stefano Bartolini, 'The Membership of Mass Parties: The Social Democratic Experience, 1889–1978', in Hans Daalder and Peter Mair, op. cit., pp. 177–220.
6. For a more extended discussion, see Stefano Bartolini and Peter Mair, 'The Class Cleavage in Historical Perspective: An Analytical Reconstruction and Empirical Test', paper presented to the Annual Meeting of the German Political Science Association, Mannheim, 1983.
7. See Peter Mair, 'Adaptation and Control: Towards an Understanding of Party and Party System Change', in Hans Daalder and Peter Mair, op. cit., pp. 405–30.
8. See, for example, Francis G. Castles (ed.), *The Impact of Parties* (London: Sage, 1982).
9. Karl Dittrich and Lars Norby Johansen, 'Voting Turnout in Europe, 1945–1978: Myths and Realities', in Hans Daalder and Peter Mair, op. cit., pp. 95–114.
10. For a discussion of the Eurobarometer question wording, see Richard S. Katz, 'Measuring Party Identification with Eurobarometer Data: A Warning Note' *West European Politics* (forthcoming January 1985).
11. The percentages here, as when cited elsewhere in this paper, have been re-computed to exclude non-respondents.
12. Rudy B. Andeweg, *Dutch Voters Adrift: On Explanations of Electoral Change, 1963–1977* (Leiden: the author, c/o Department of Political Science, University of Leyden, 1982).
13. See, for example, Francis G. Castles (ed.), *The Future of Party Government* (forthcoming), especially the chapter by Gordon Smith, 'The Futures of Party Government: A Framework for Analysis'.
14. For a similar discussion, see Peter Mair, 'Adaptation and Control', op. cit., pp. 419–25.

15. See, for example, Ian McAllister, 'Party Organisation and Minority Nationalism: A Comparative Study of the United Kingdom', *European Journal of Political Research*, Vol. 9, No. 3 (1981), pp. 237–56.

16. See Gordon Smith, 'Social Movements and Party Systems in Western Europe', in Martin Kolinsky and William E. Patterson (eds.), *Social and Political Movements in Western Europe* (London: Croom Helm, 1976), pp. 331–54.

17. See, for example, Philippe Schmitter and Gerhard Lehmbruch (eds.), *Trends Towards Corporatist Intermediation* (London: Sage, 1979).

DATE DUE

JAN 3 0 1989			